MEN WOMEN KIDS

By

Geo Neal

Penciled Portraits

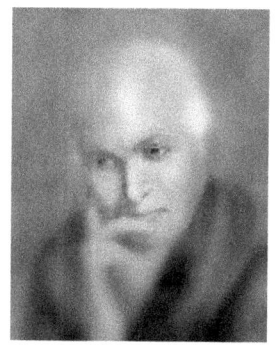

The author is a graphic designer, formerly a
Philadelphia advertising art director, illustrator,
playwright, fiction and nonfiction writer.

Men Women Kids at Amazon books.

georgeneal@aol.com

KIDS

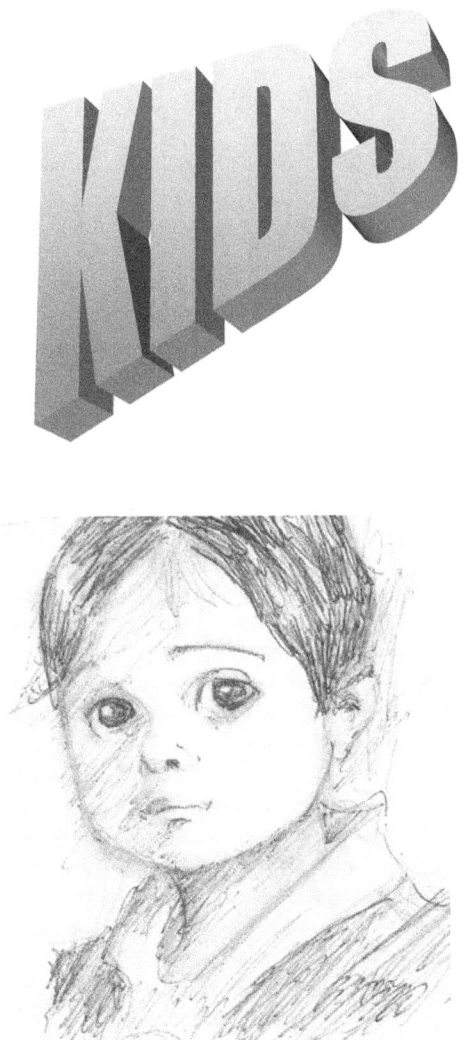

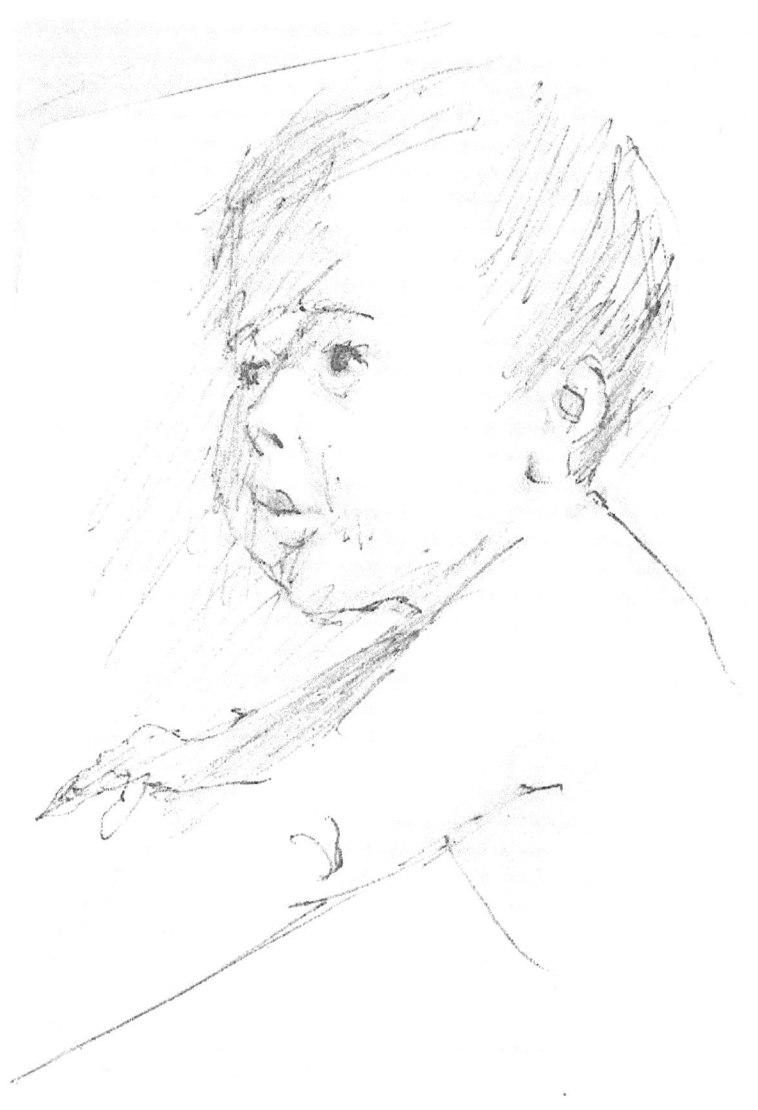

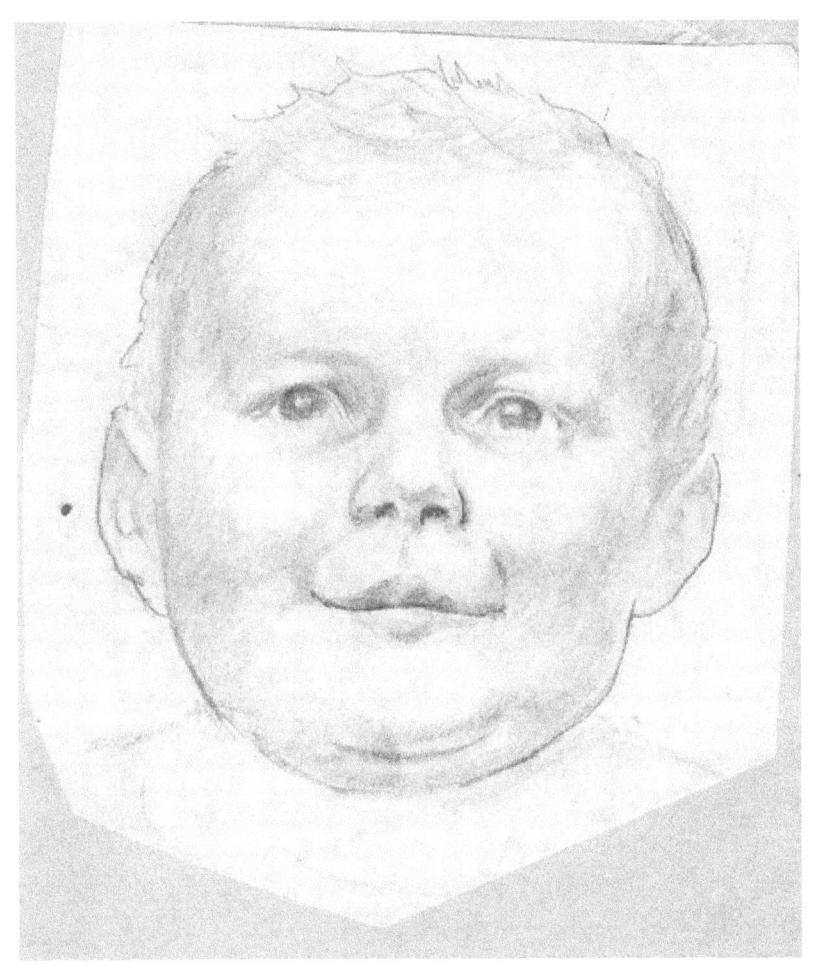

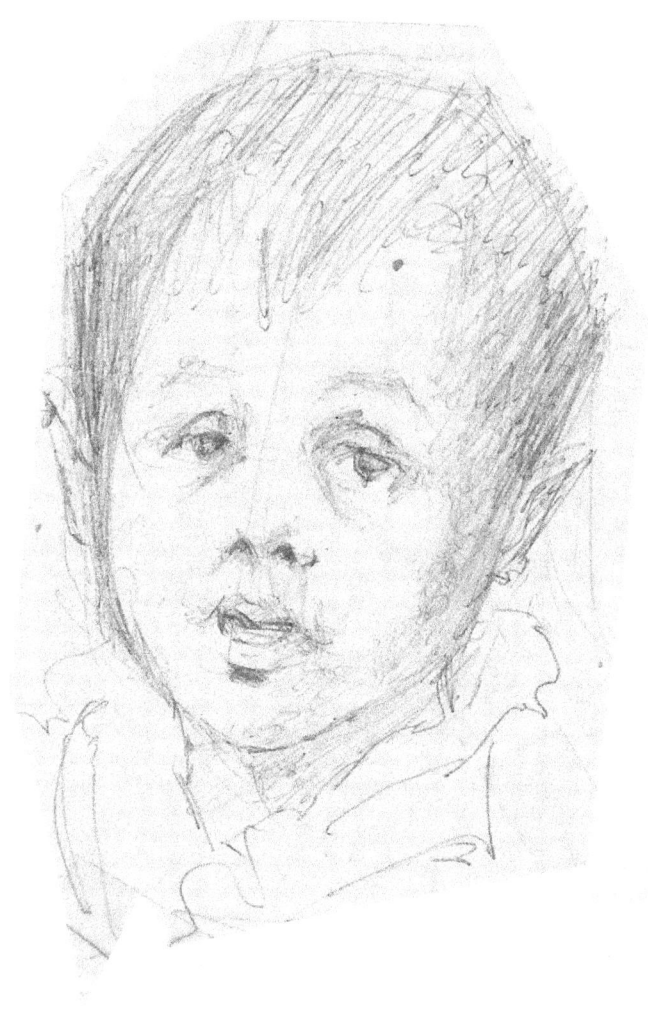

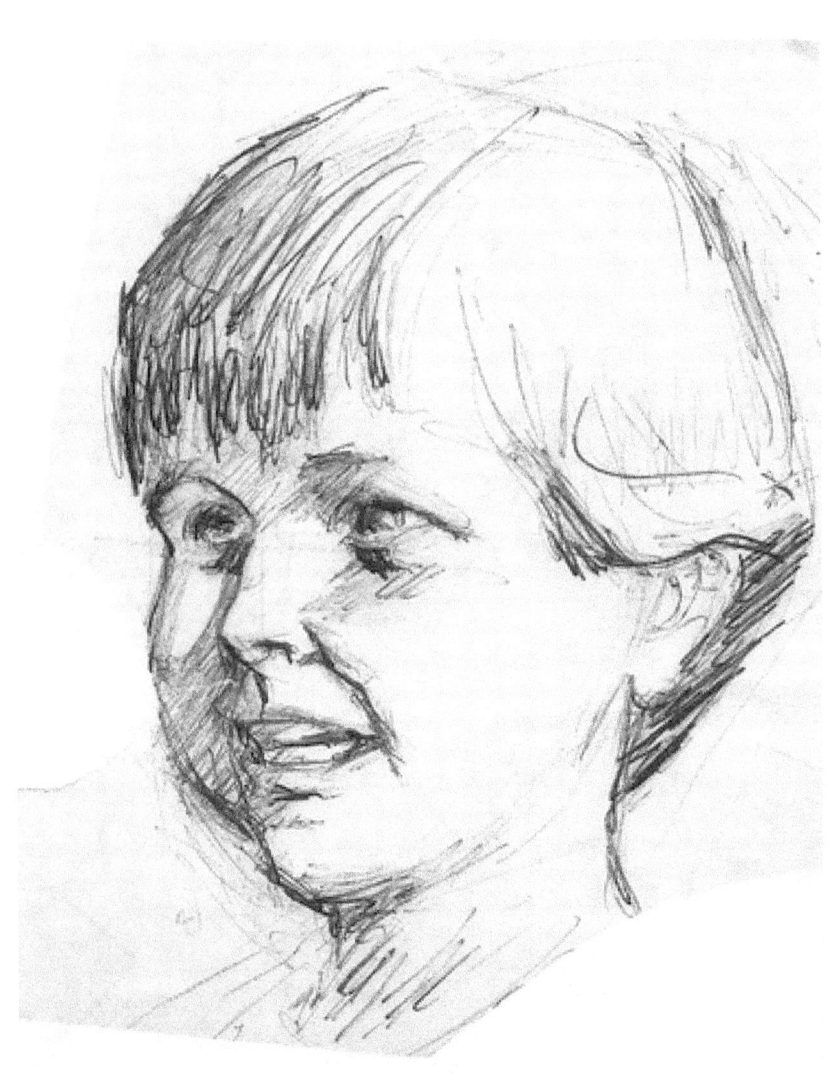

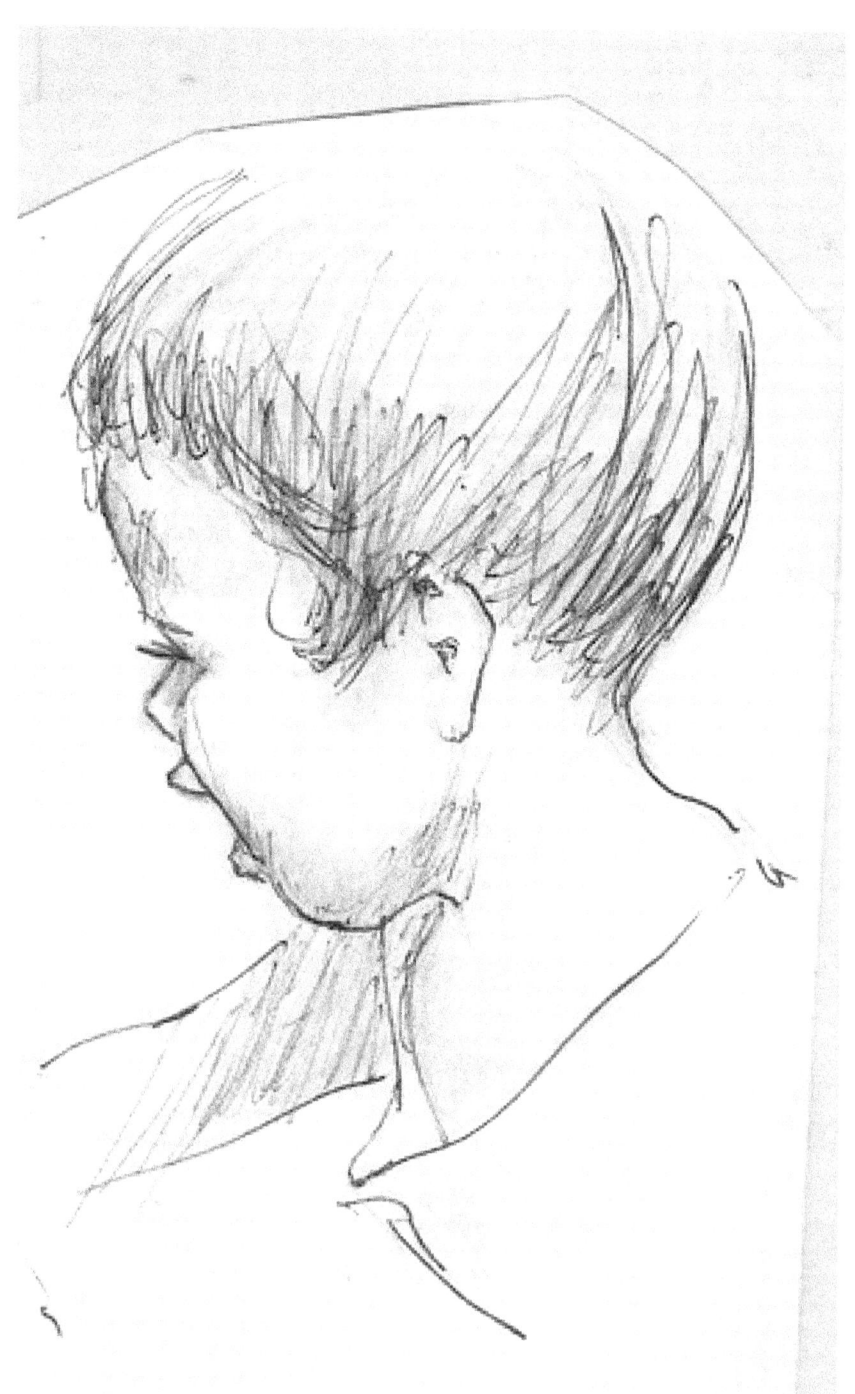

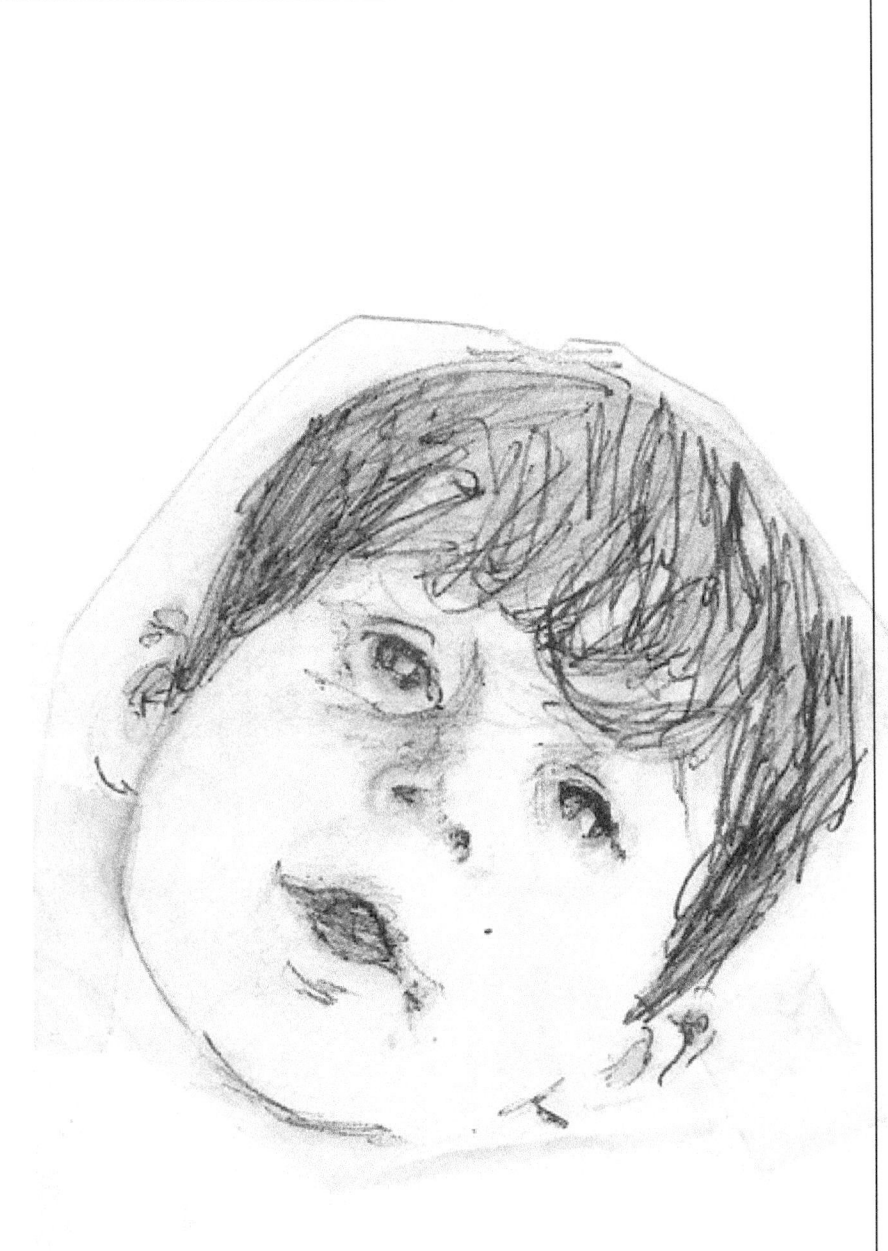

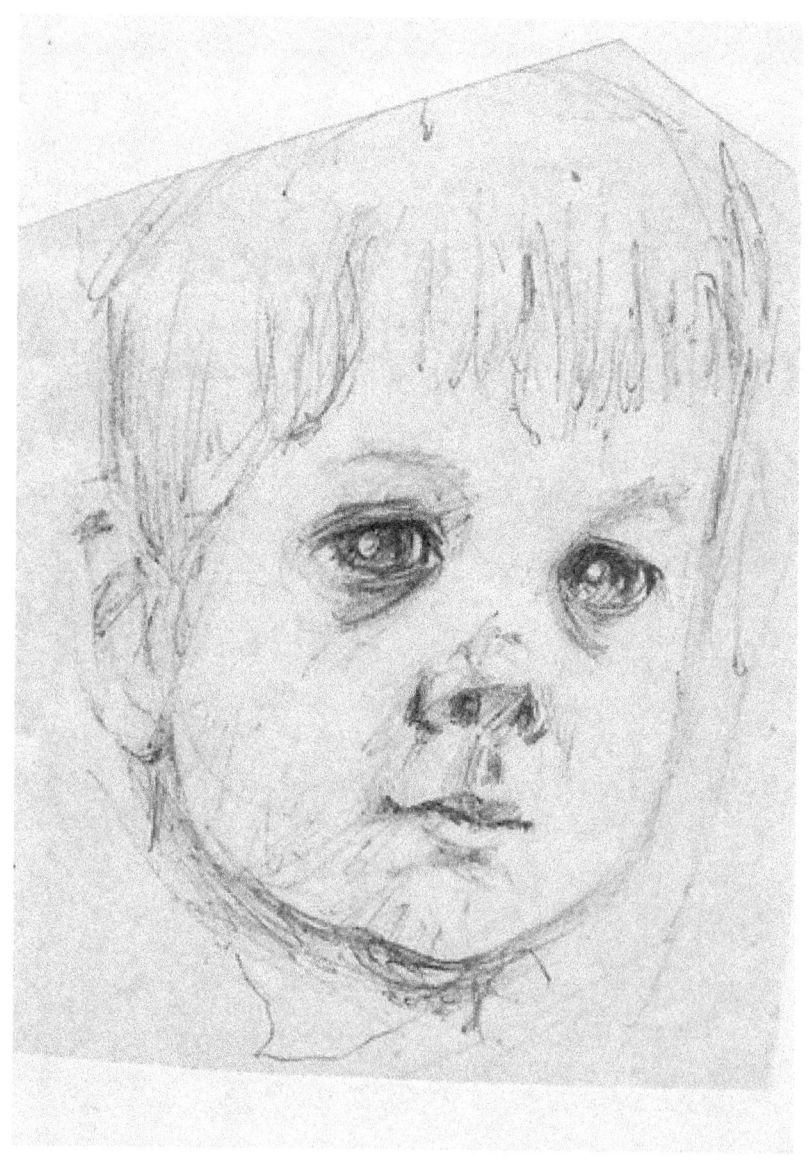

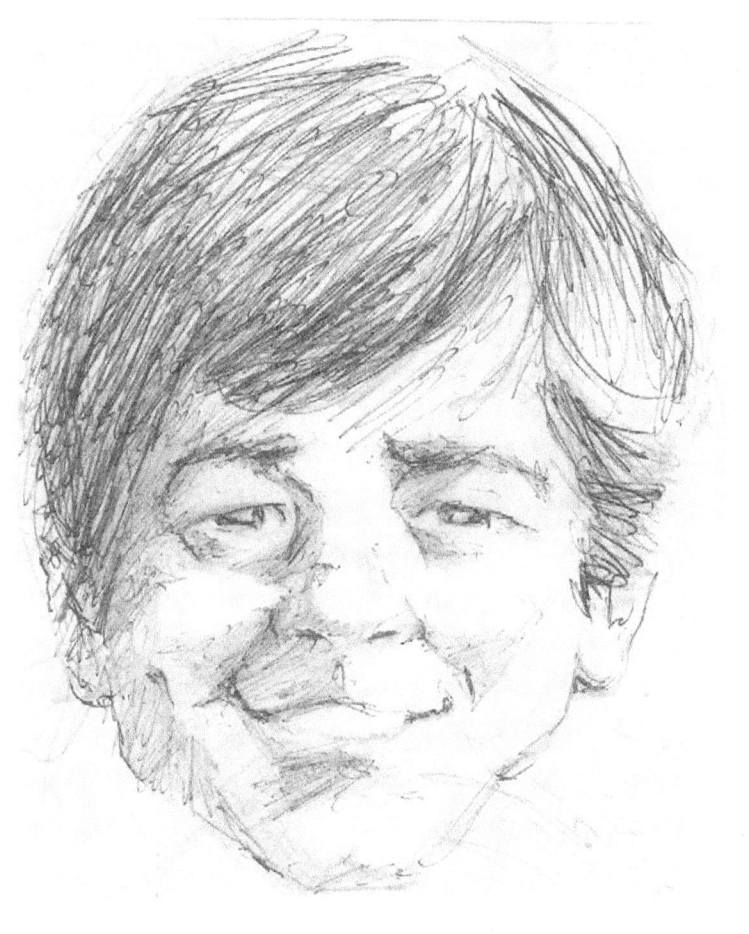

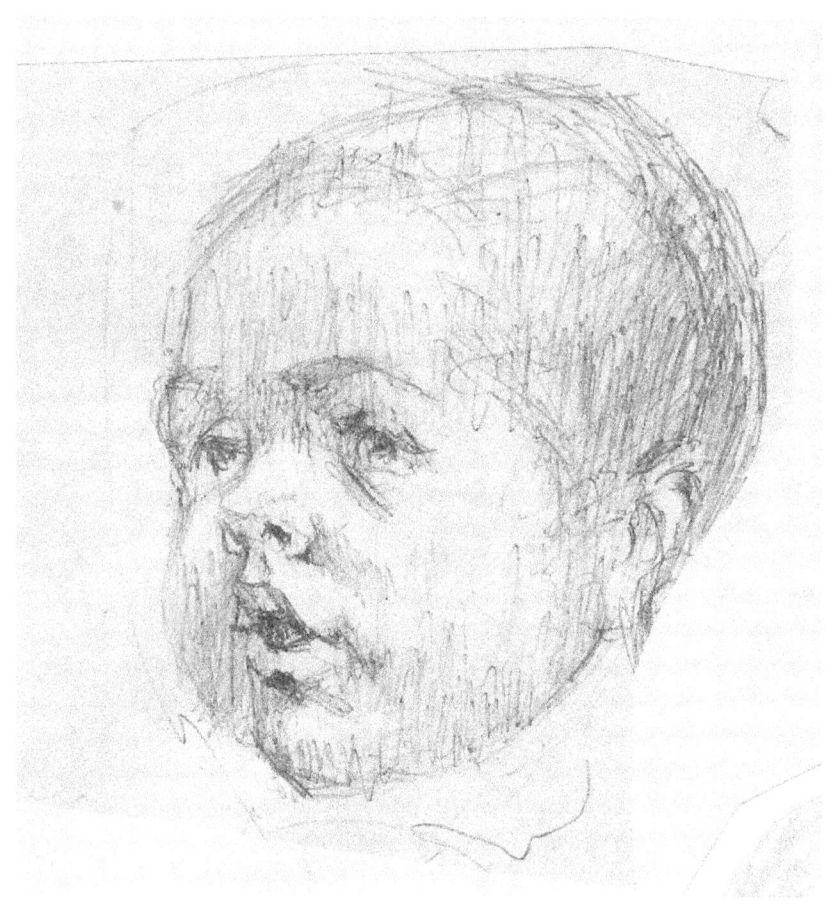

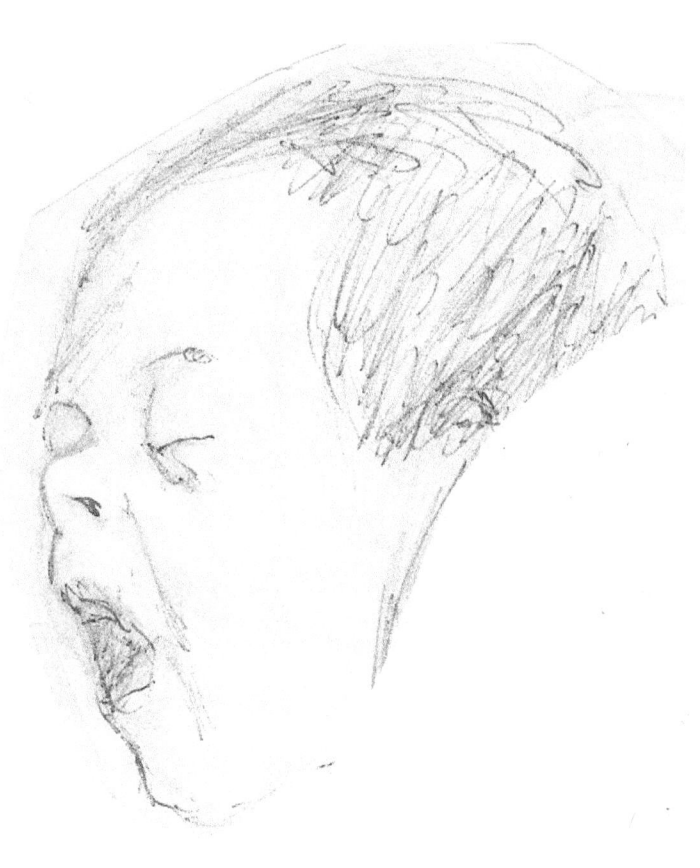

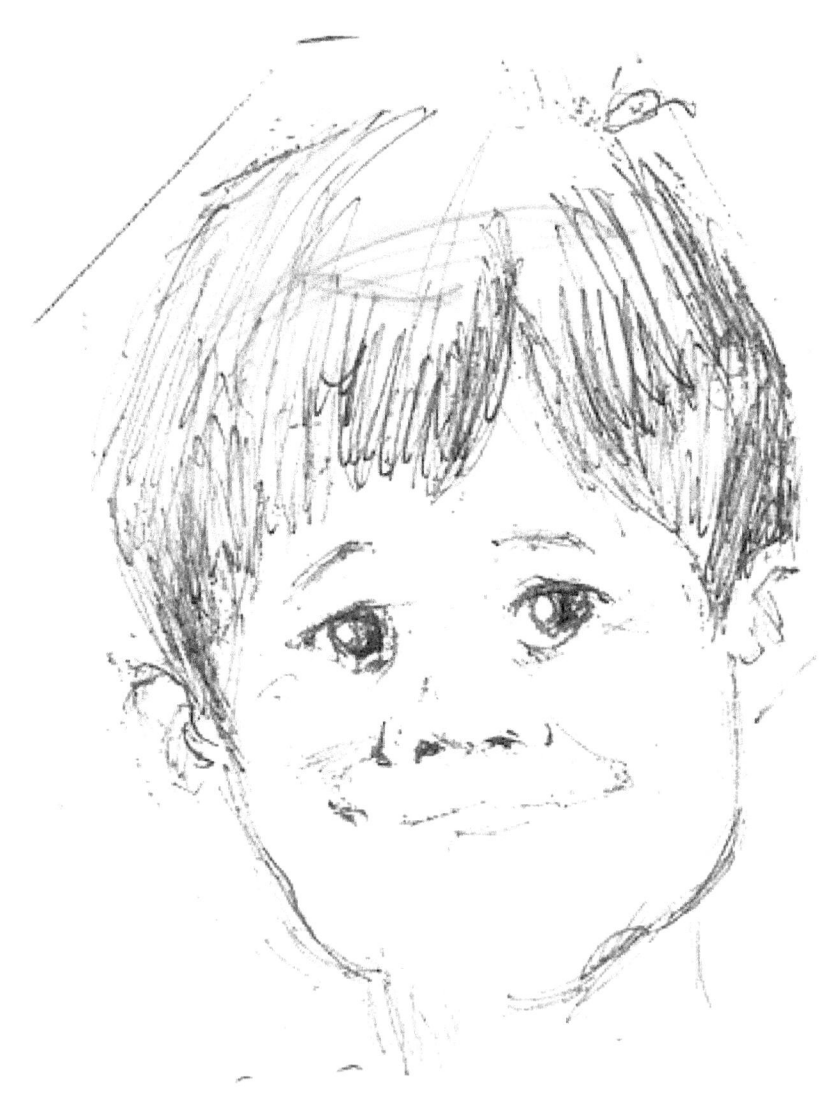

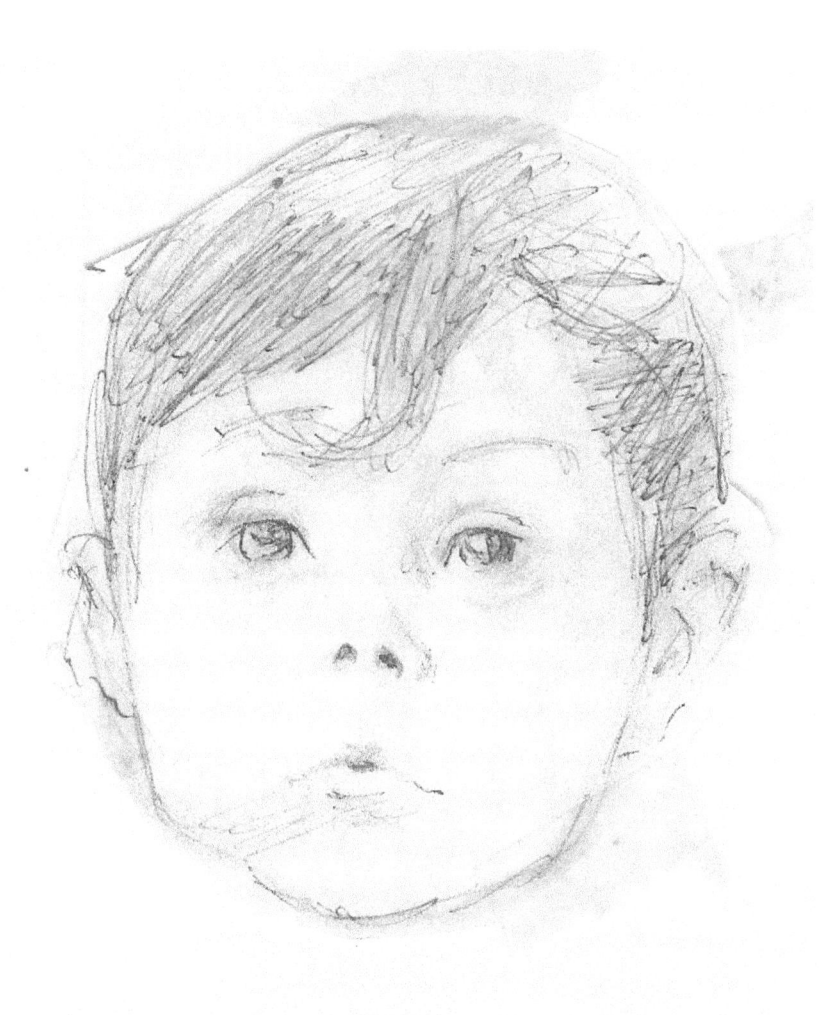

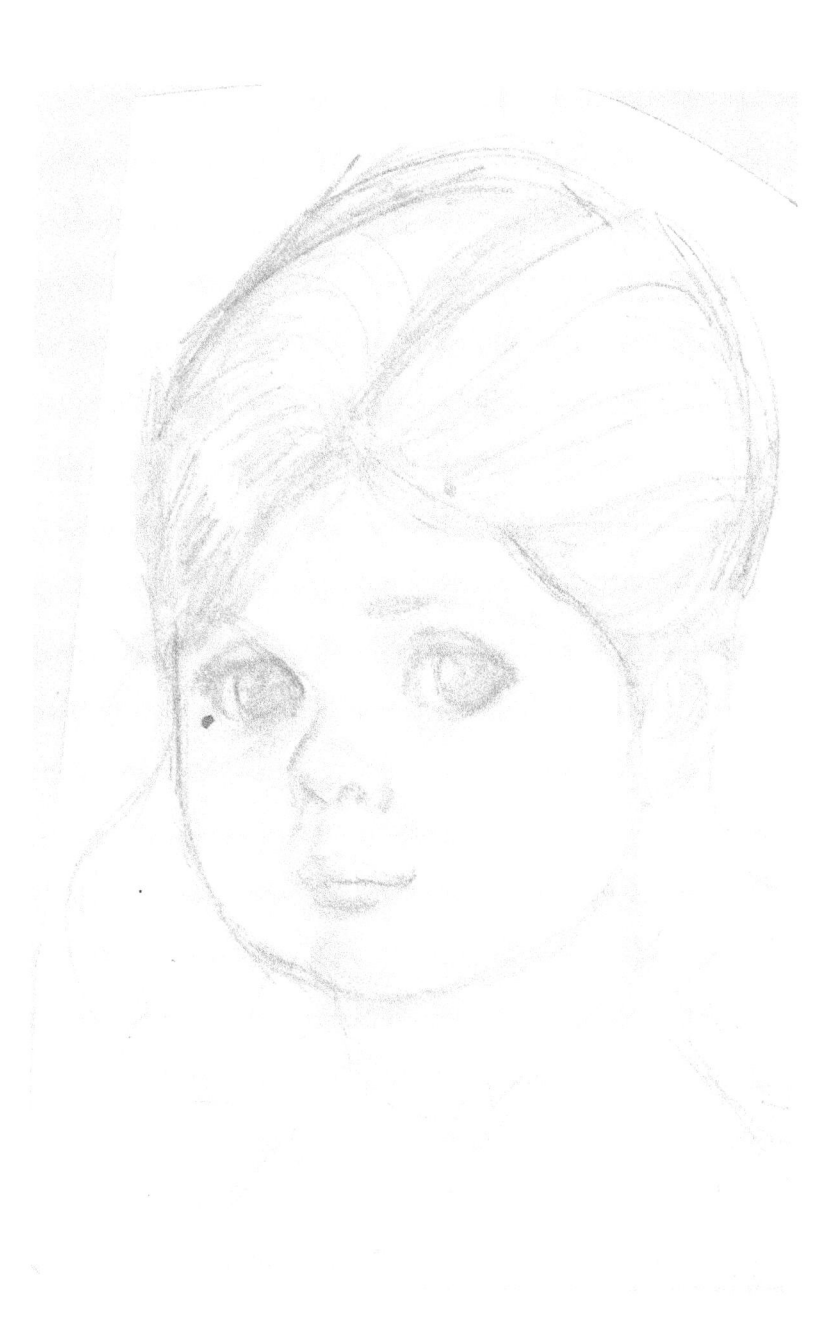

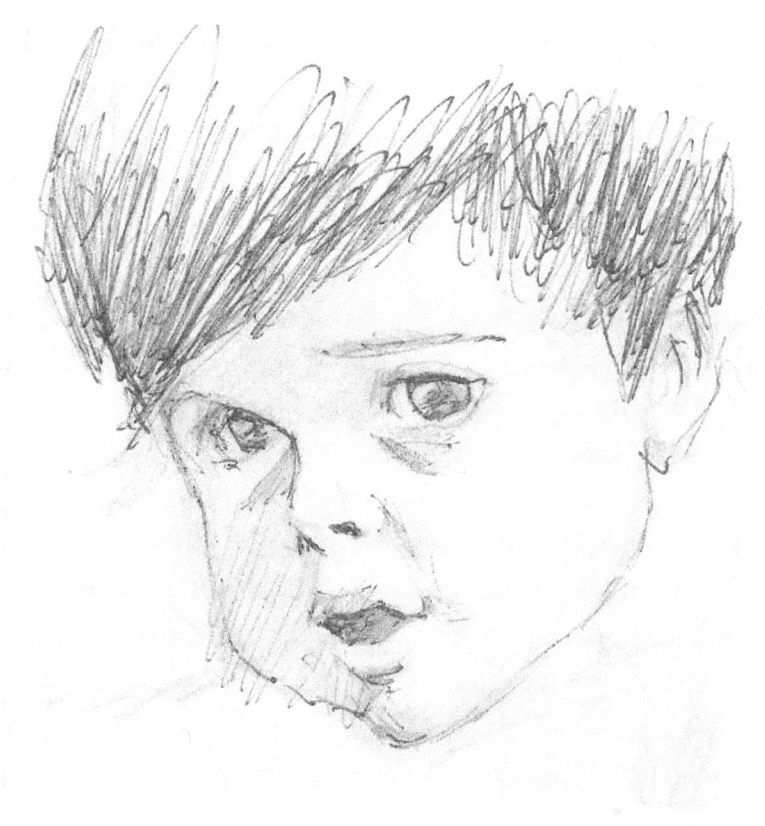

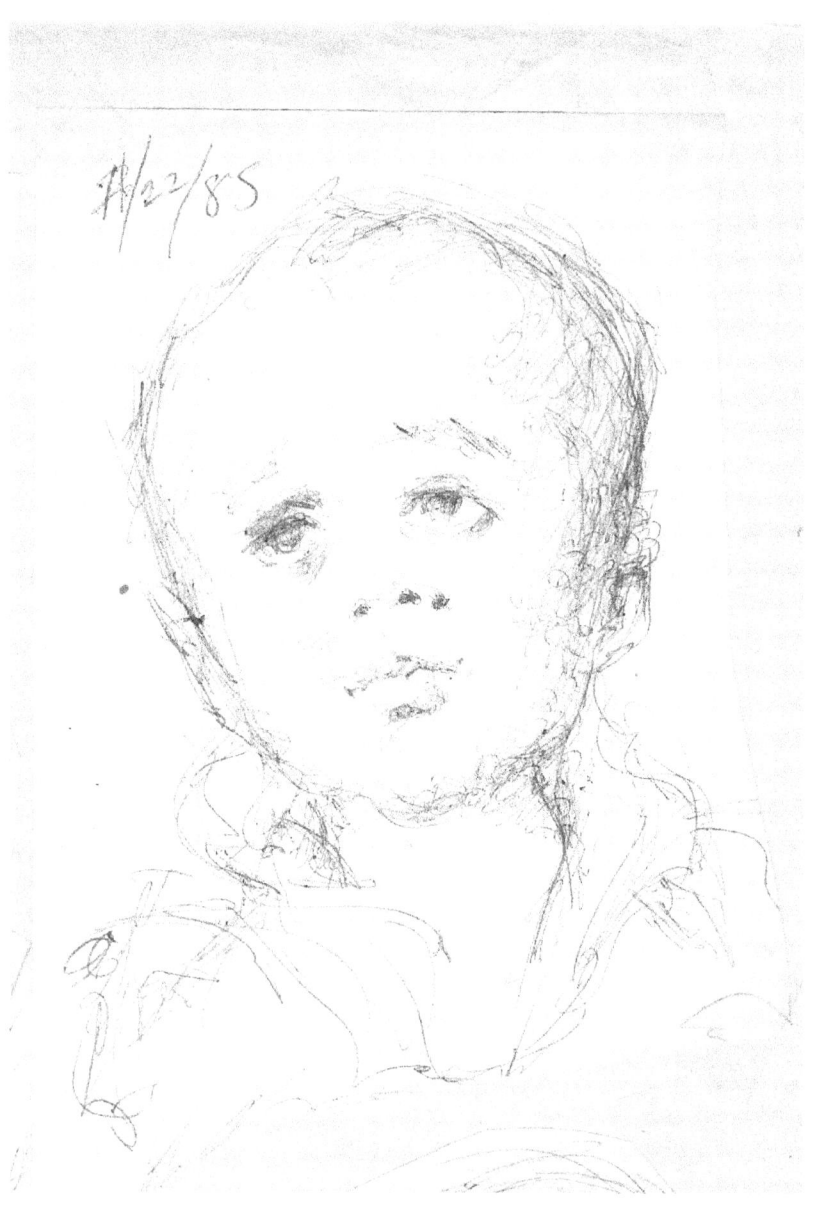

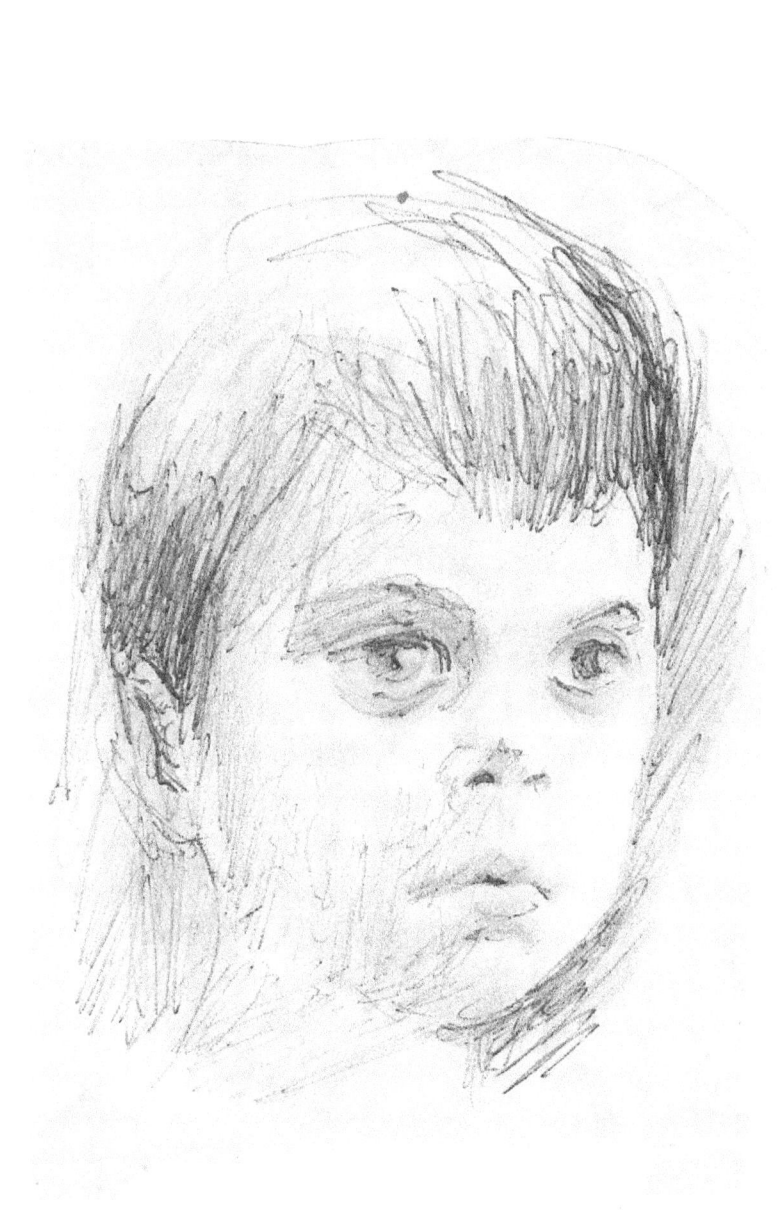

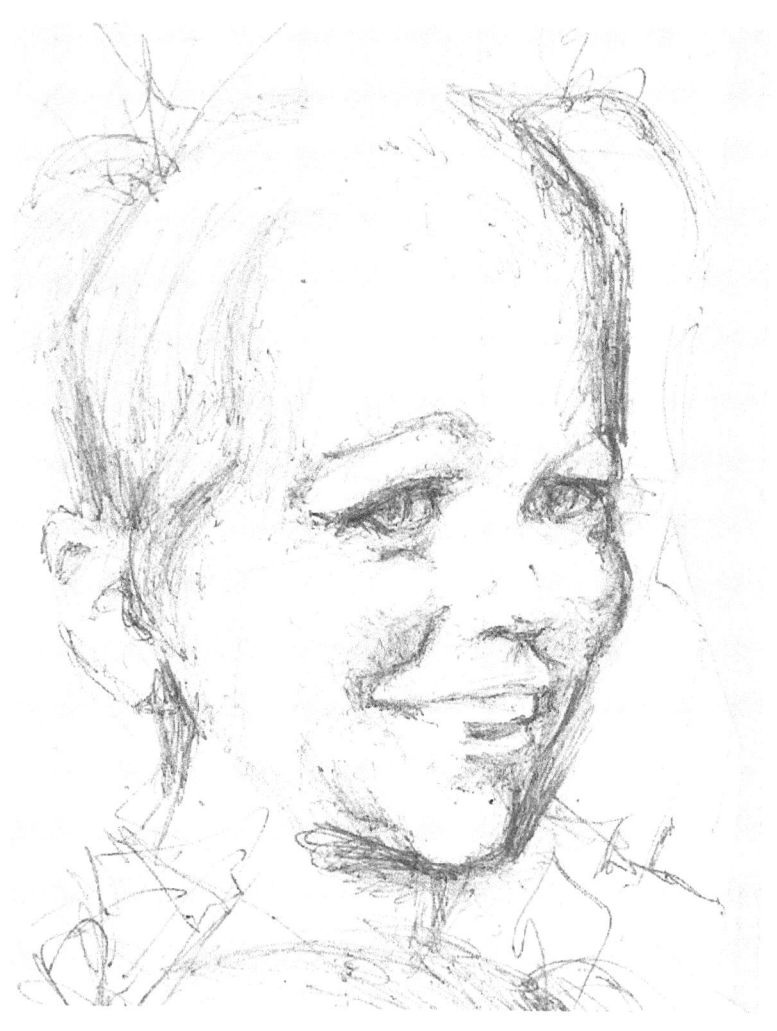

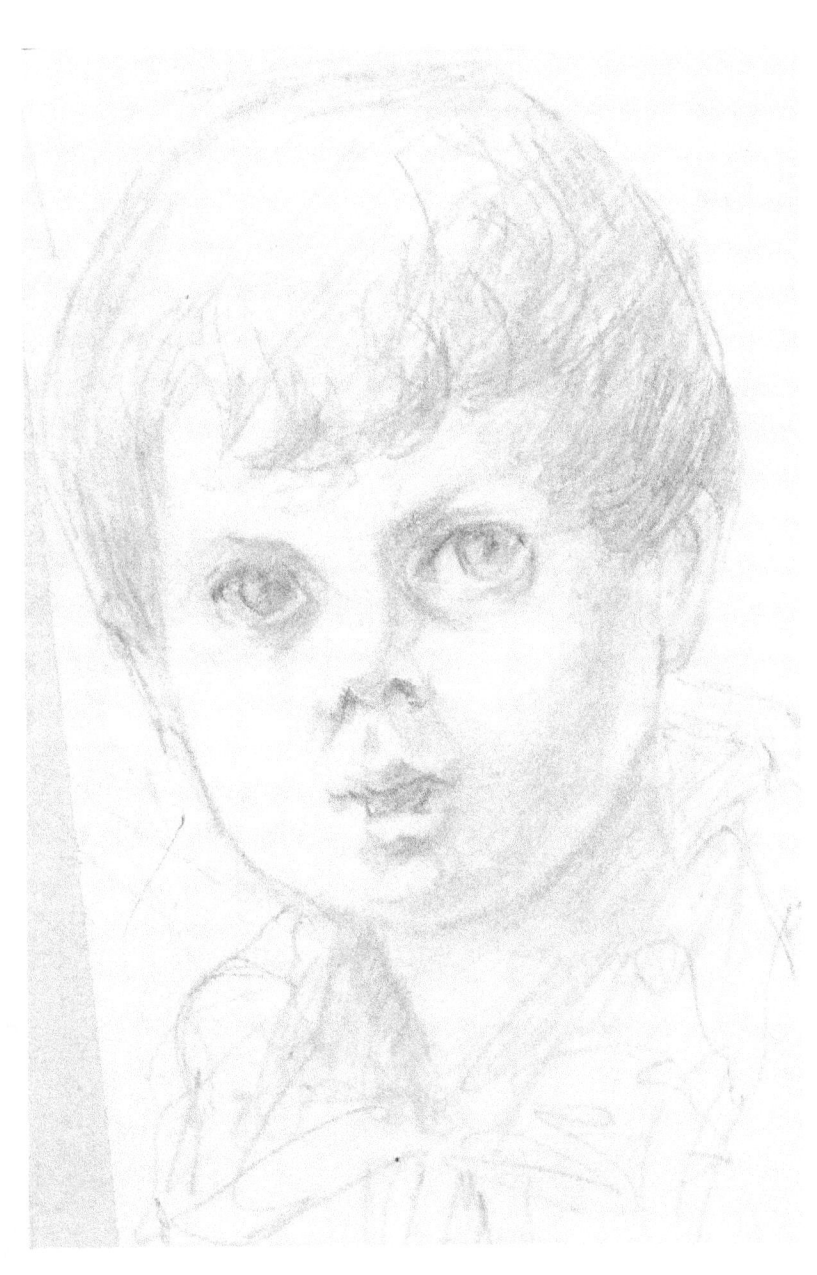

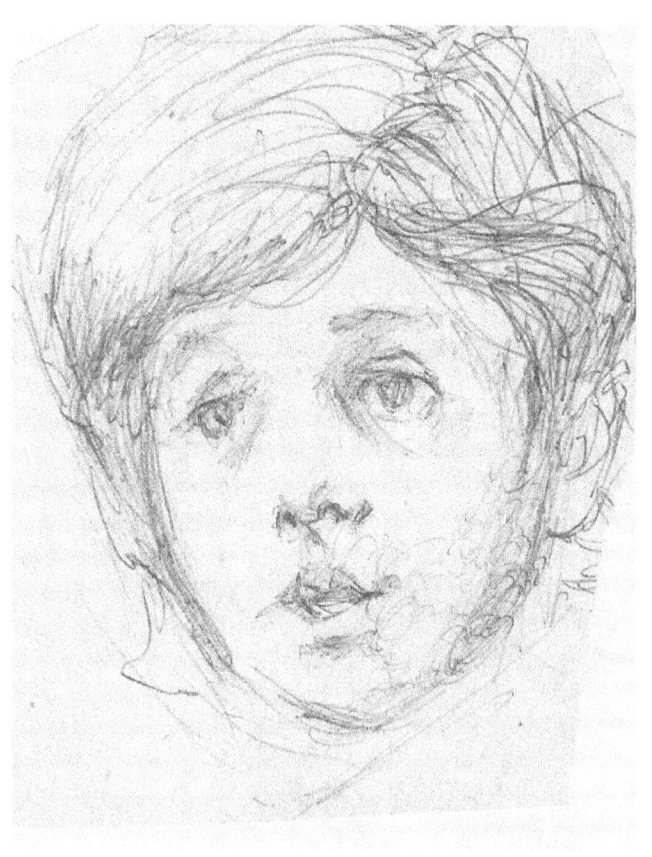

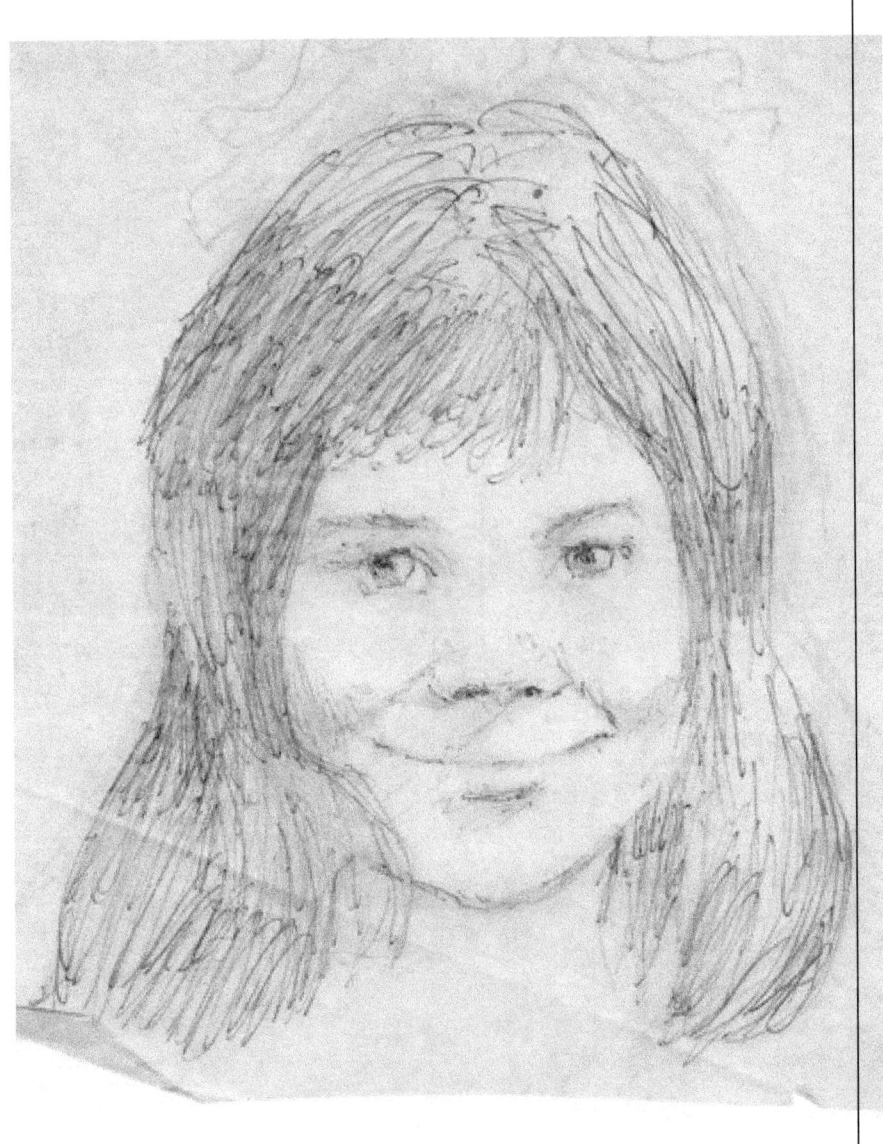

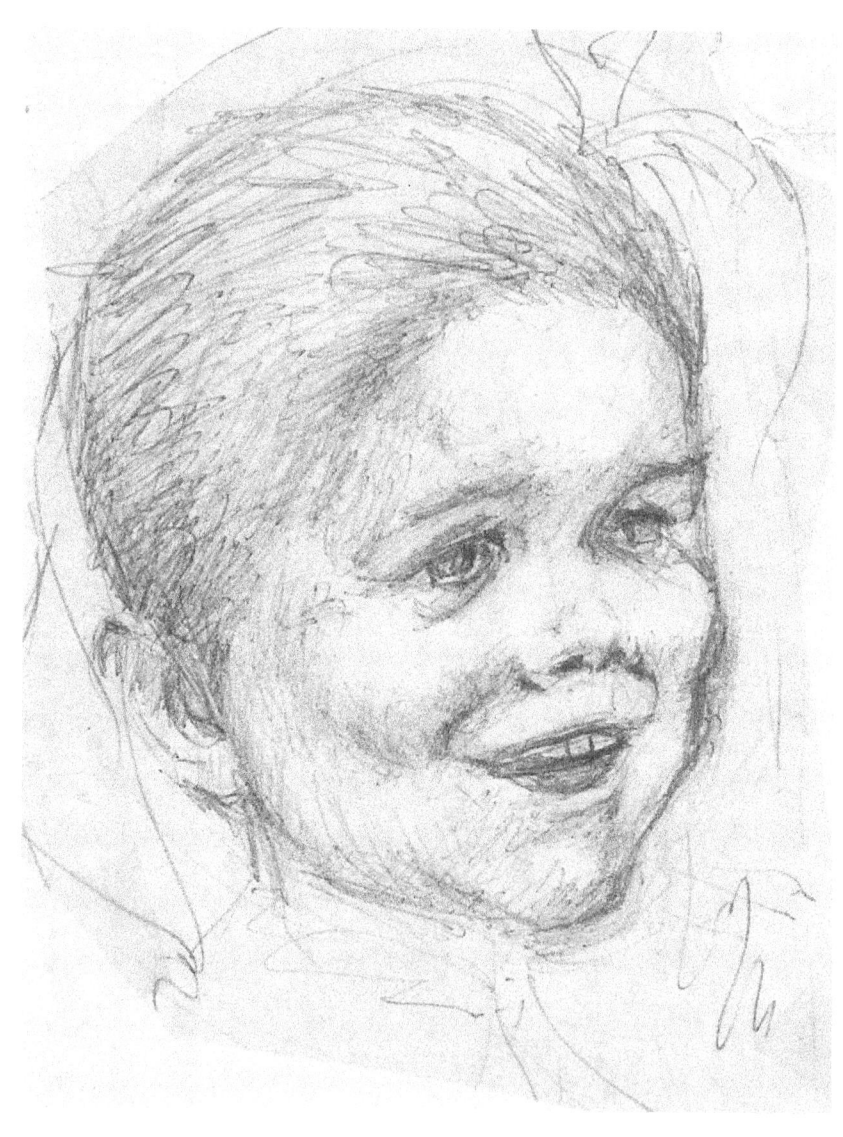

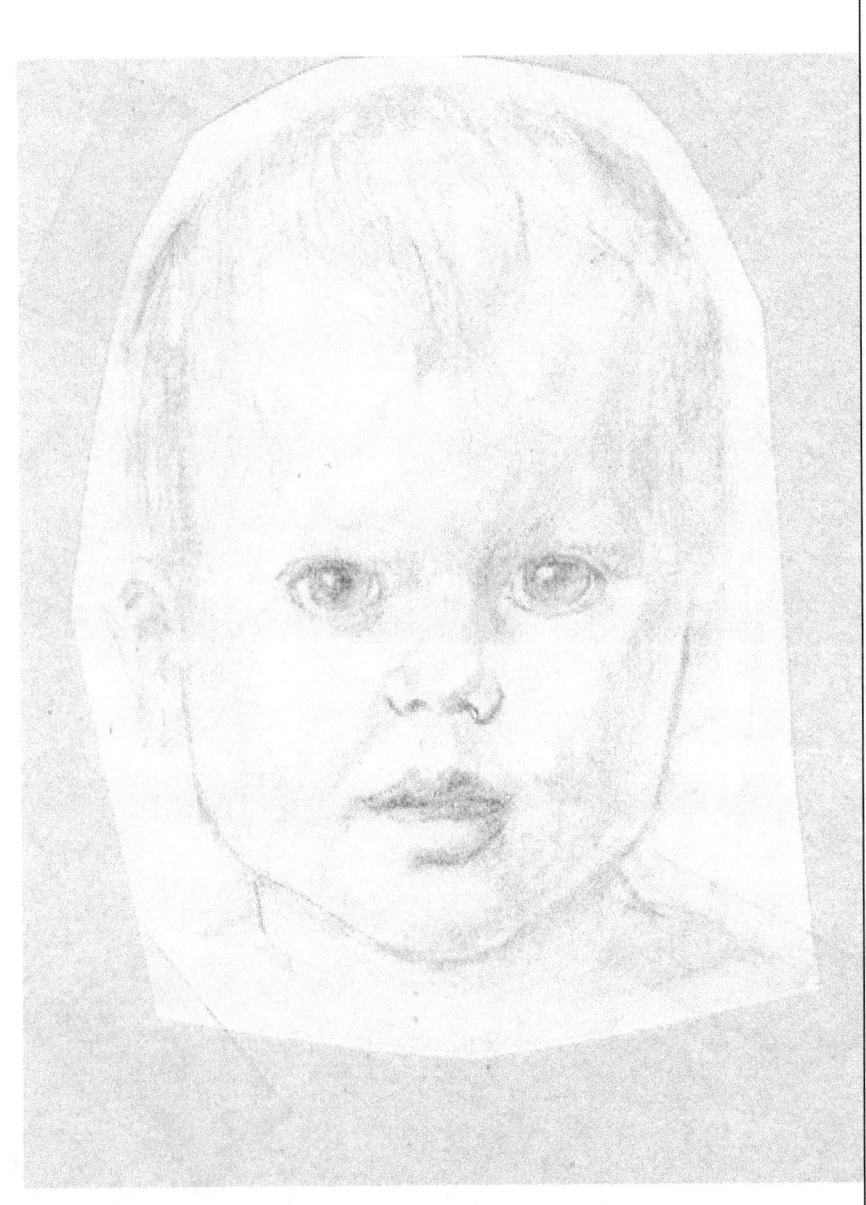

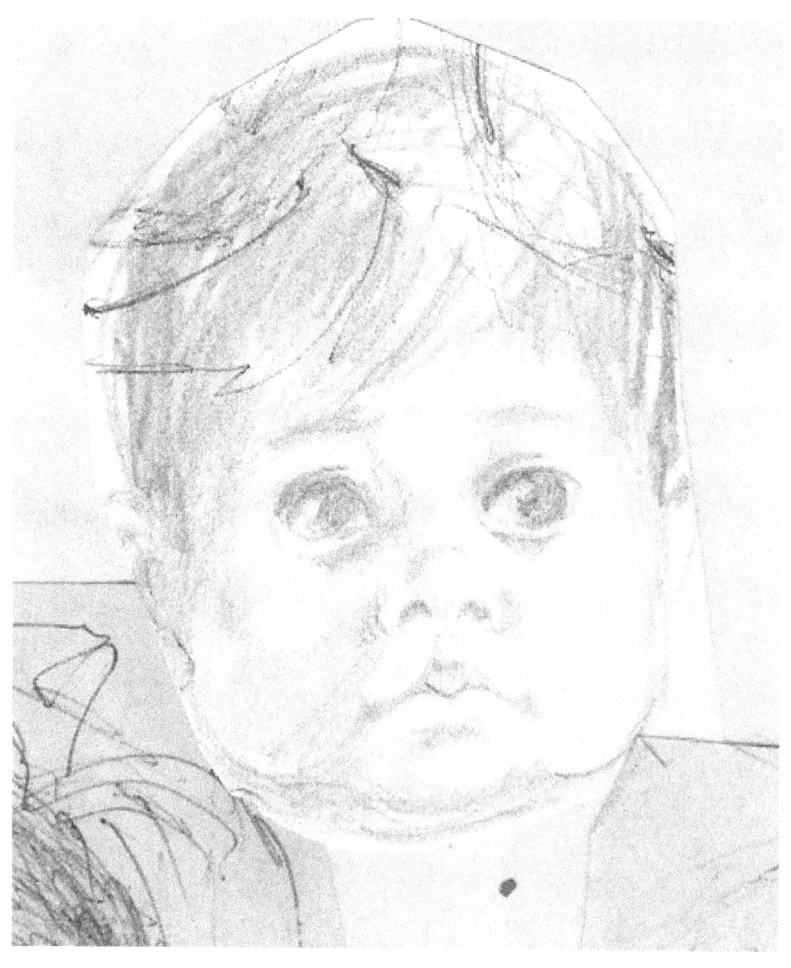

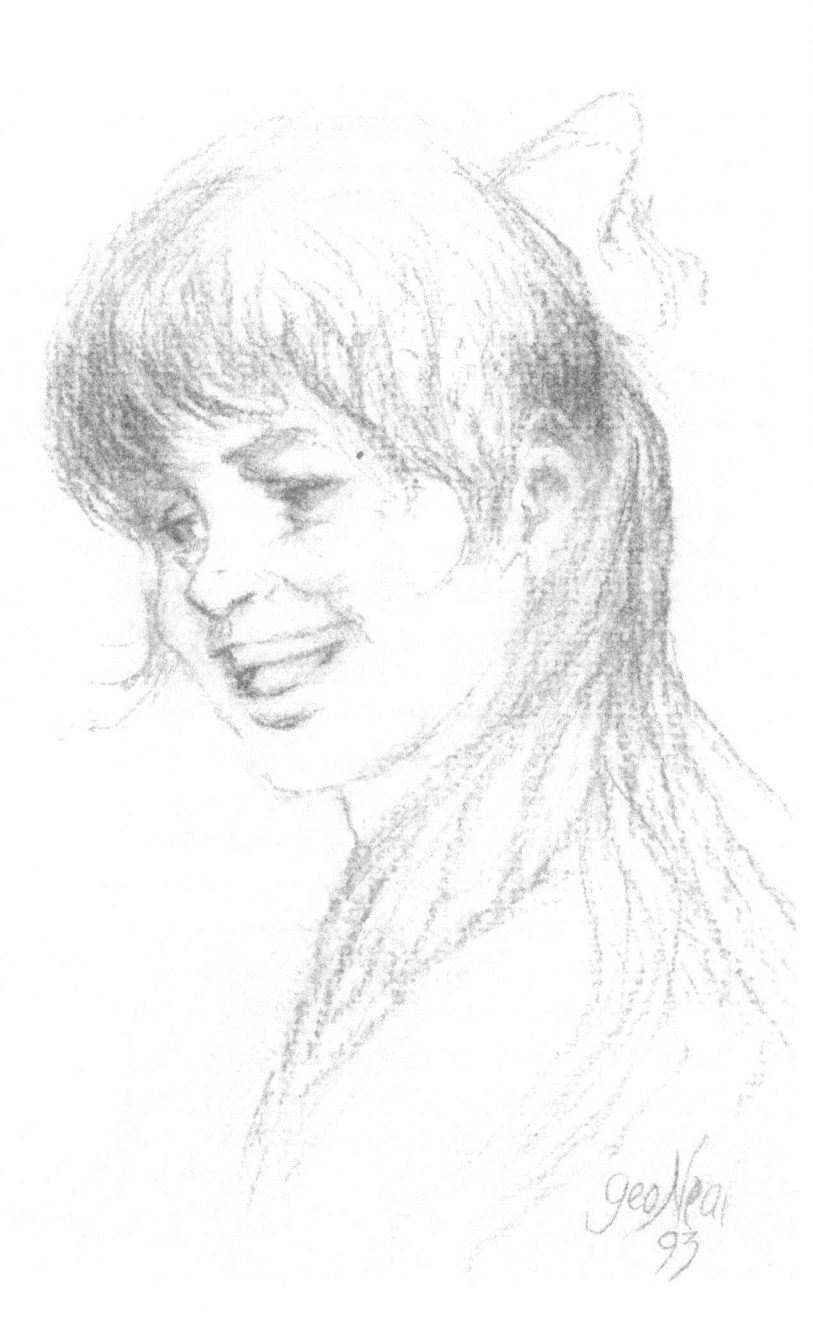

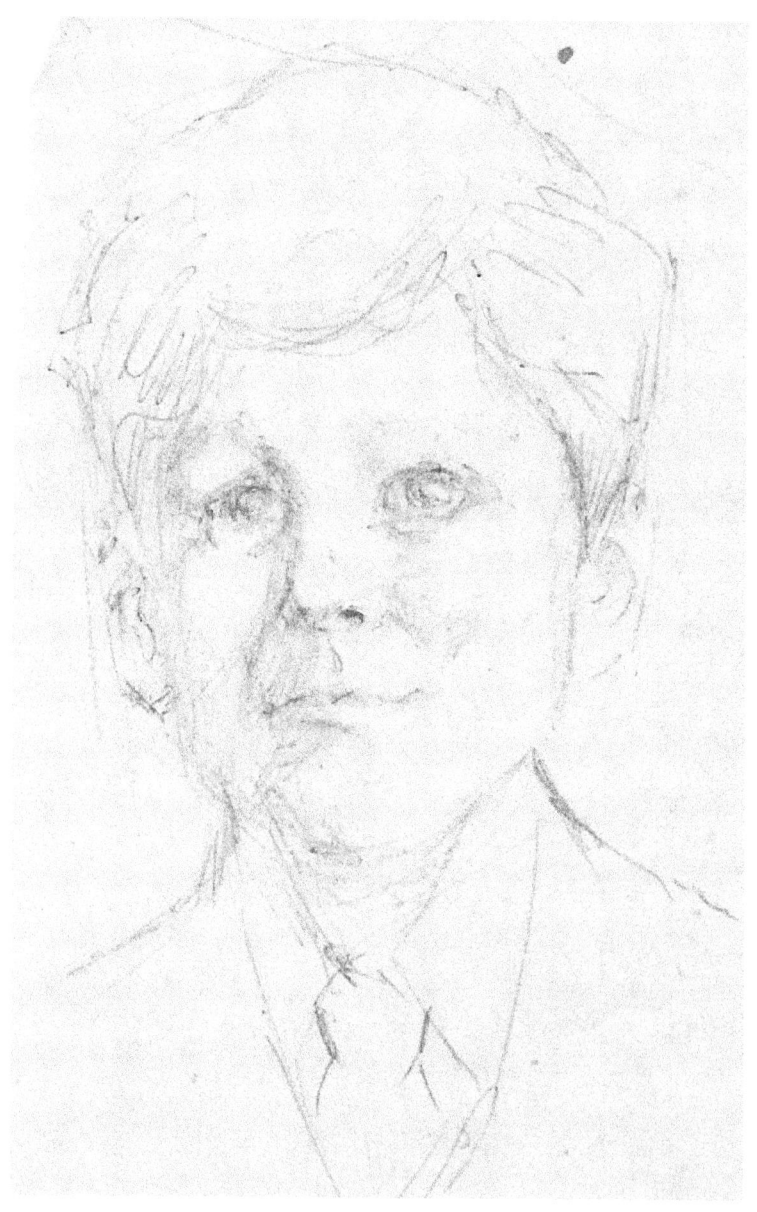

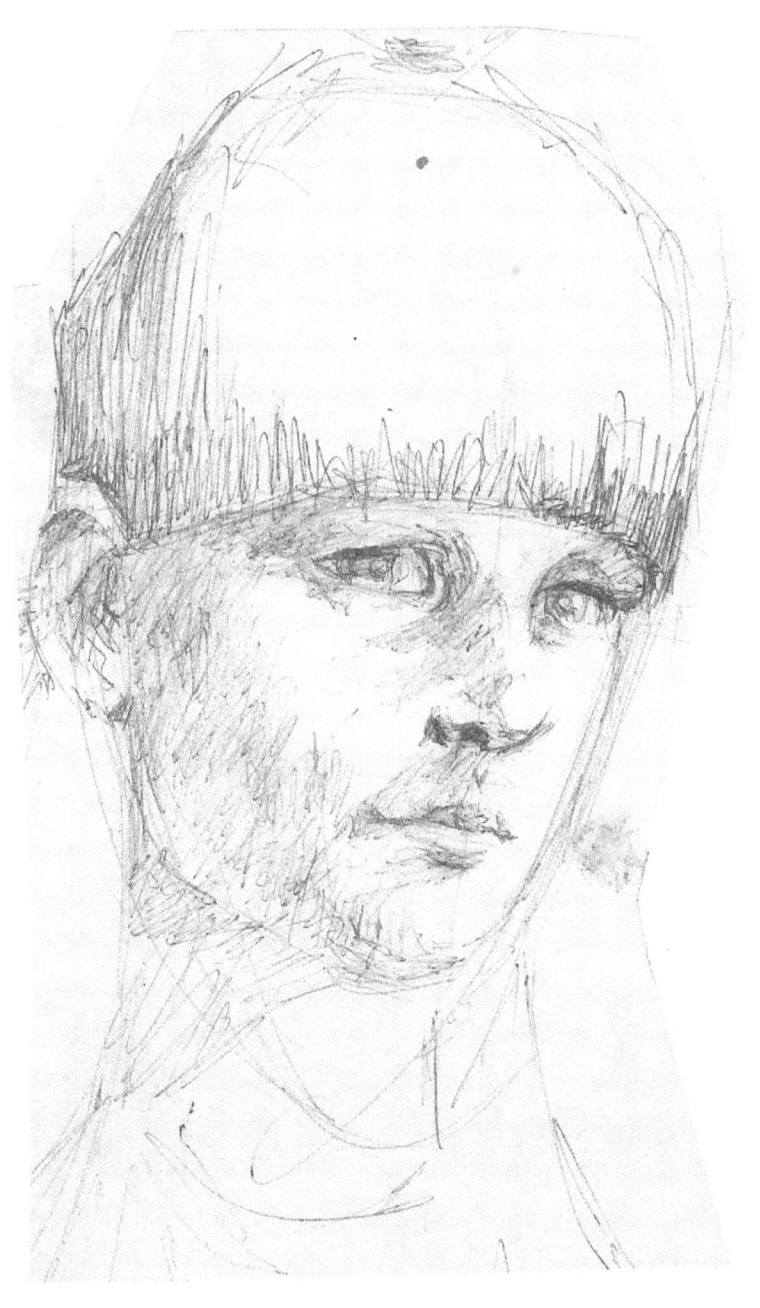

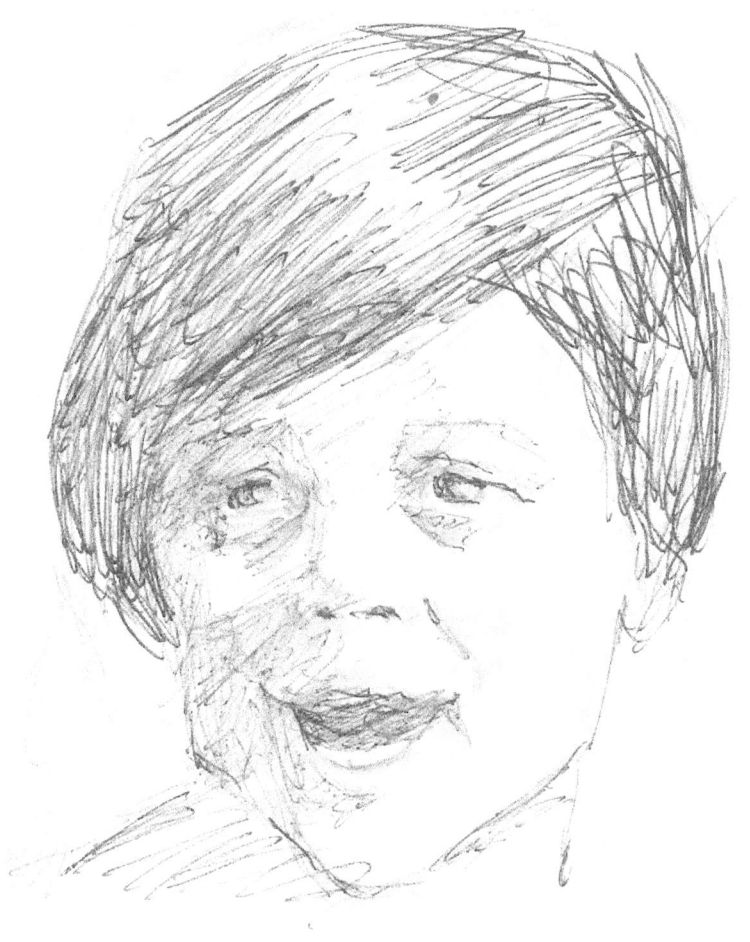

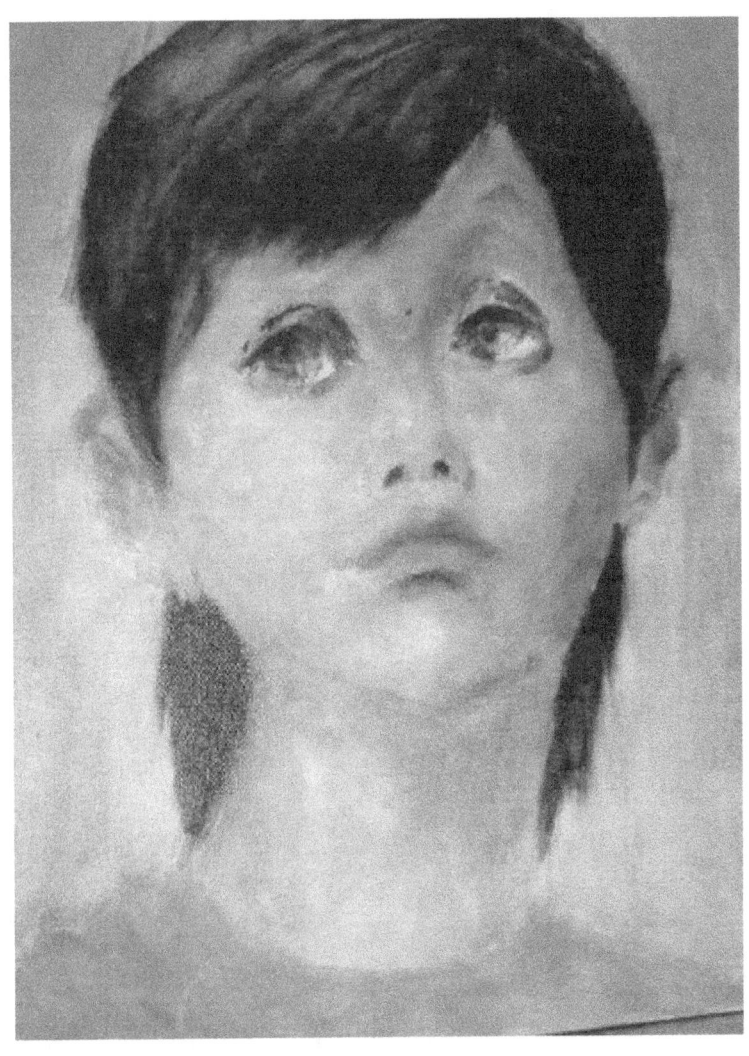

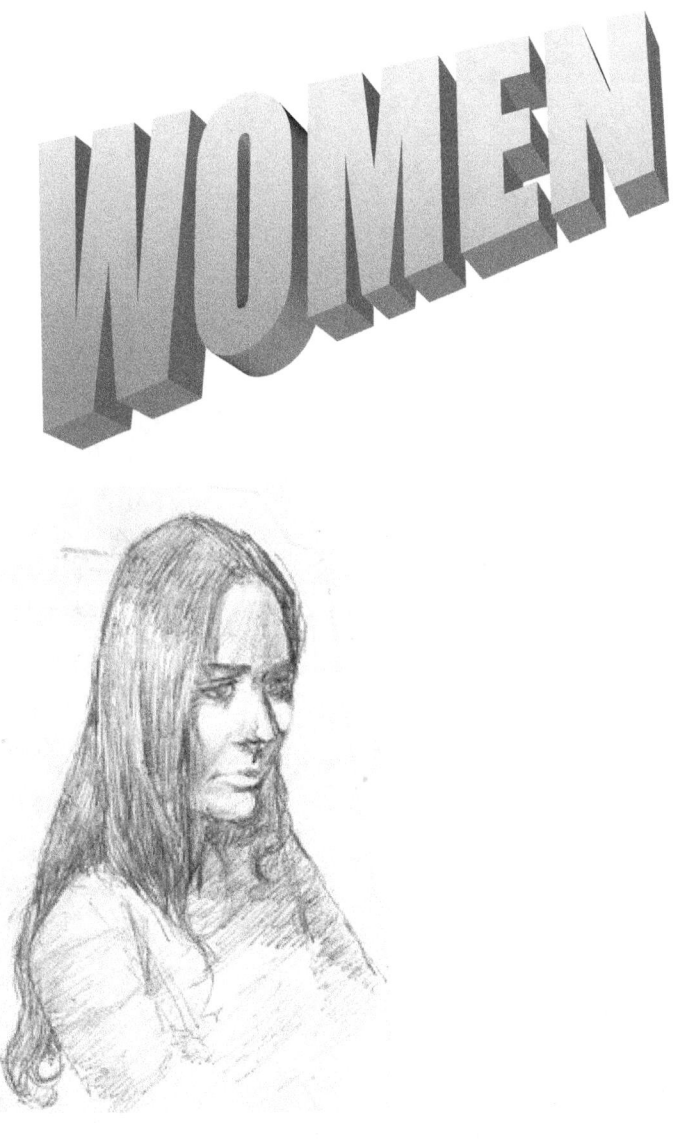

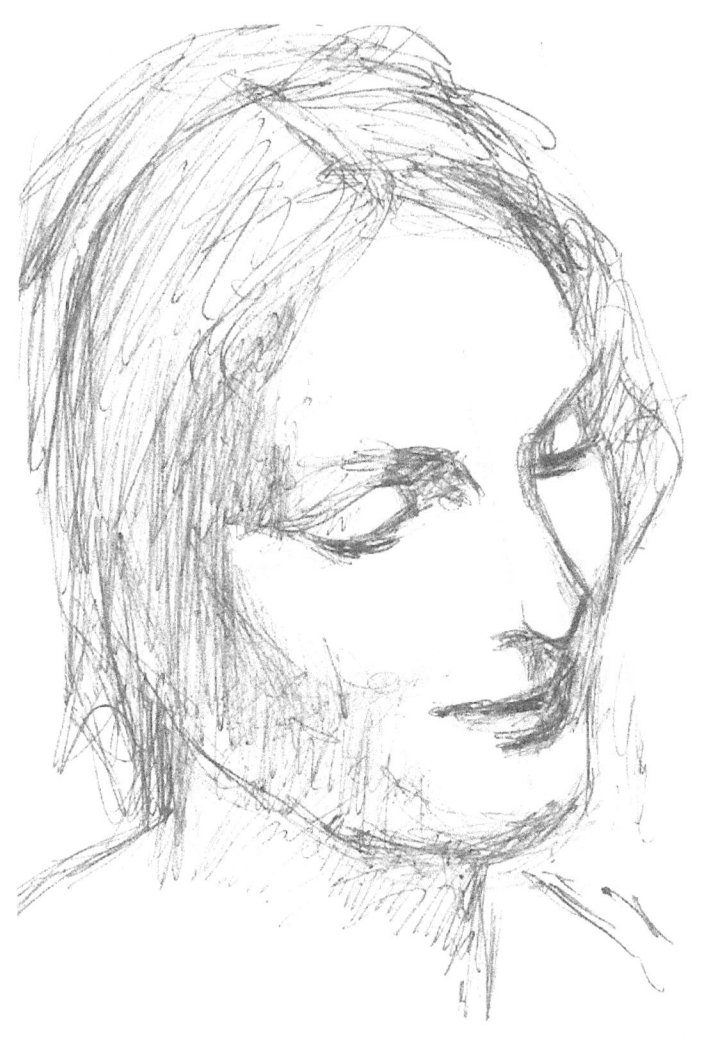

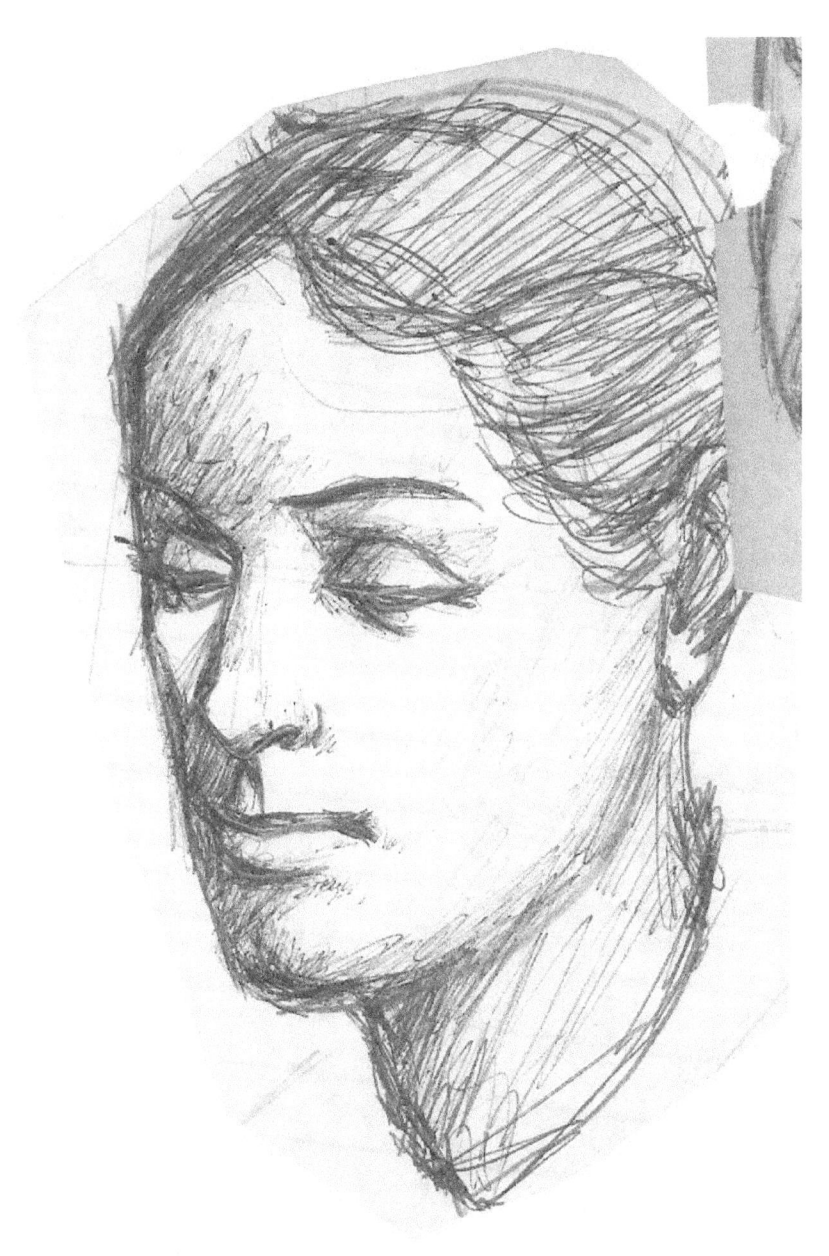

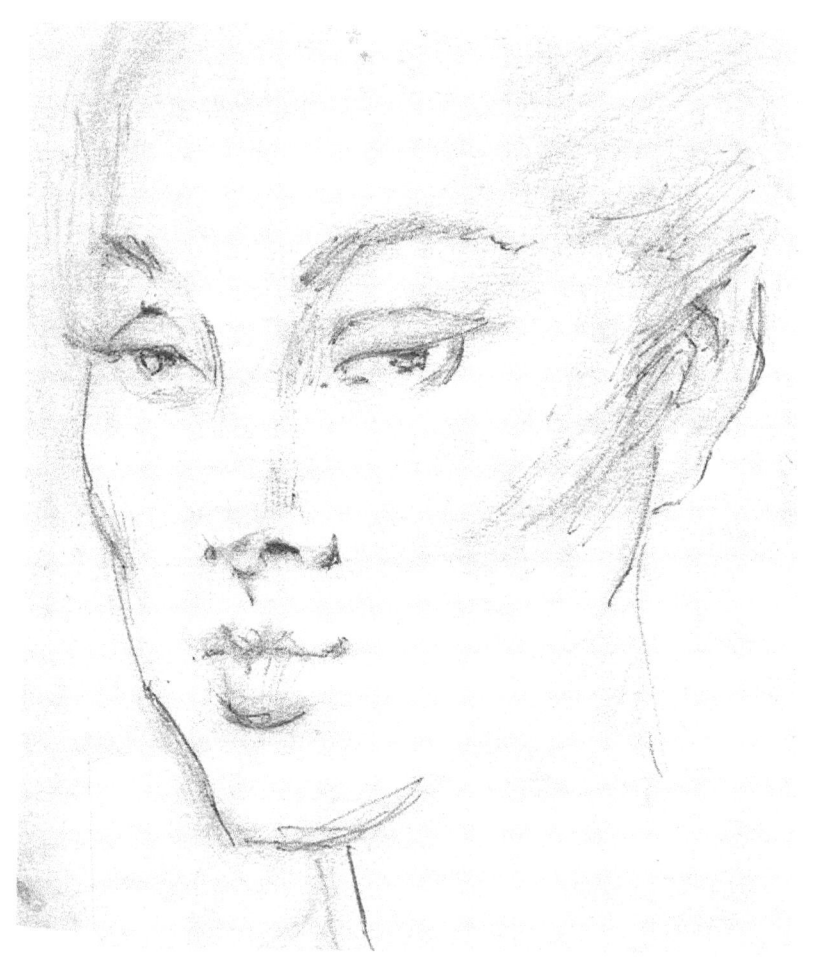

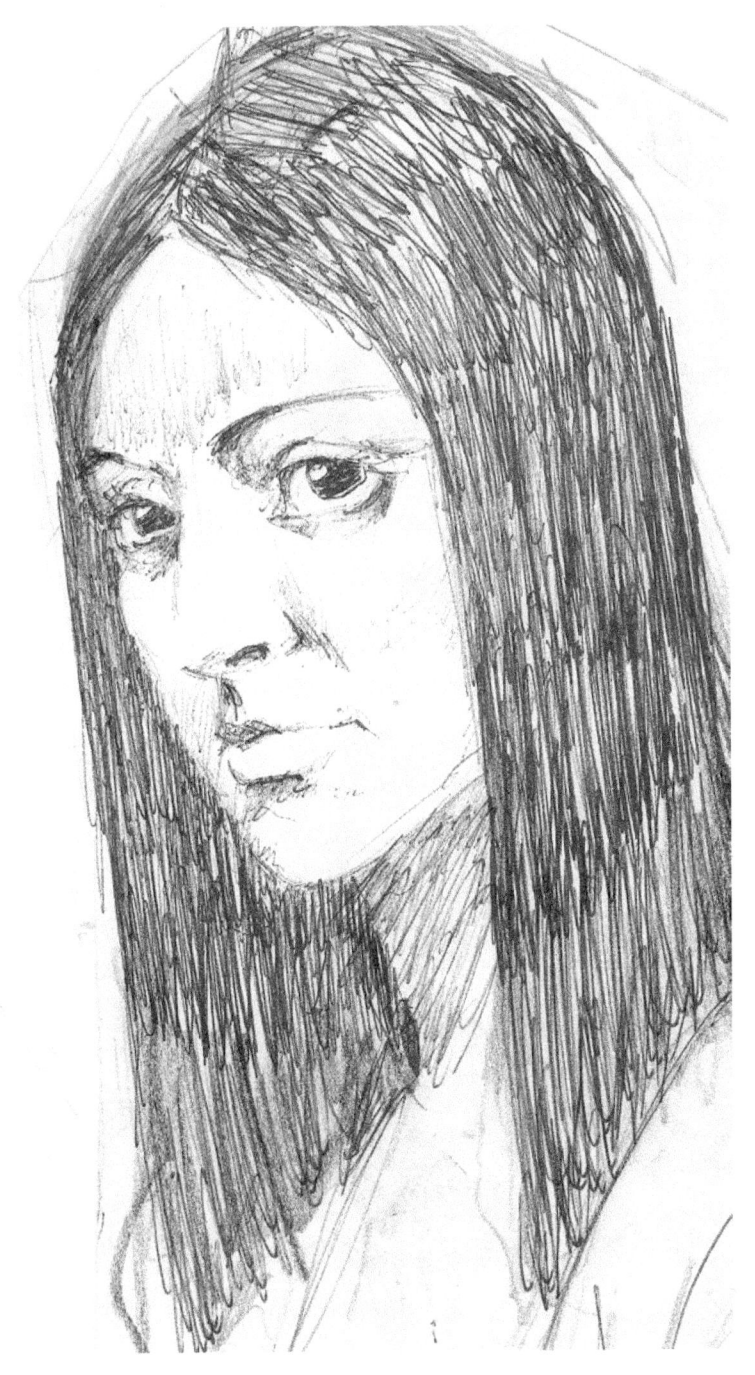

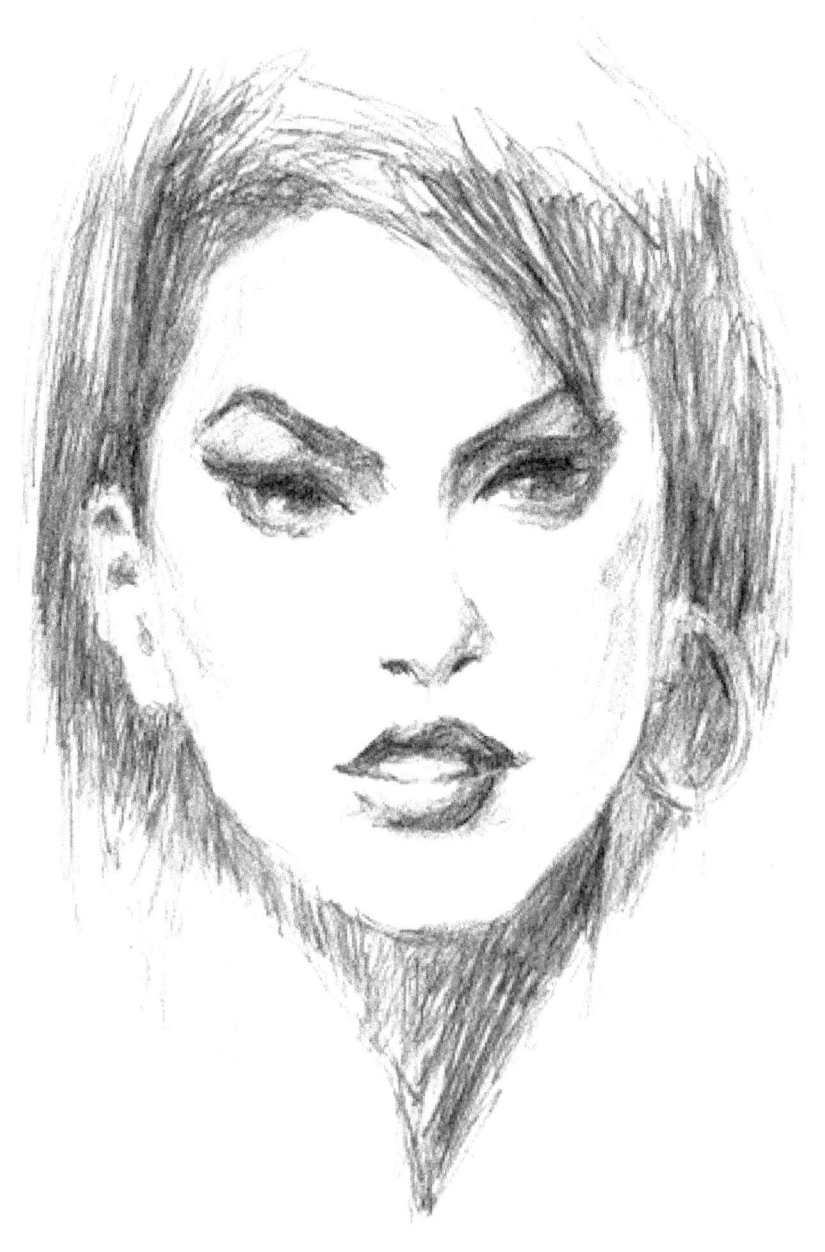

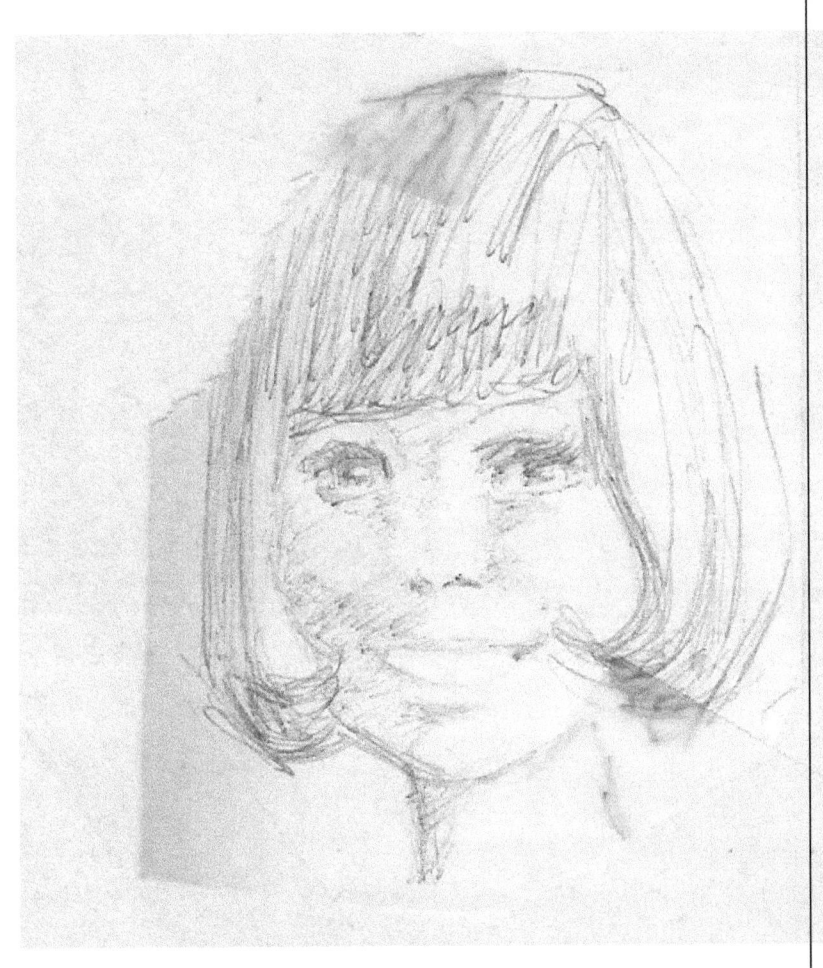

41

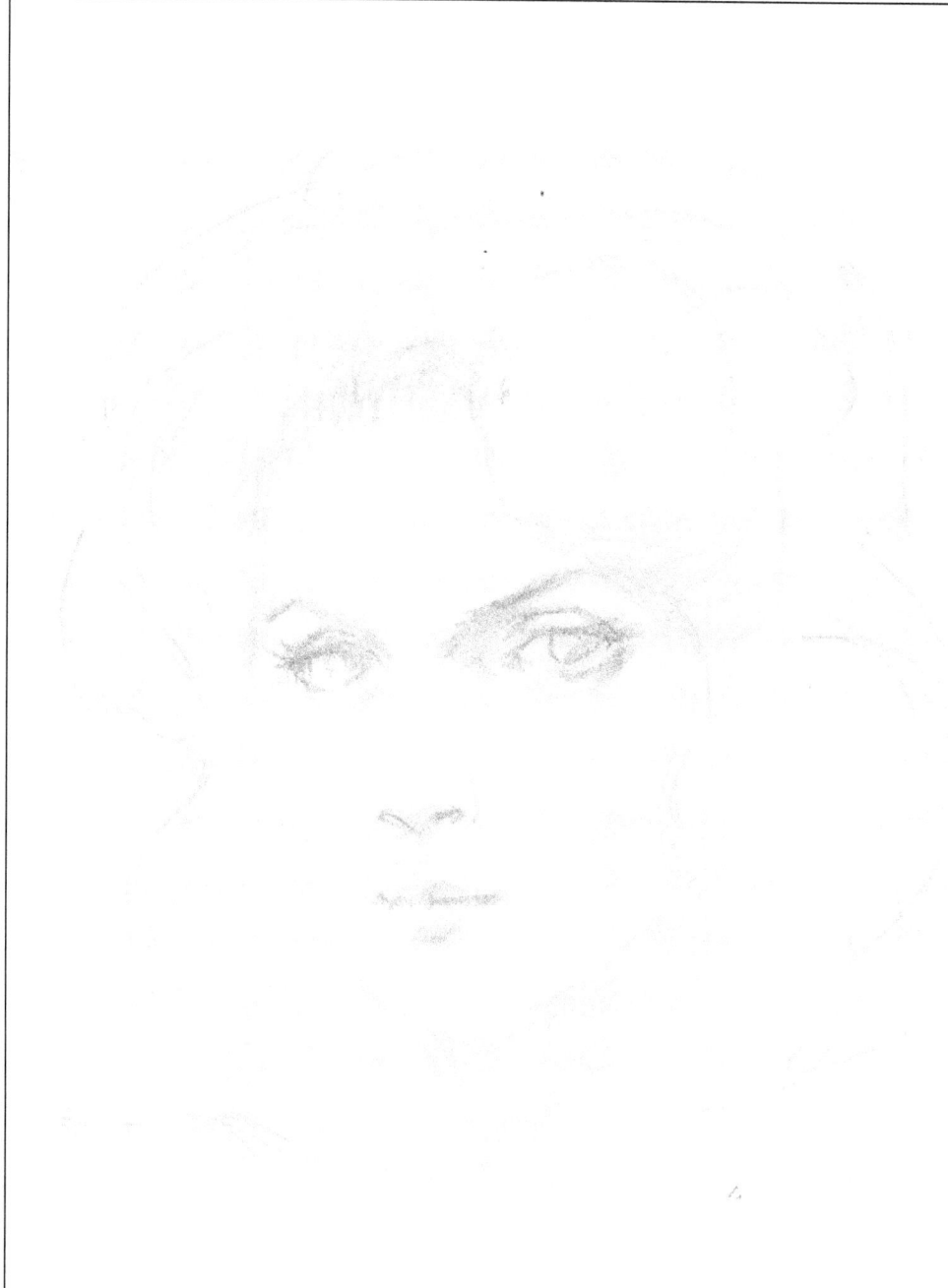

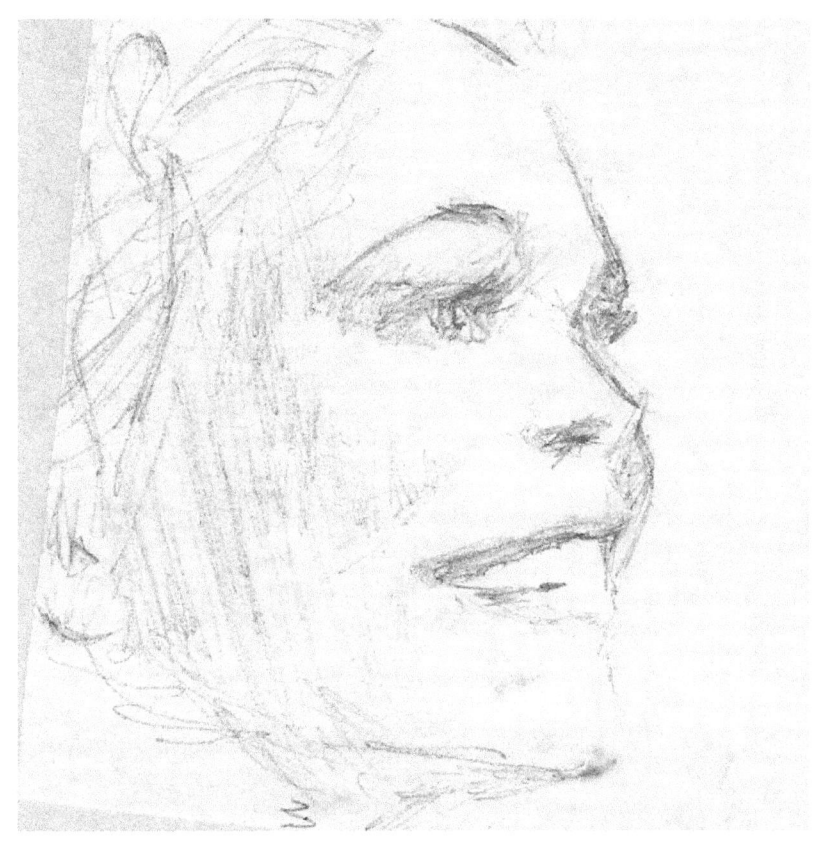

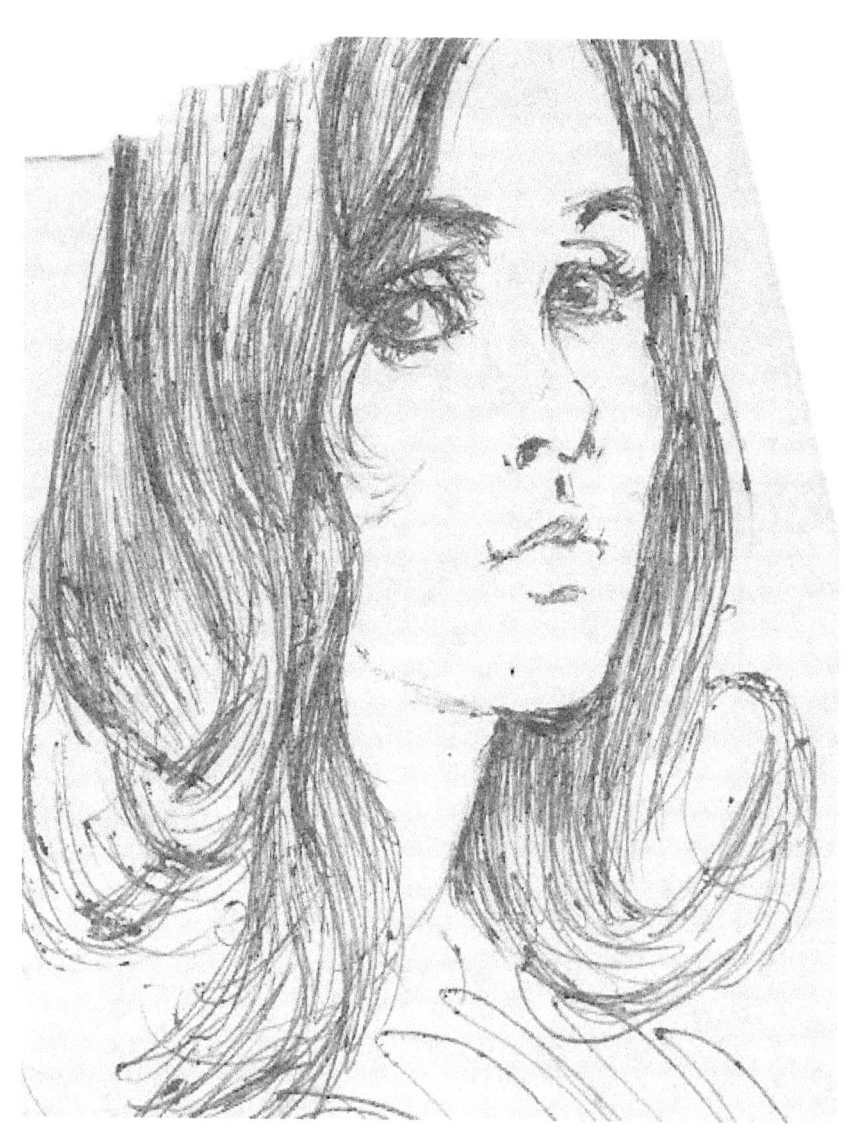

44

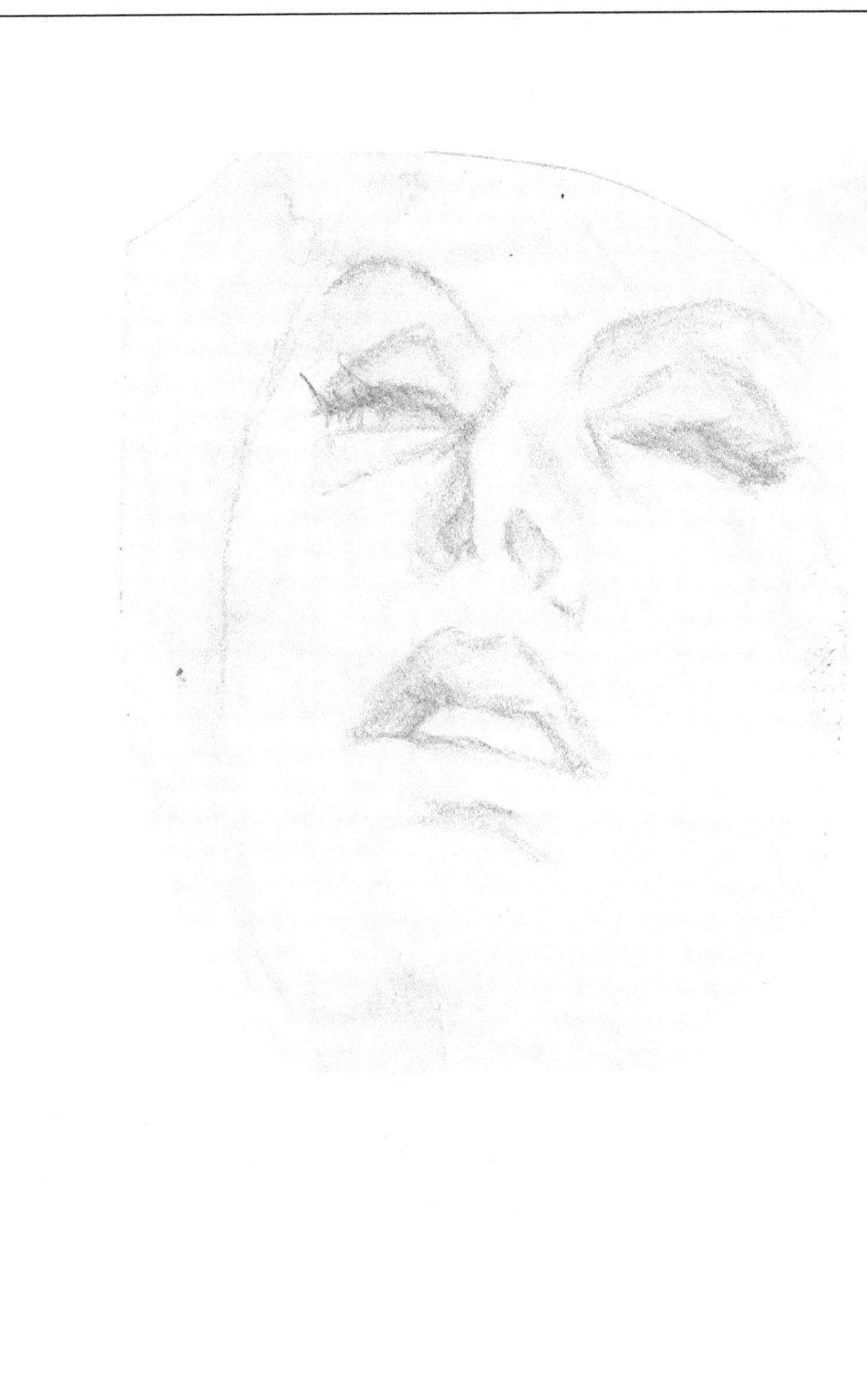

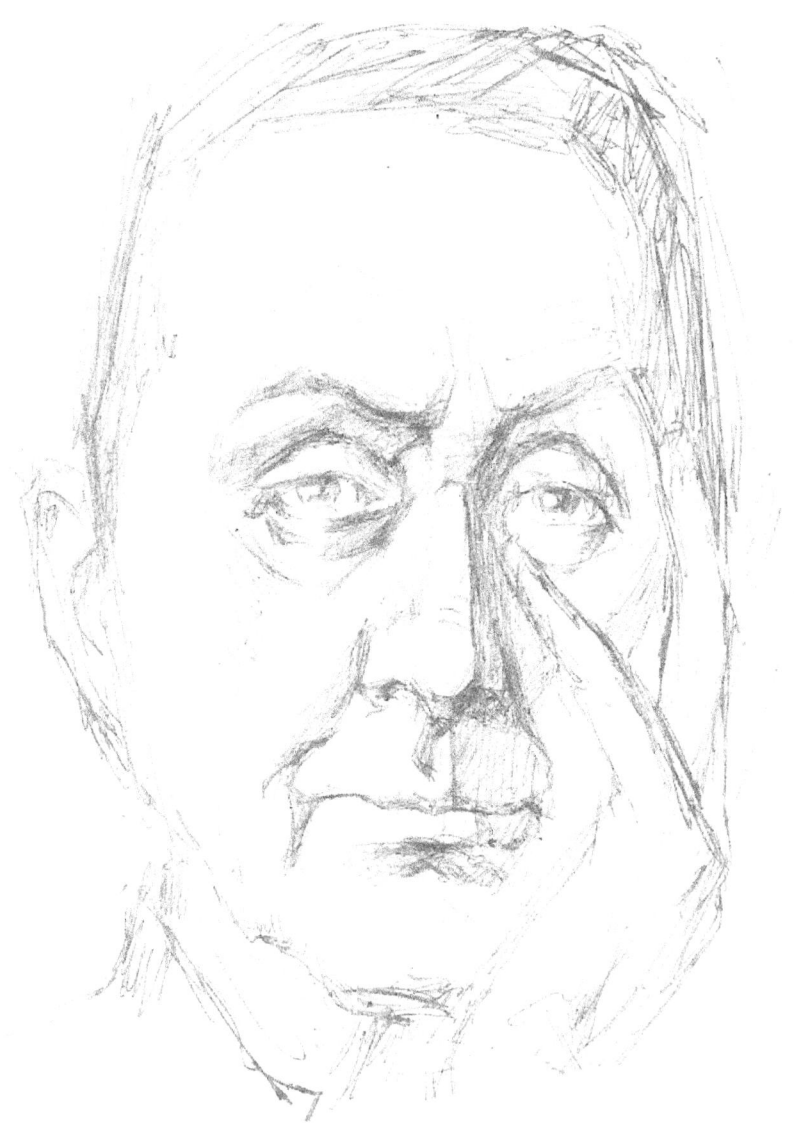

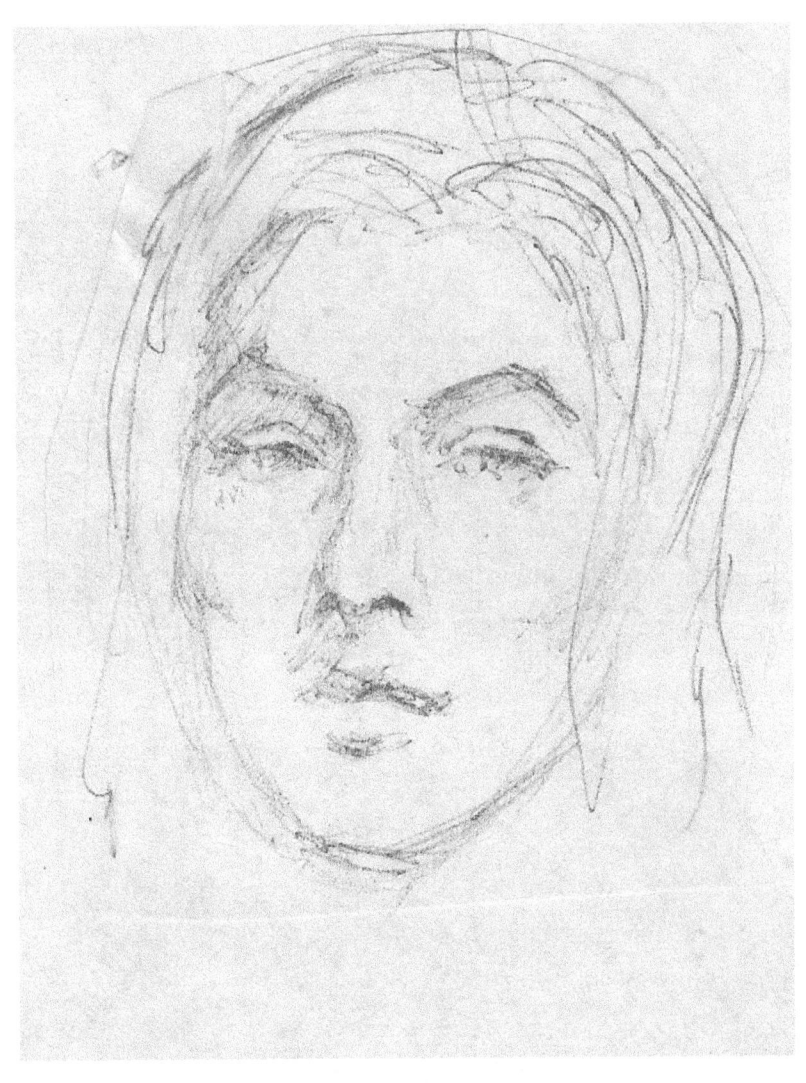

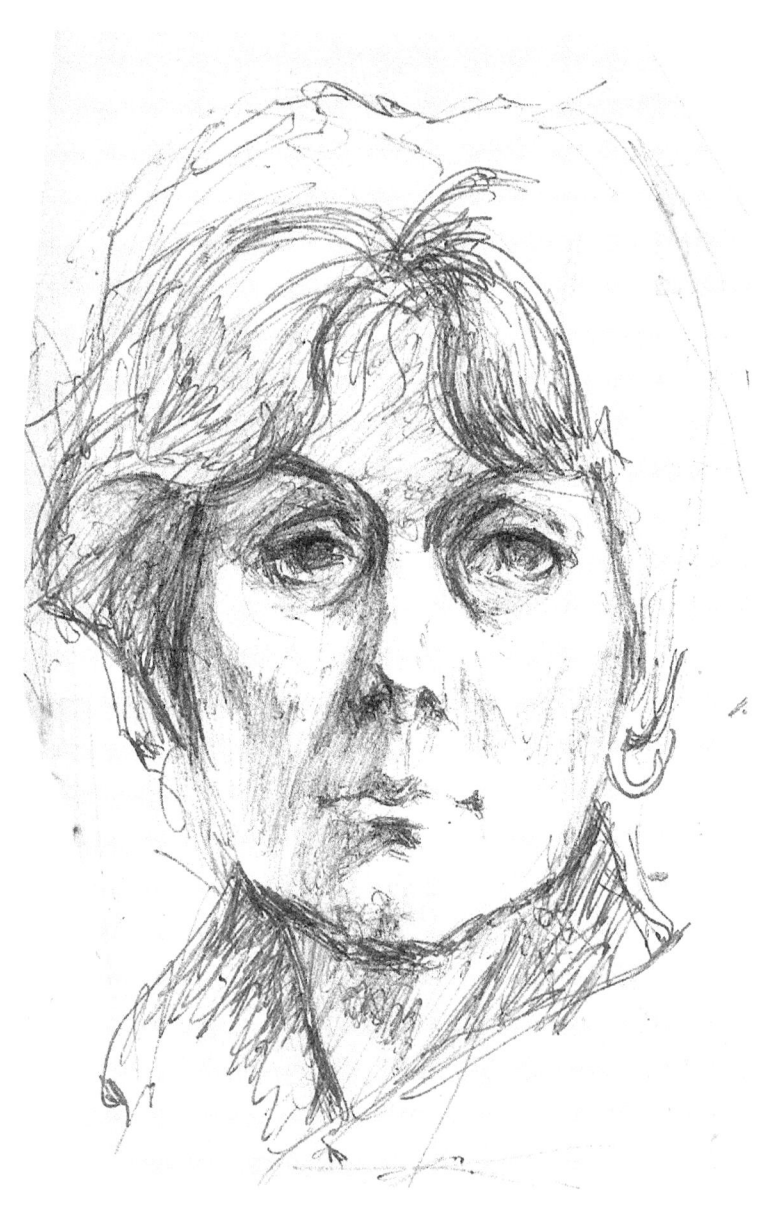

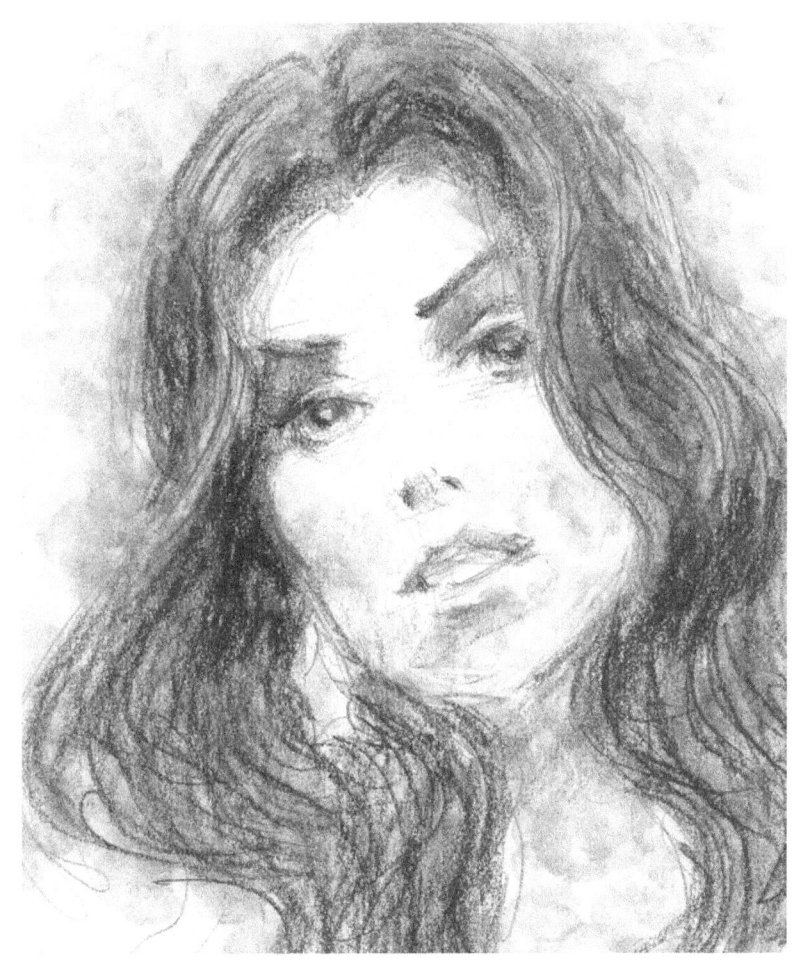

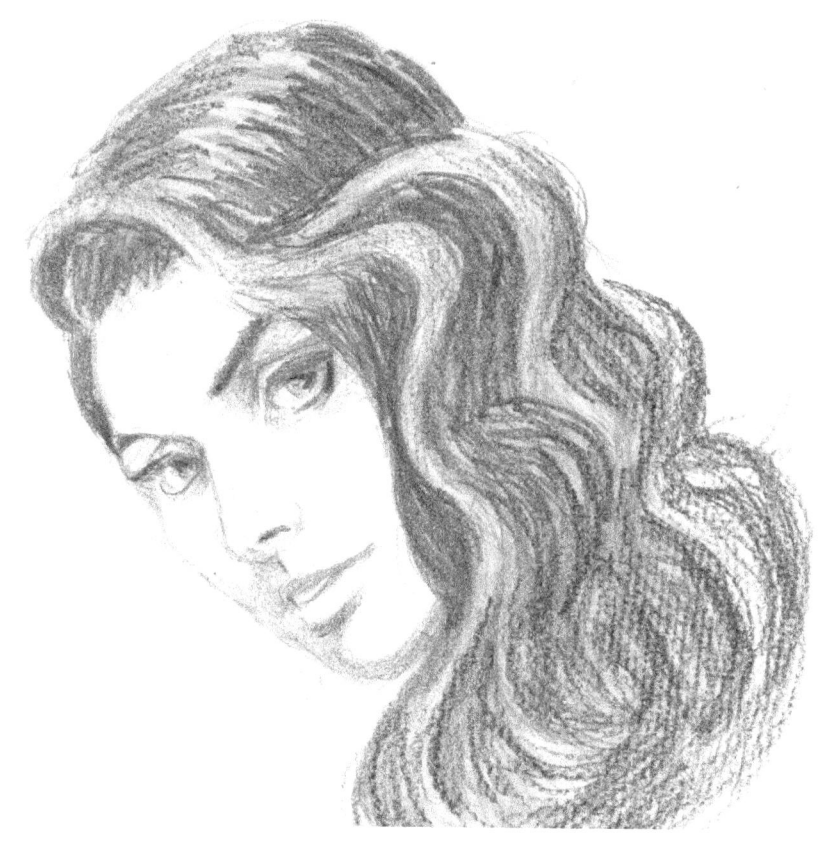

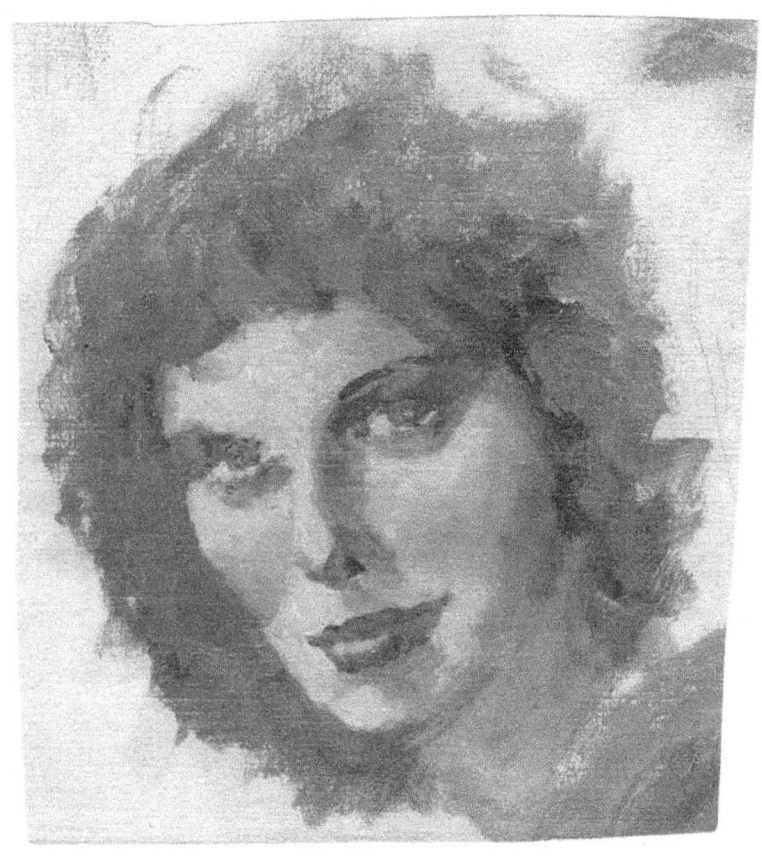

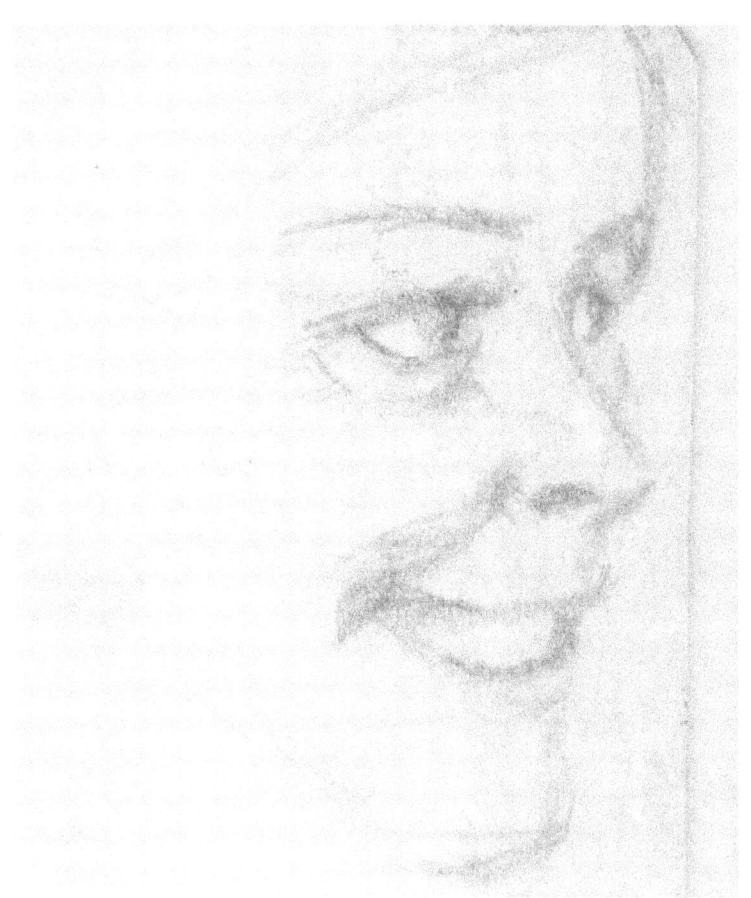

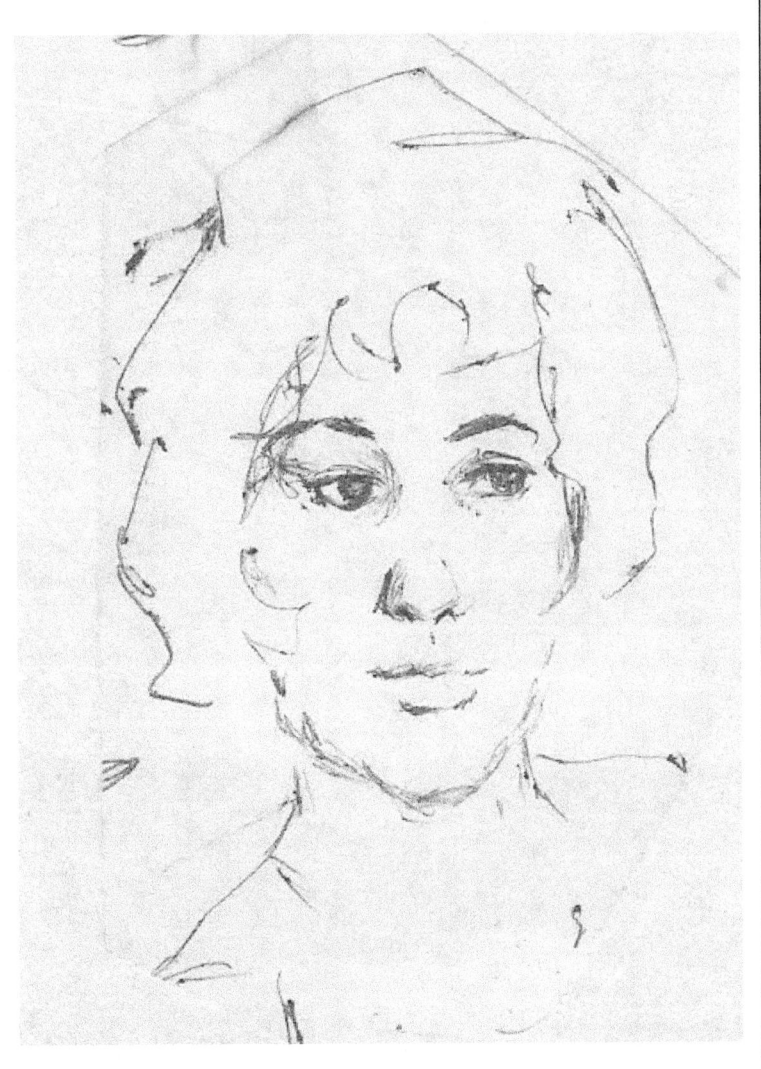

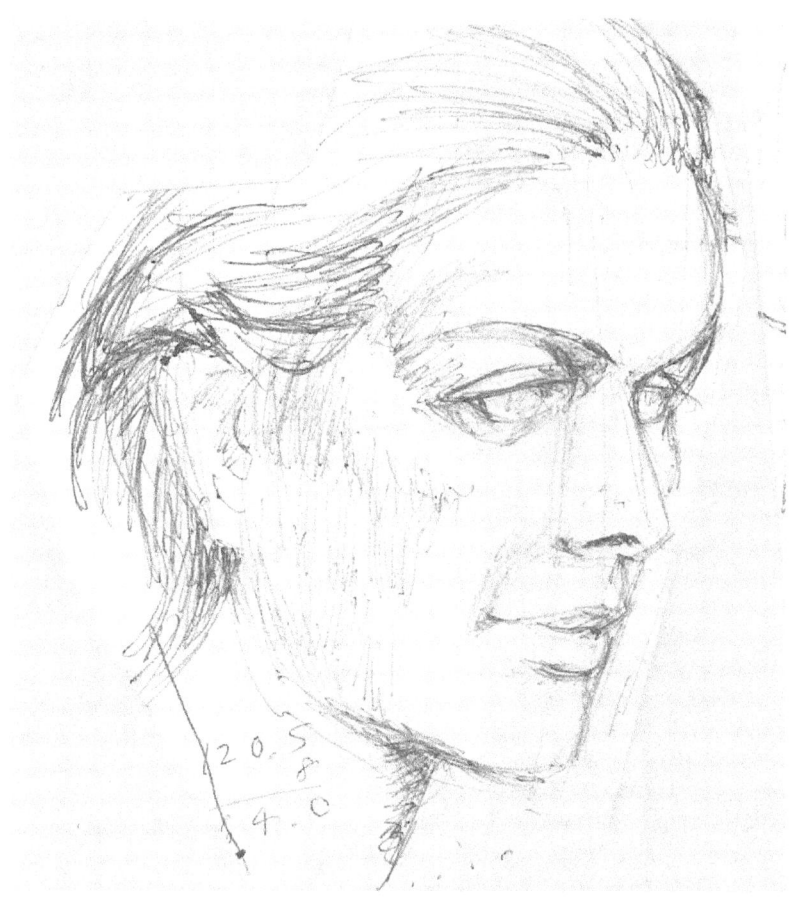

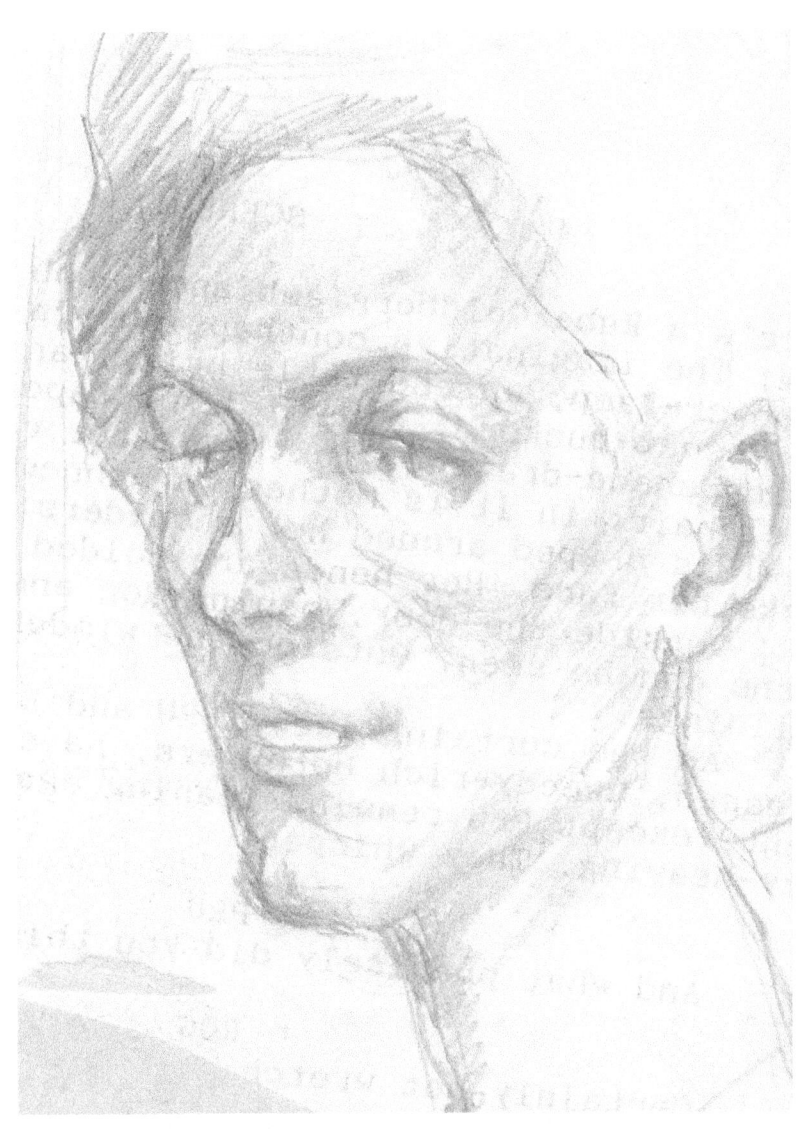

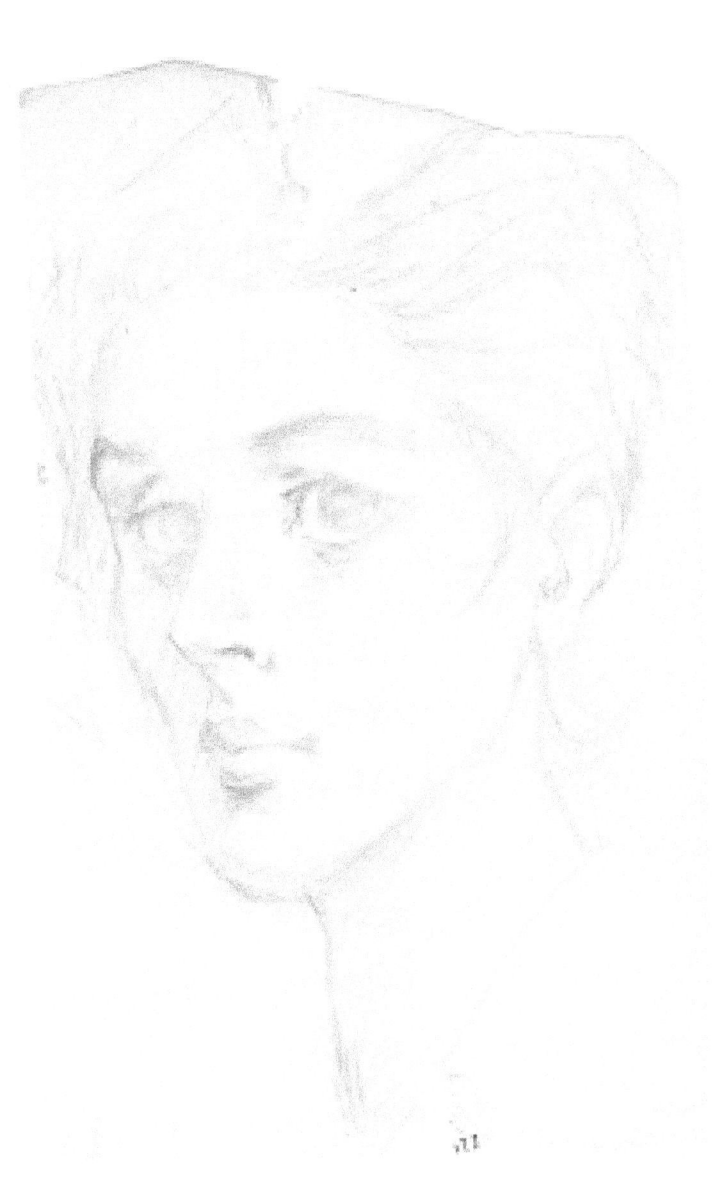

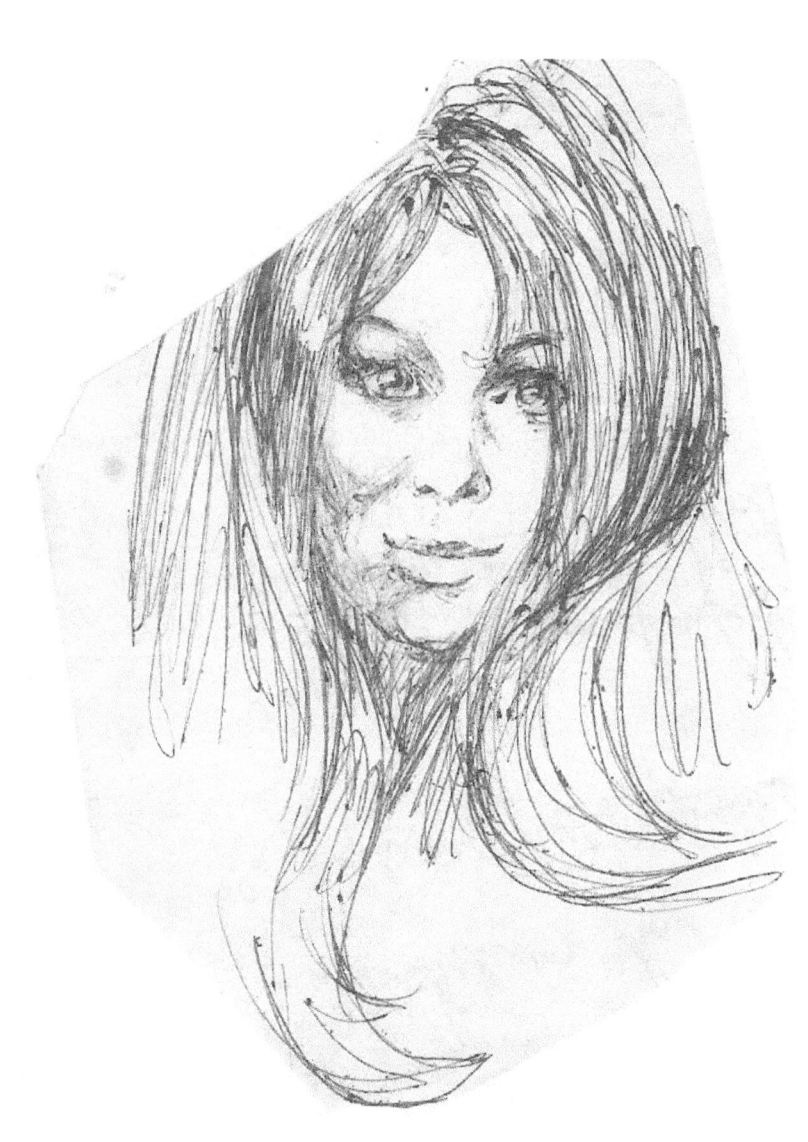

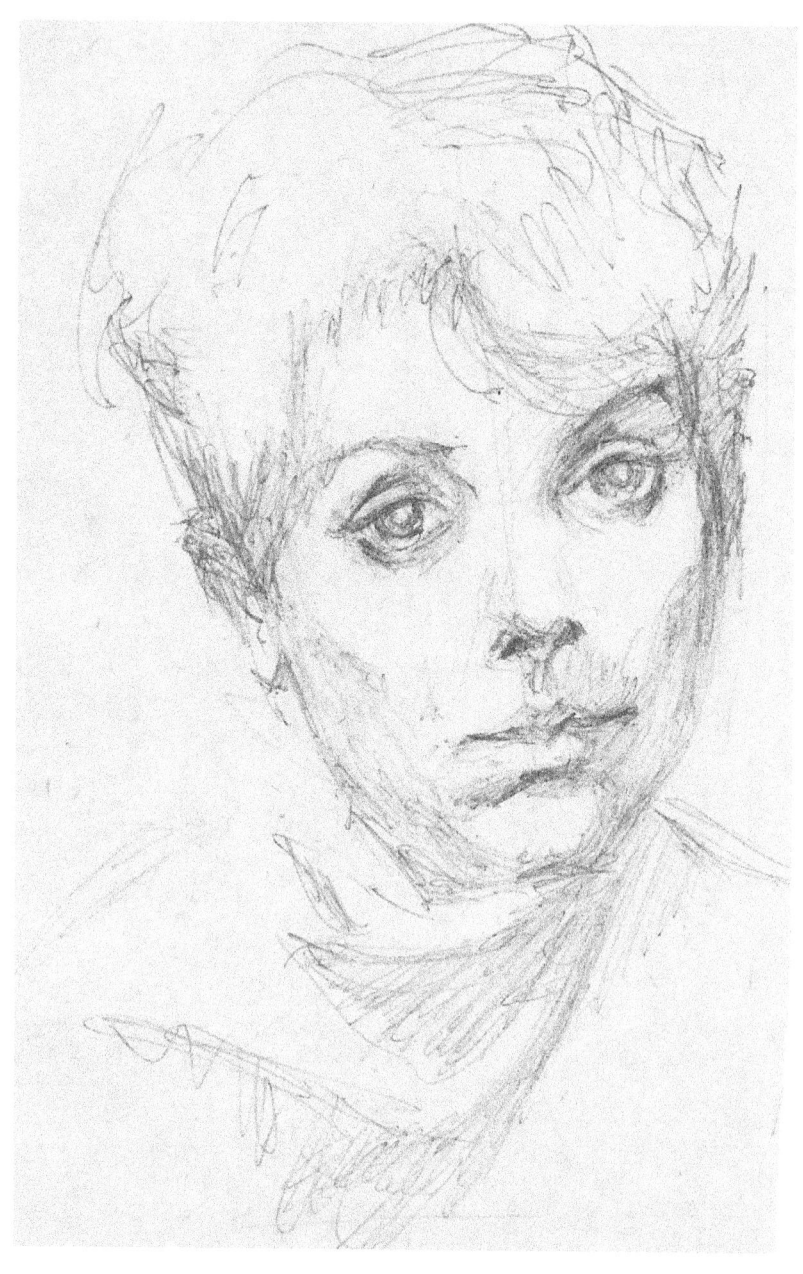

58

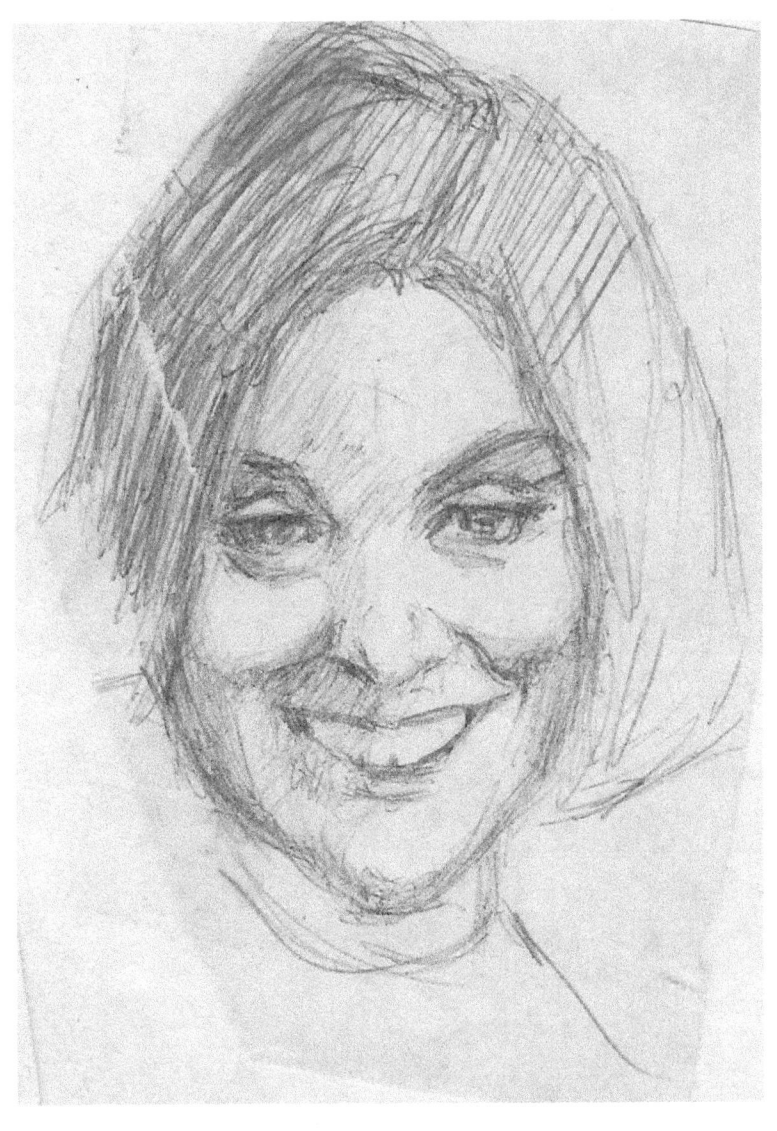

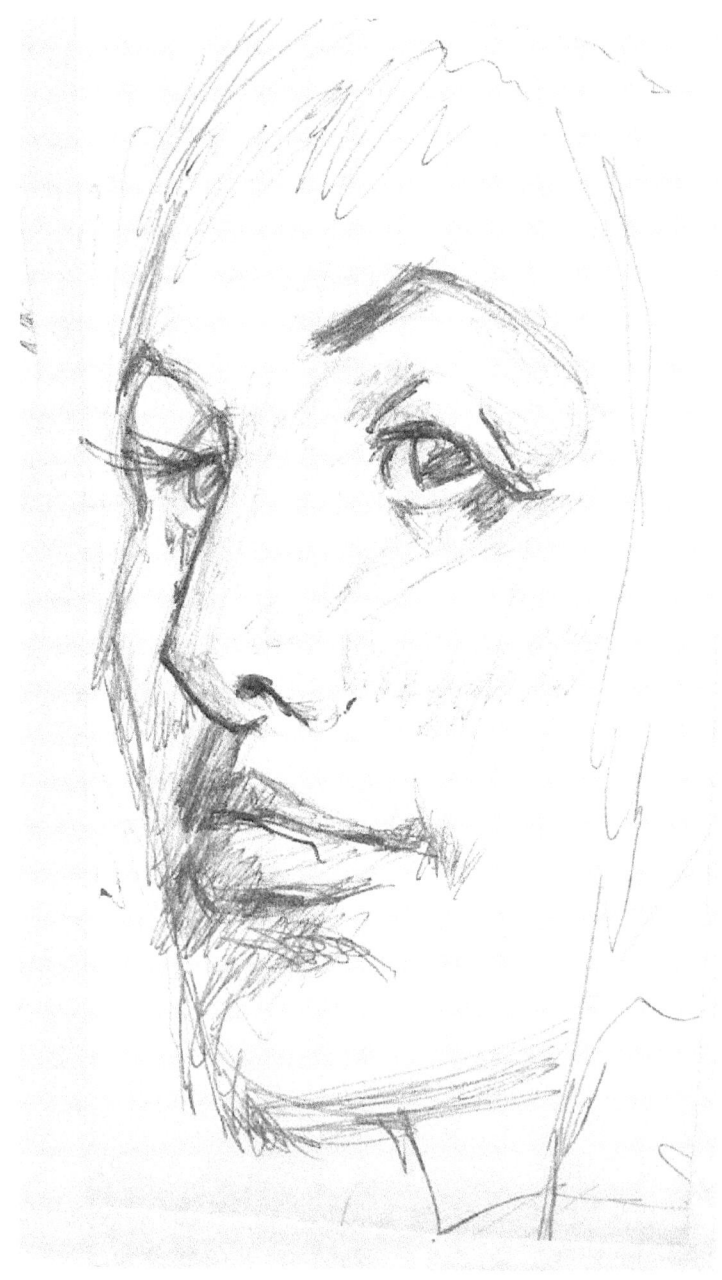

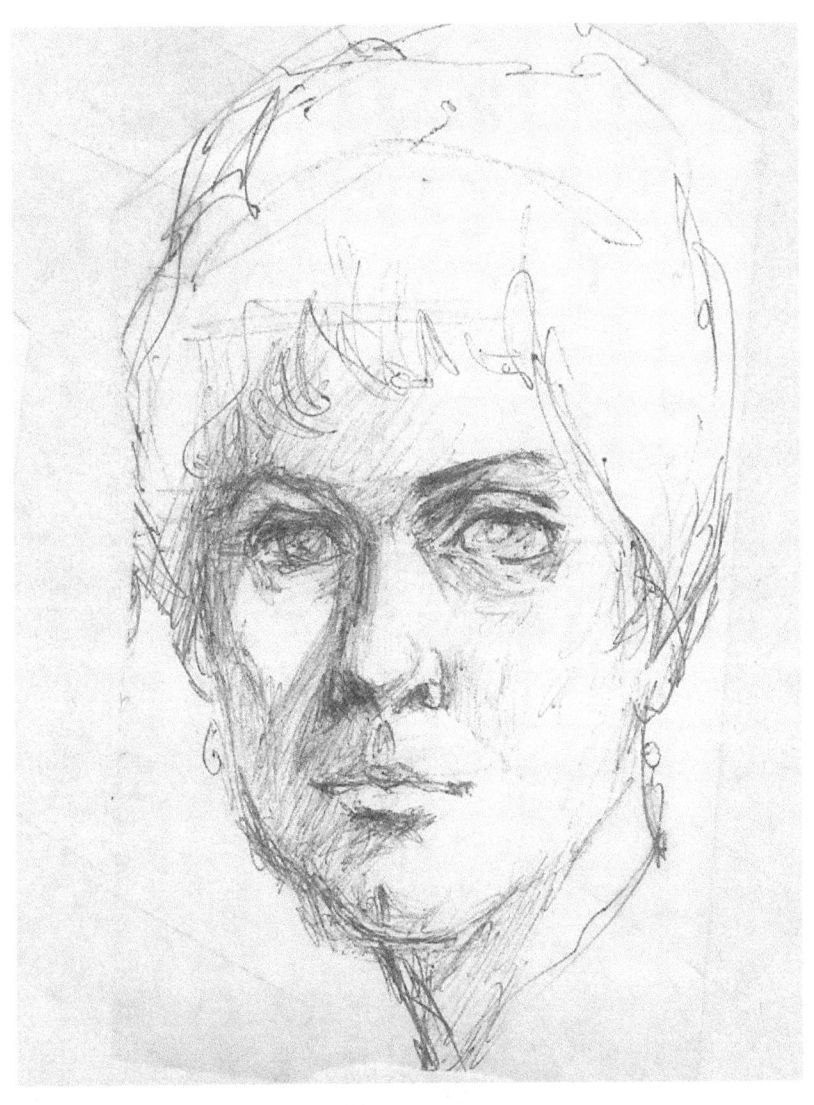

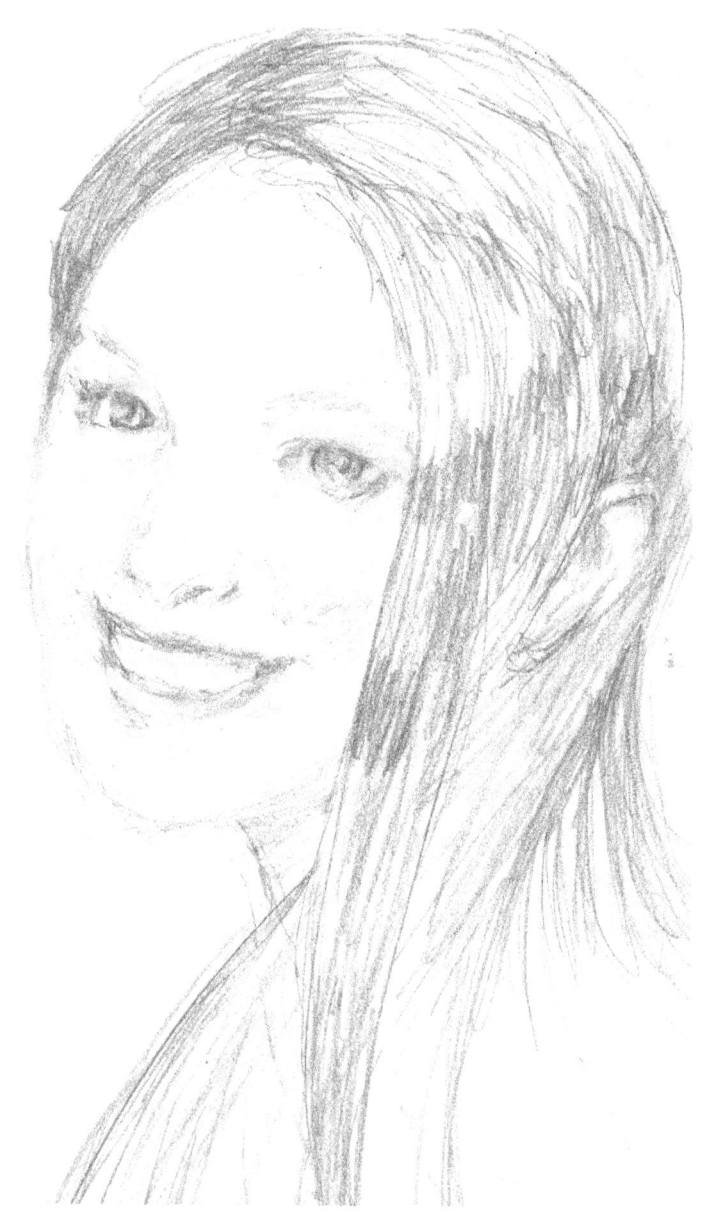

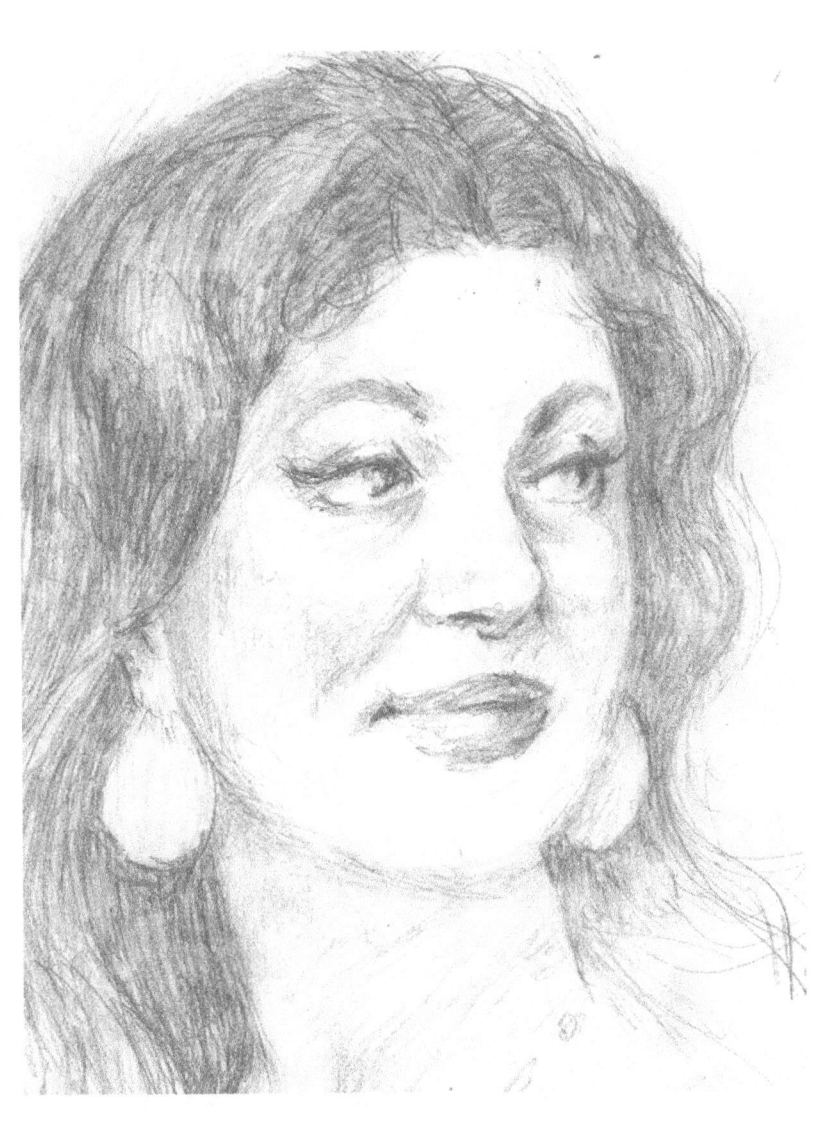

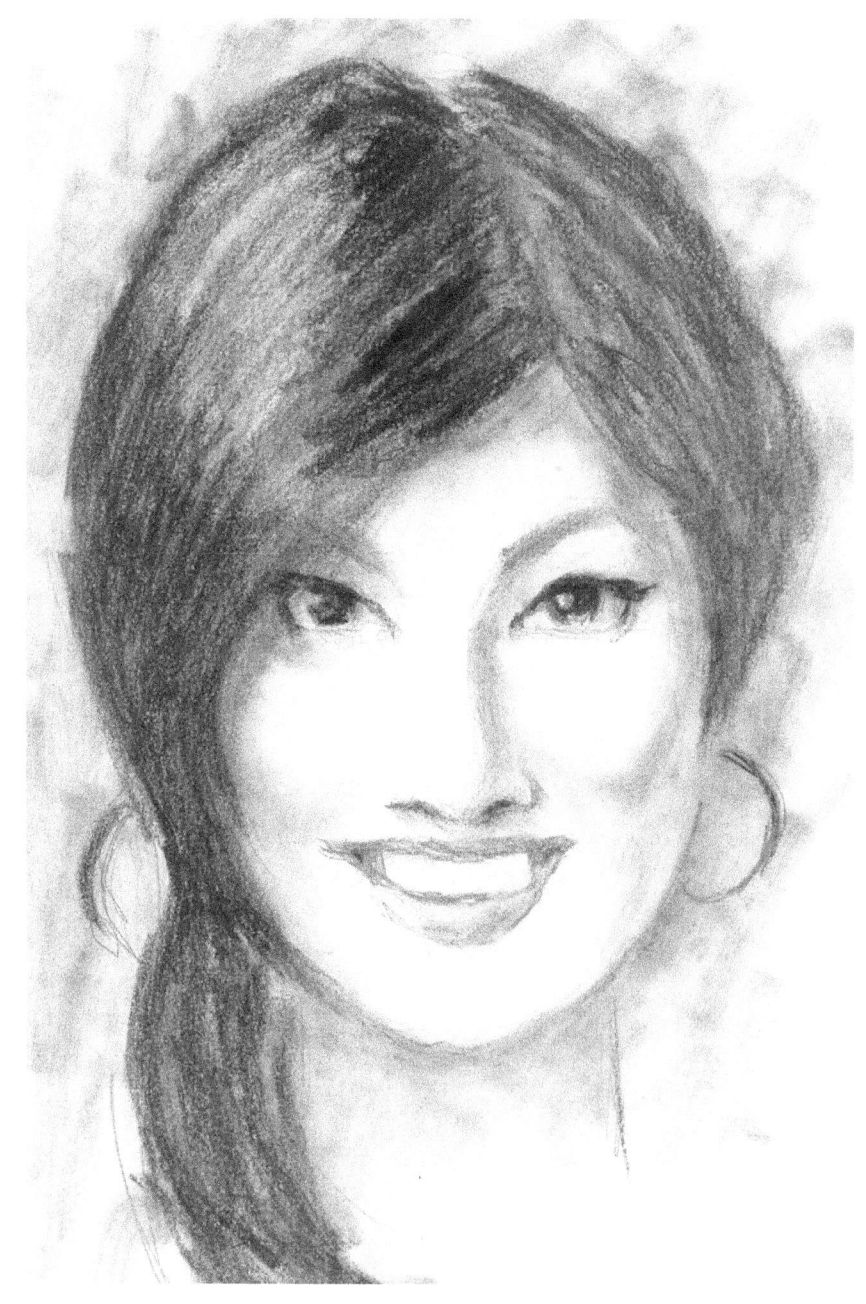

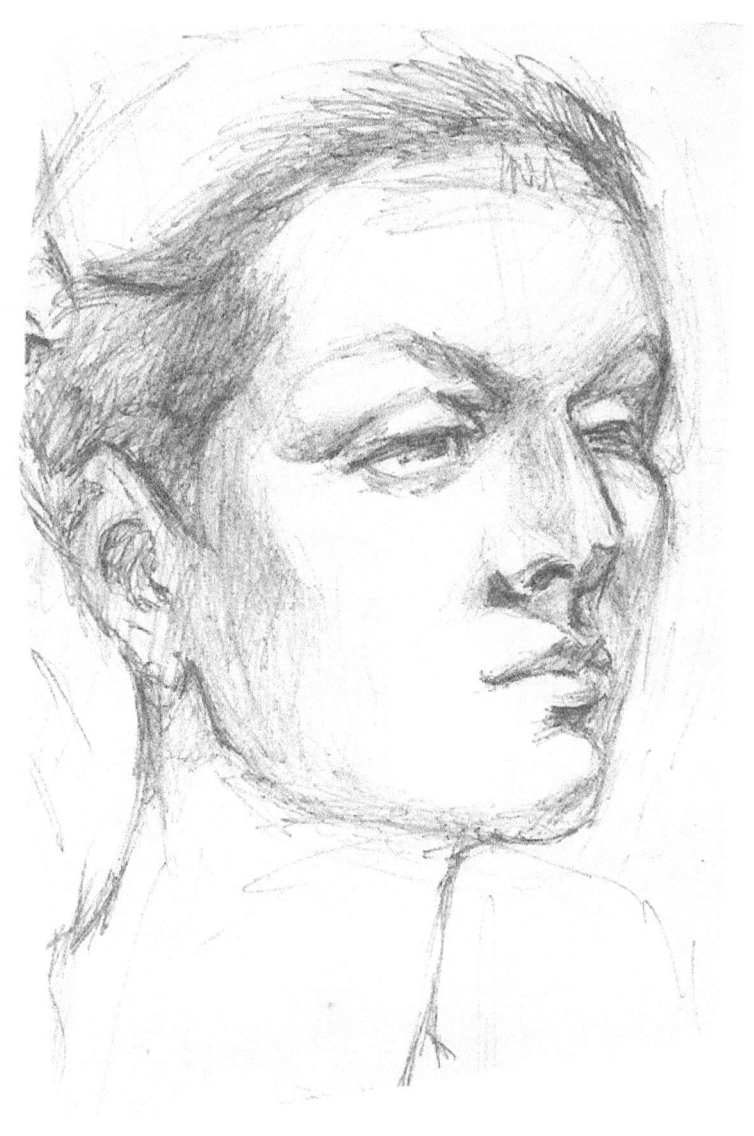

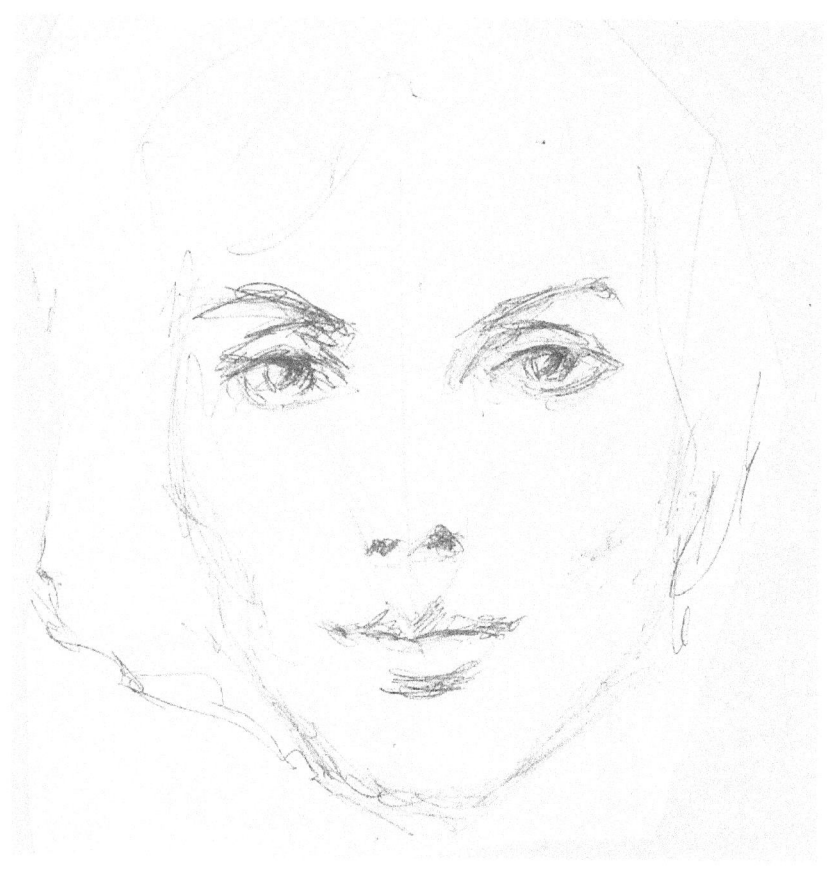

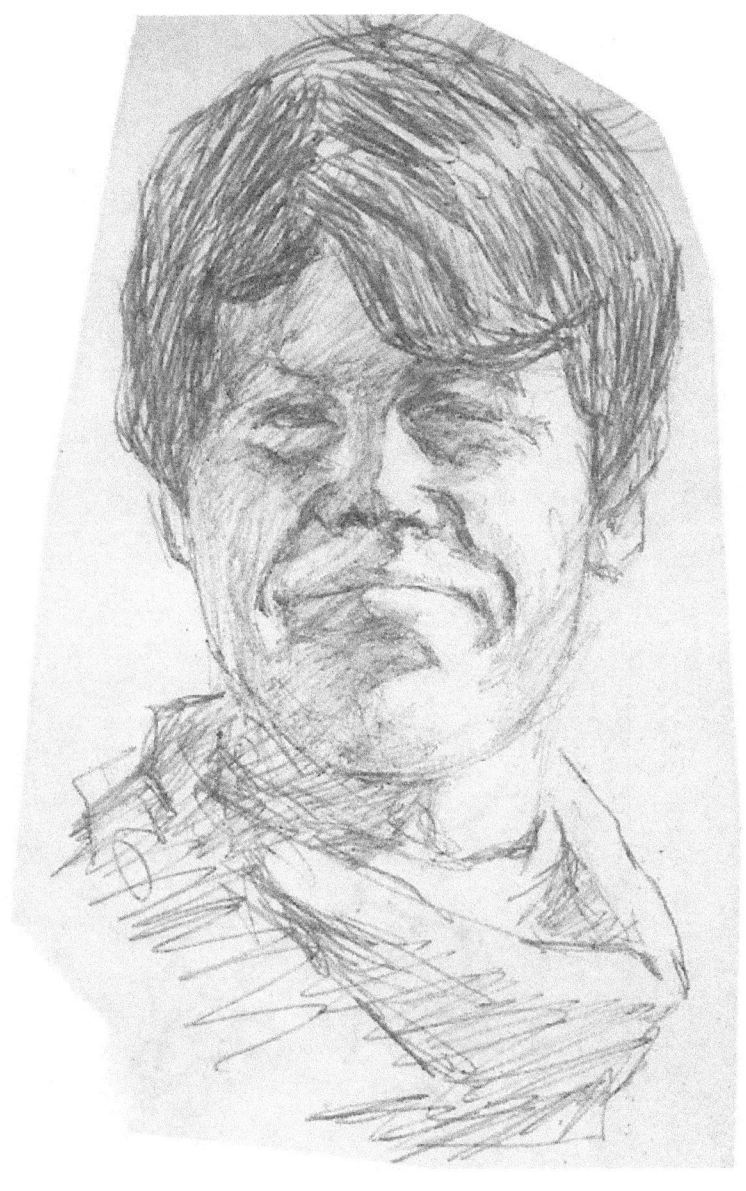

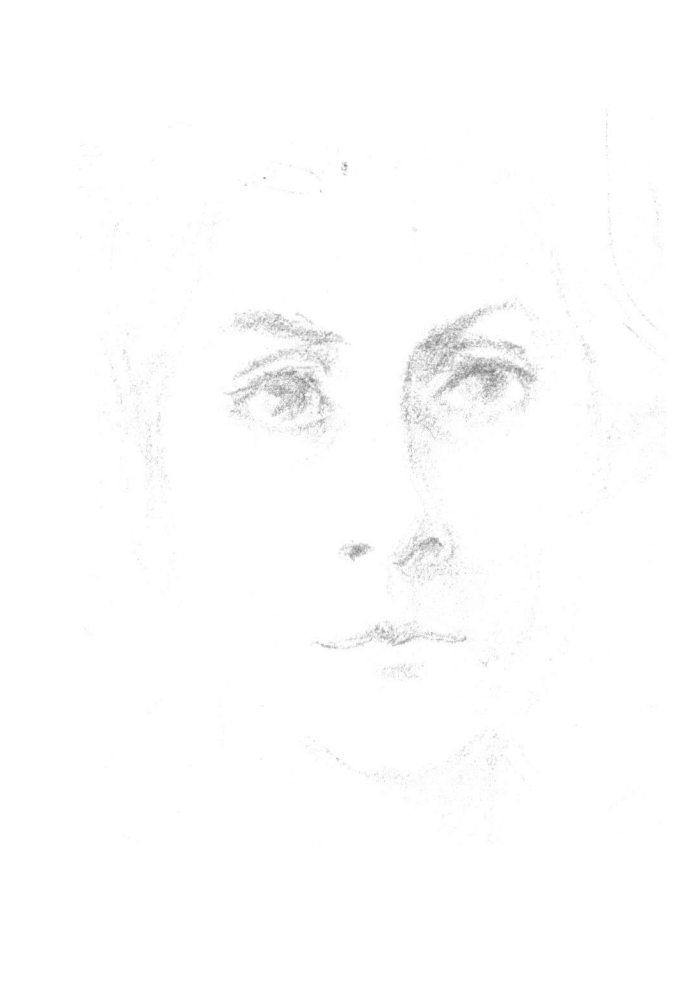

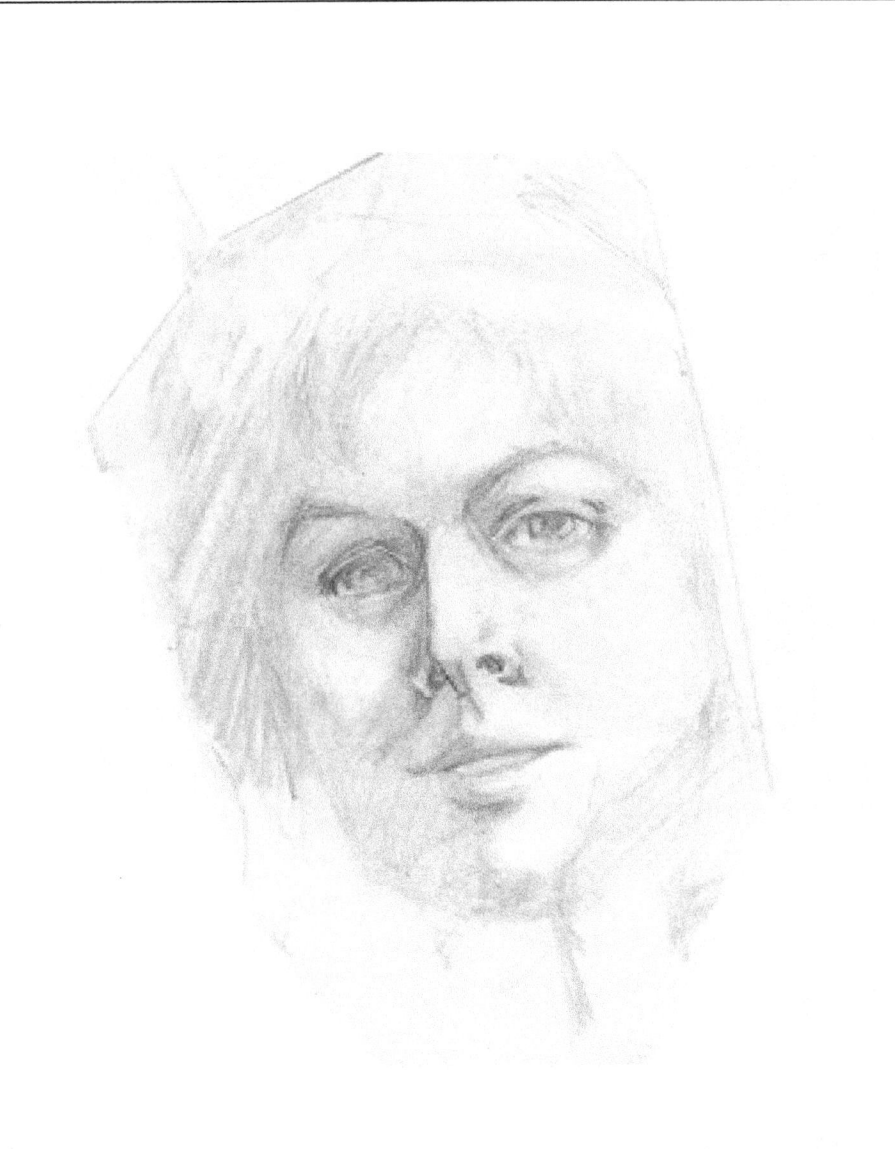

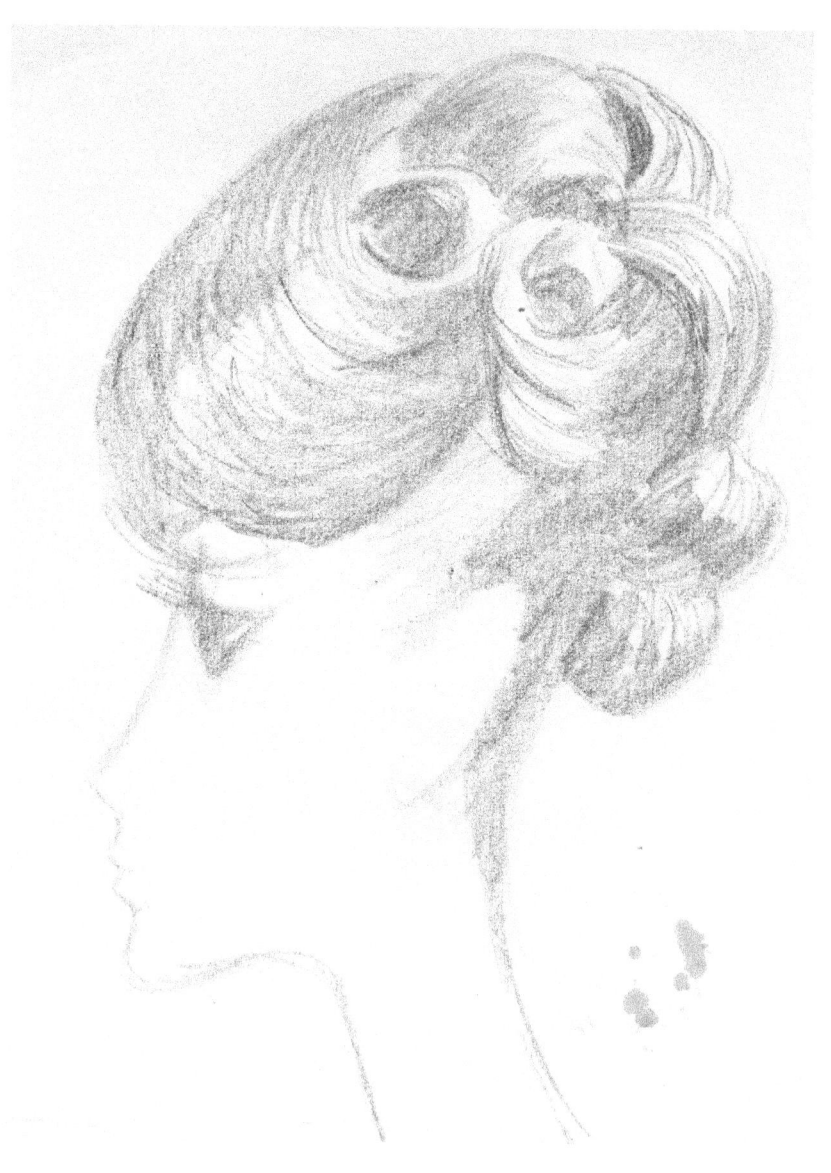

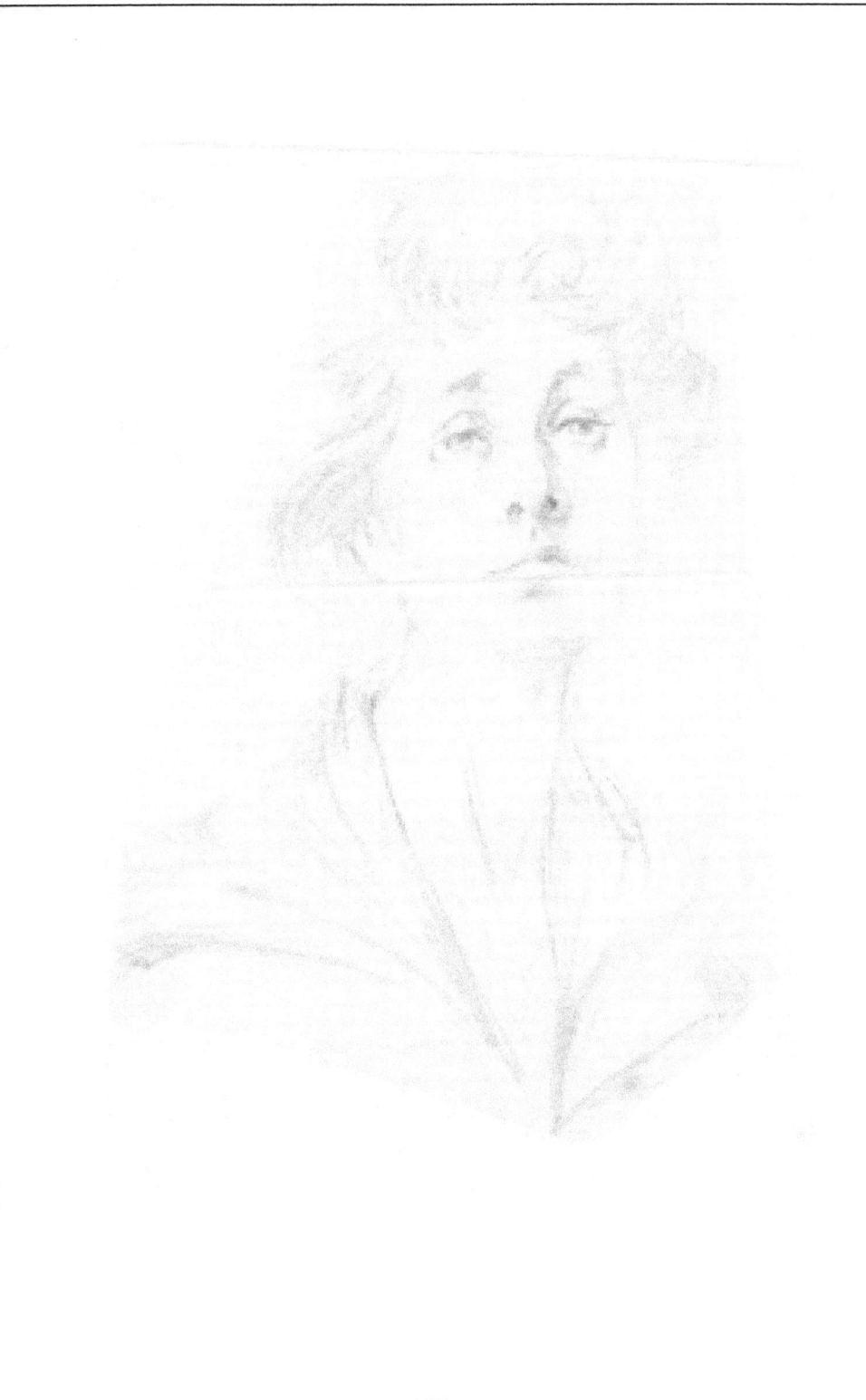

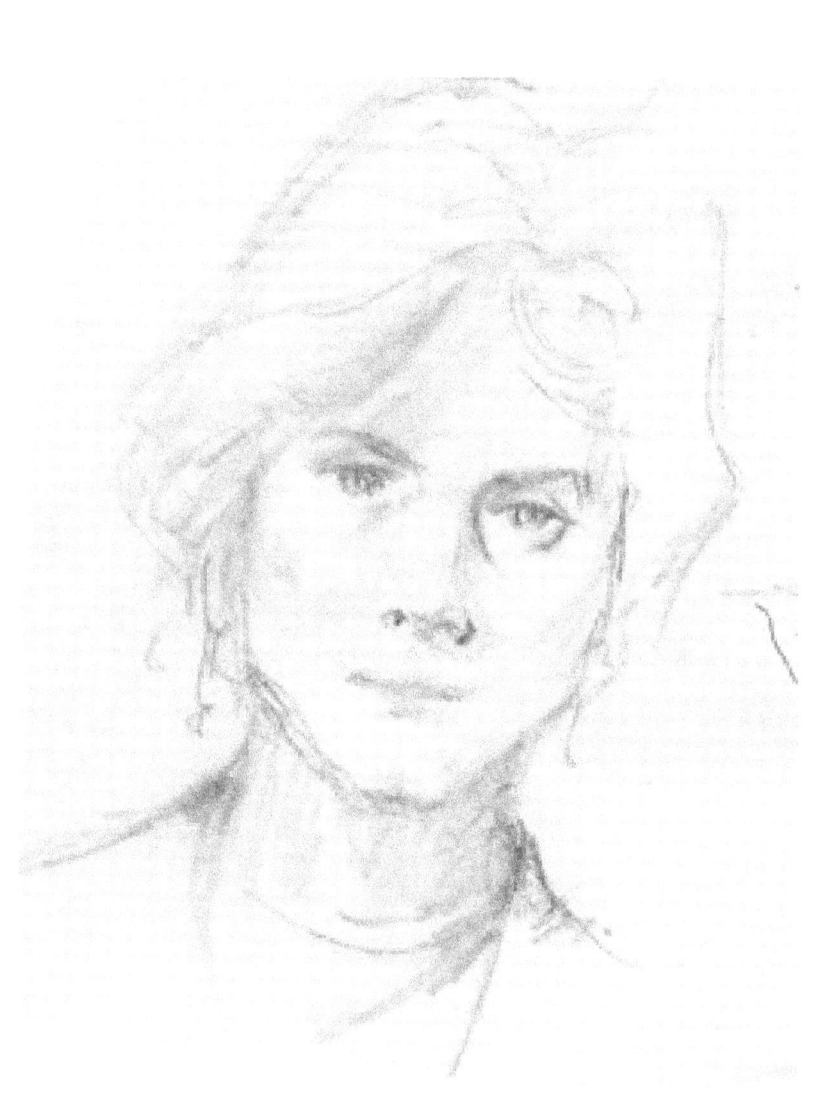

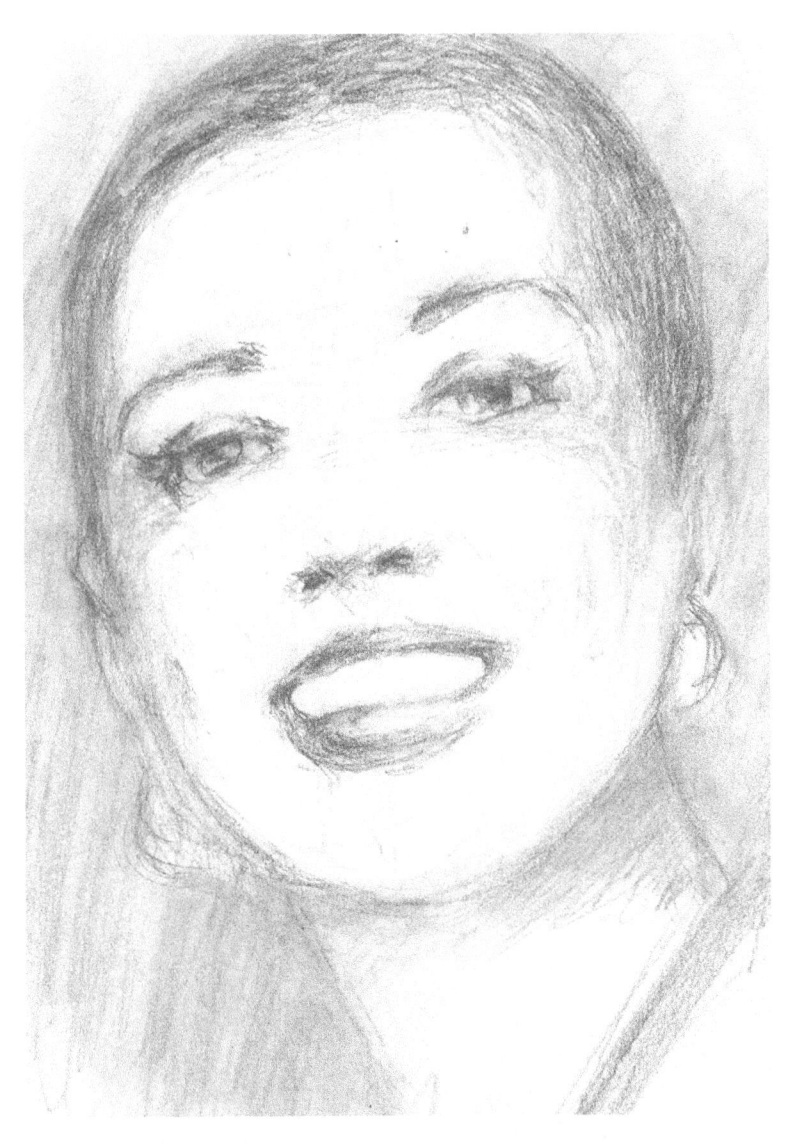

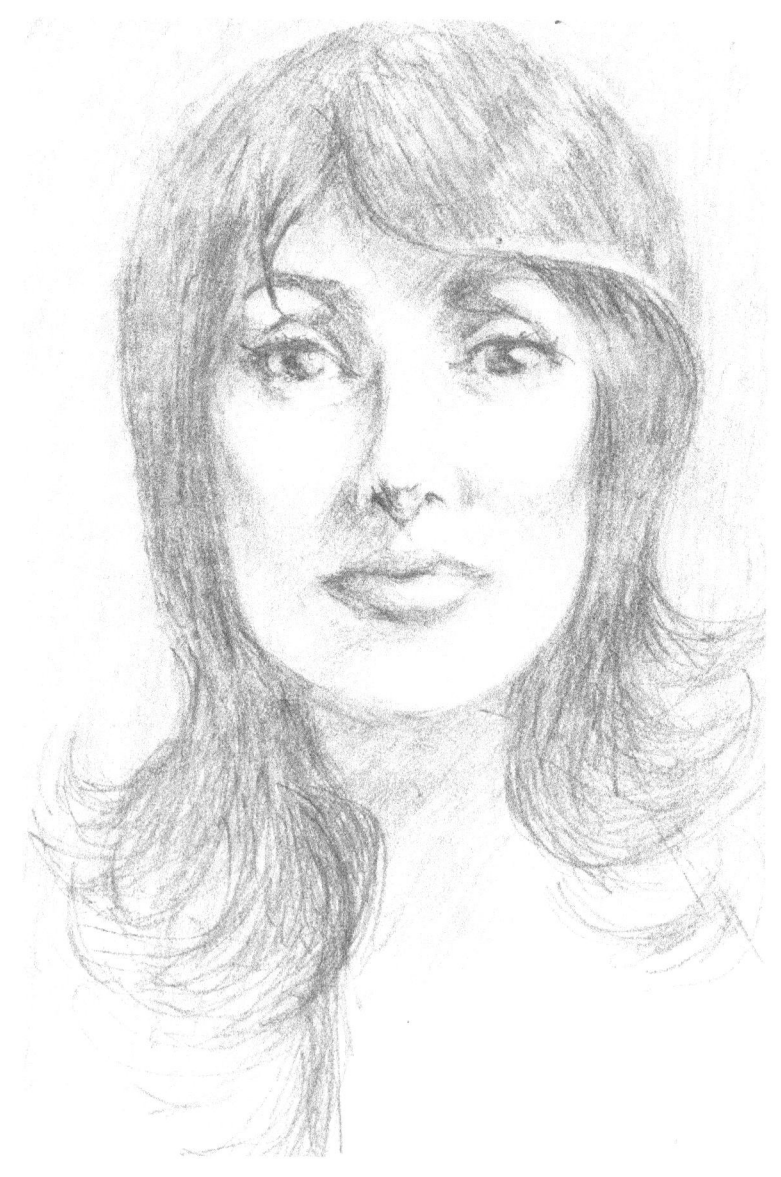

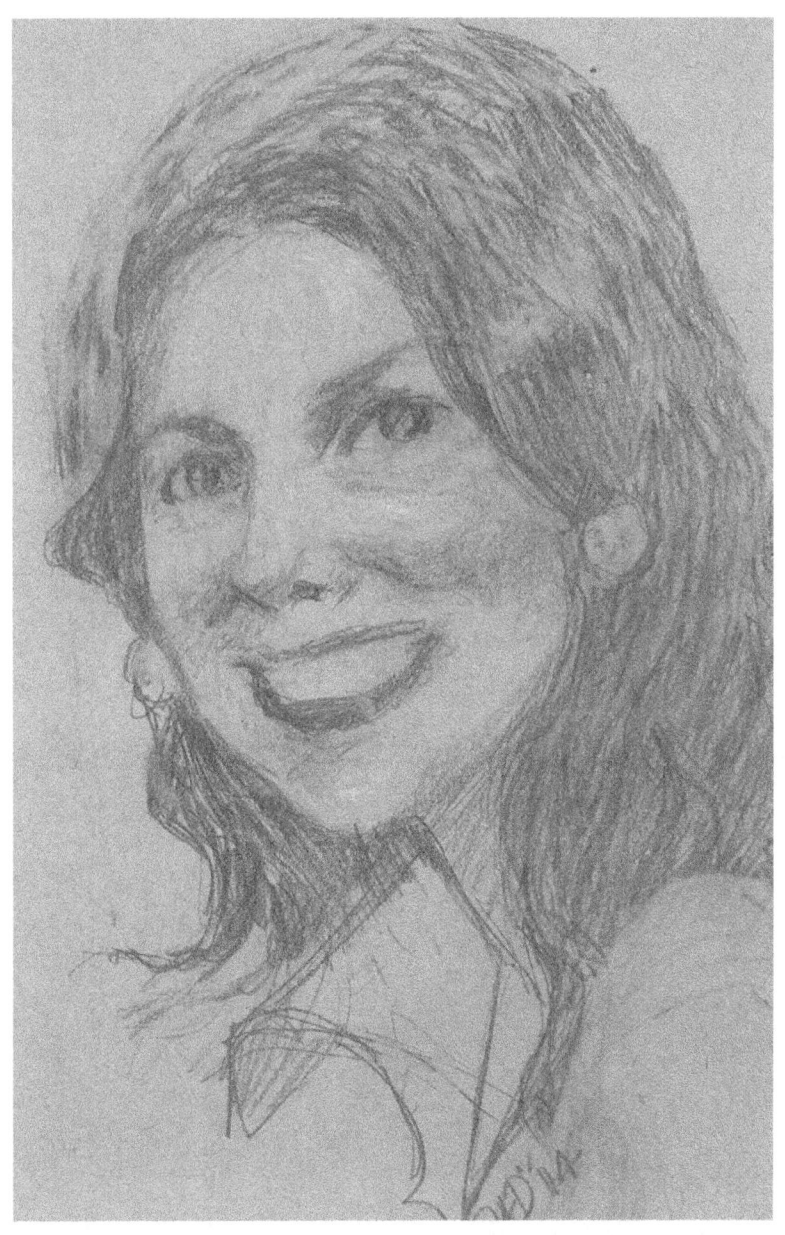

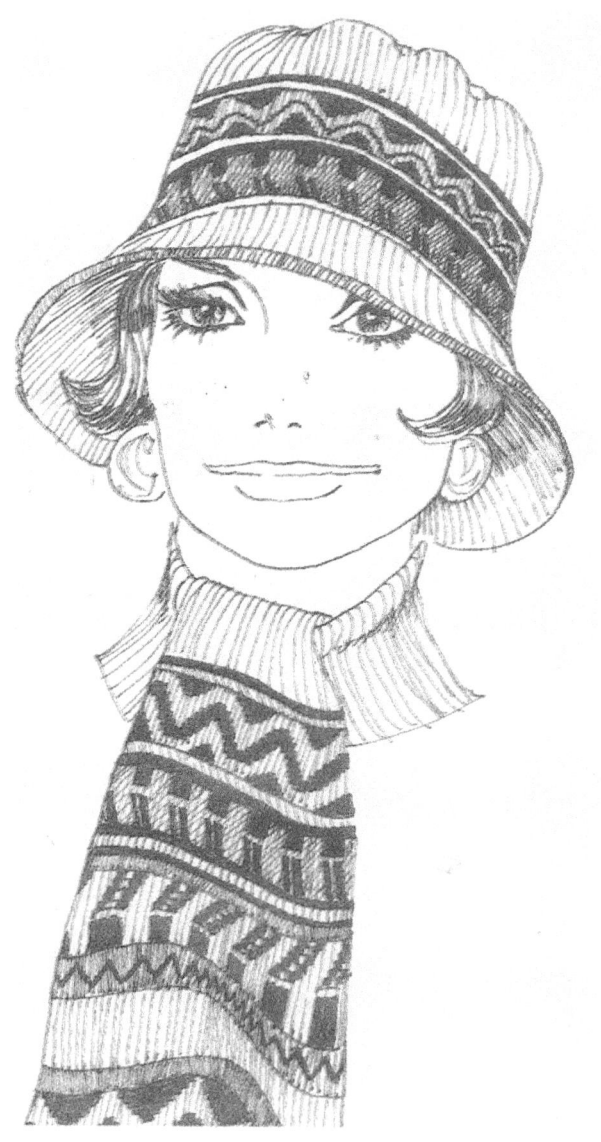

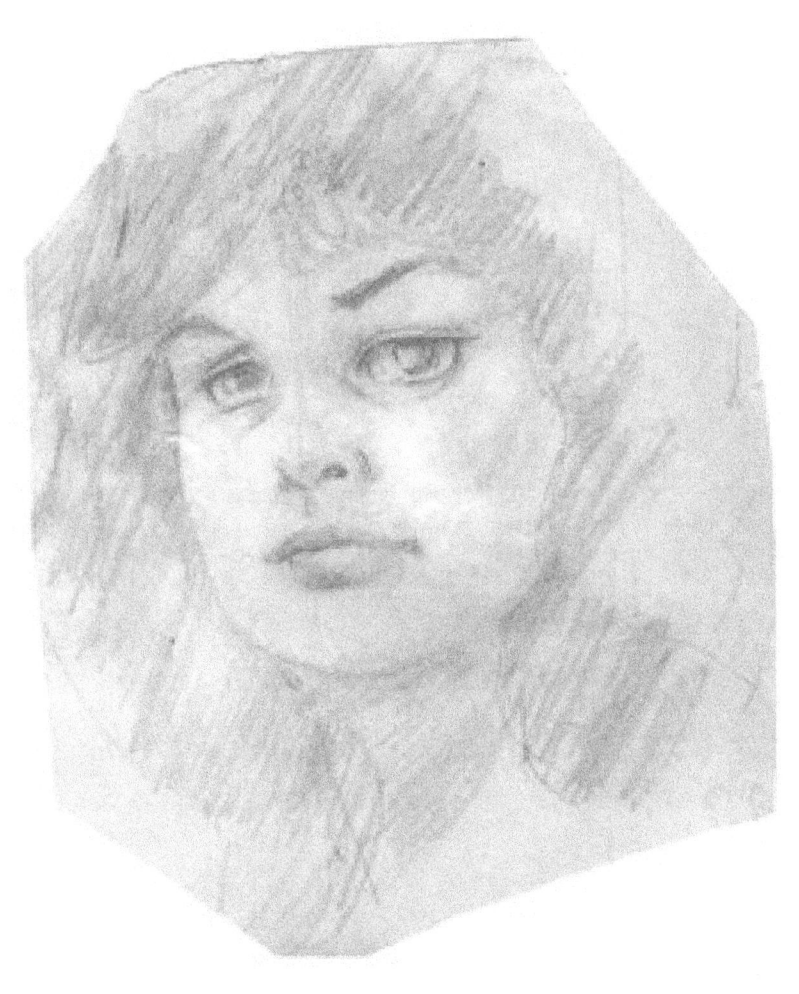

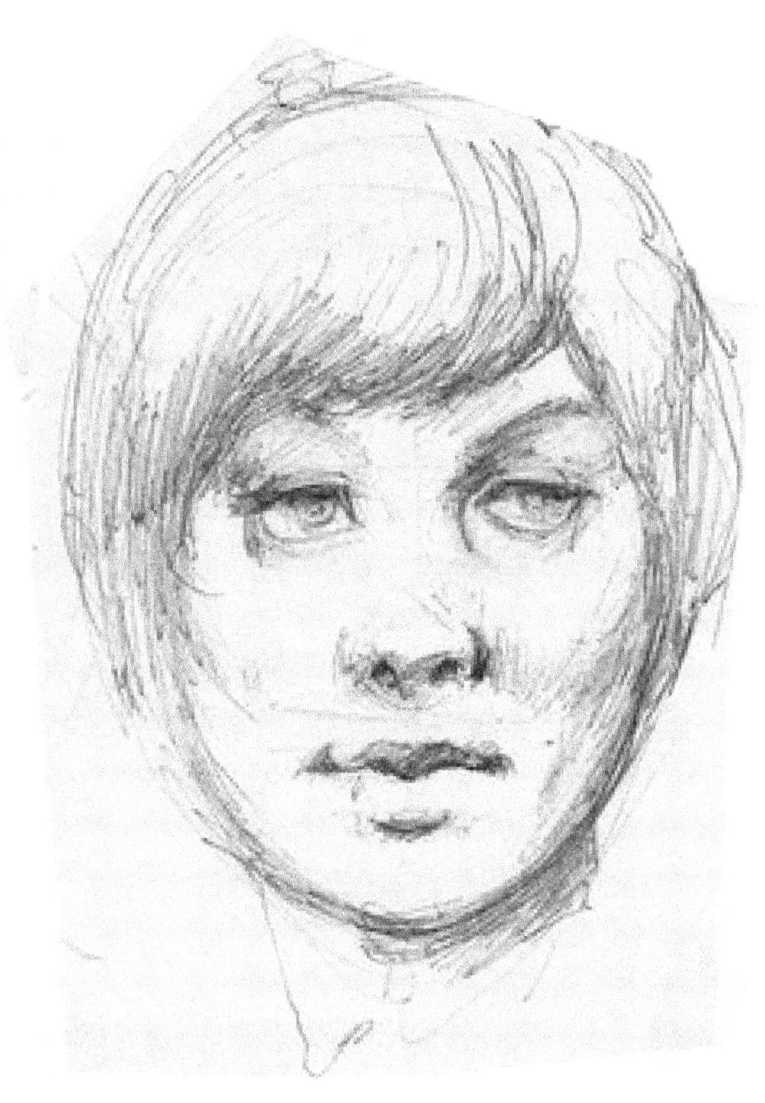

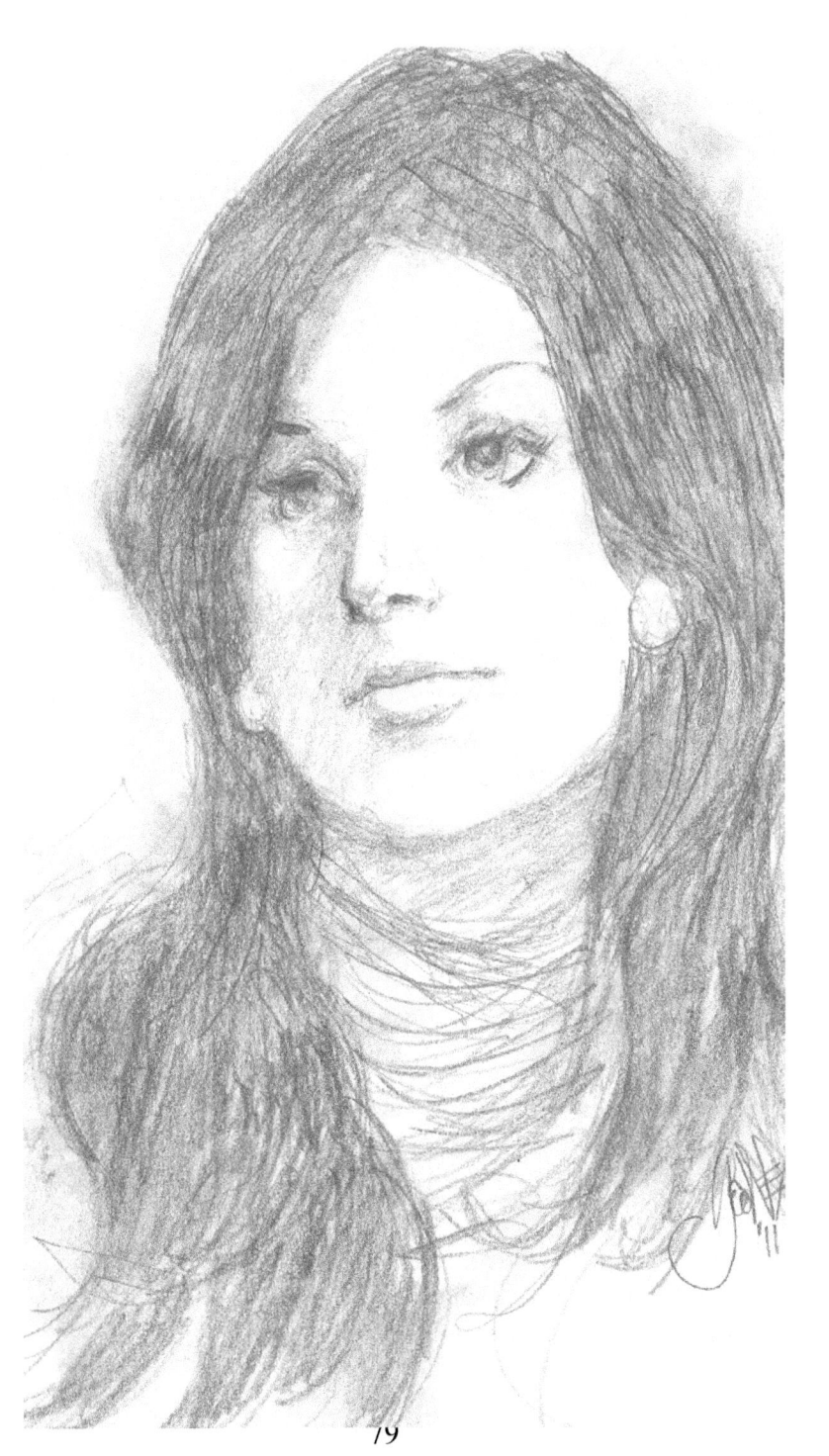

79

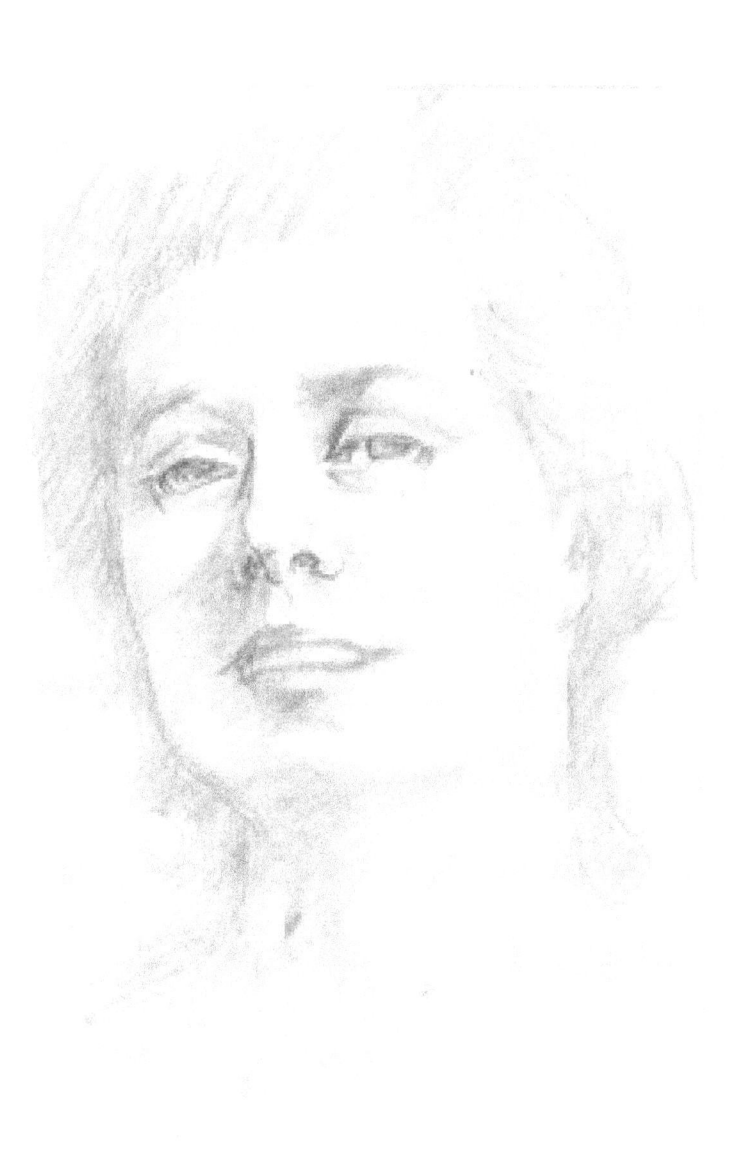

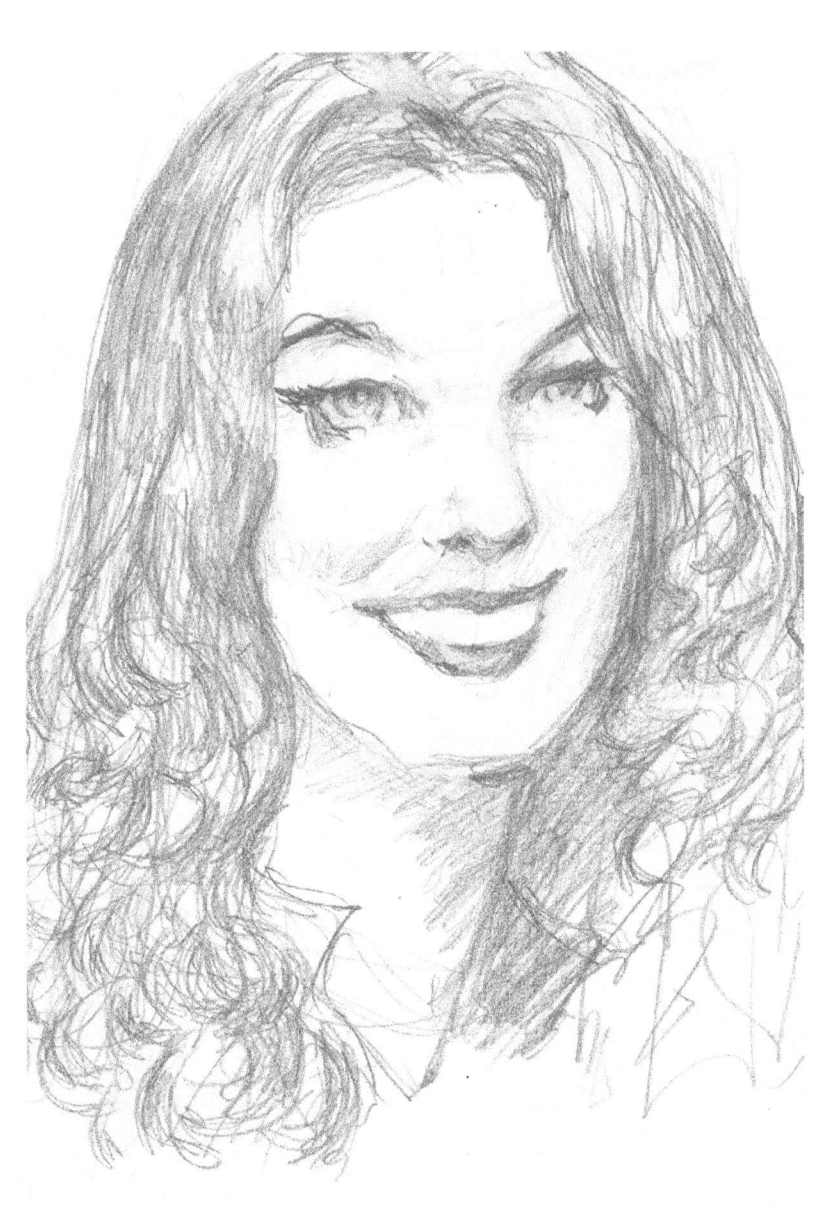

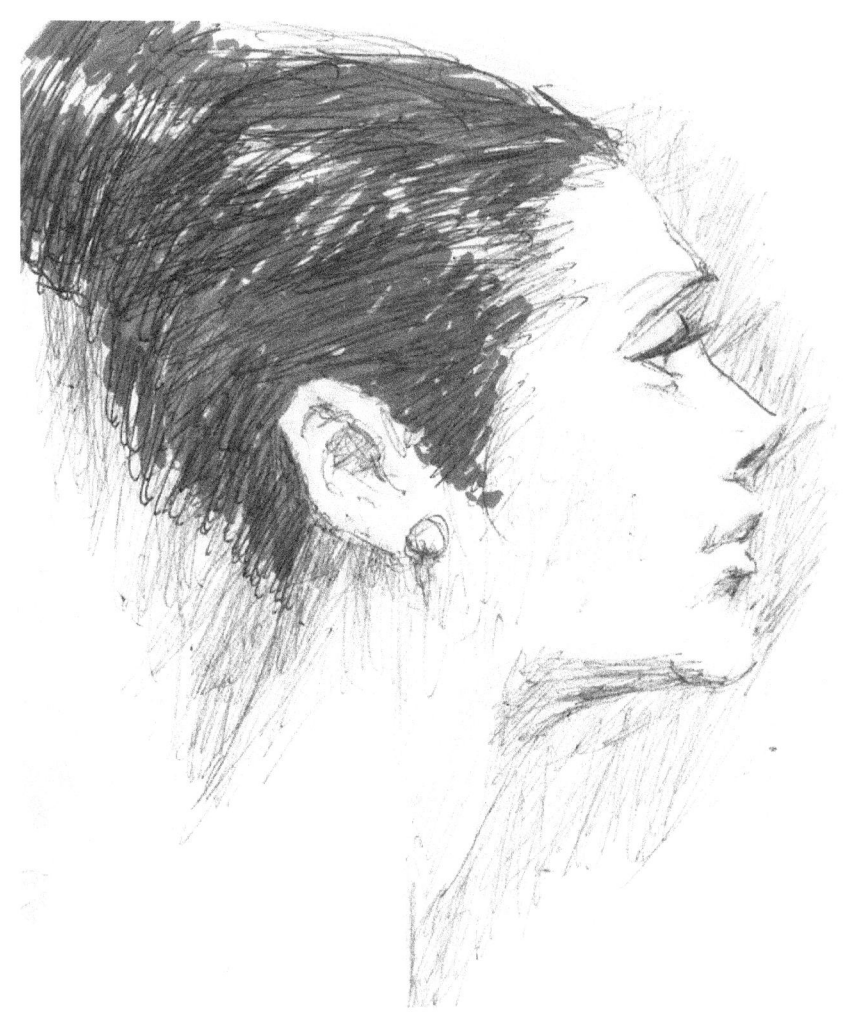

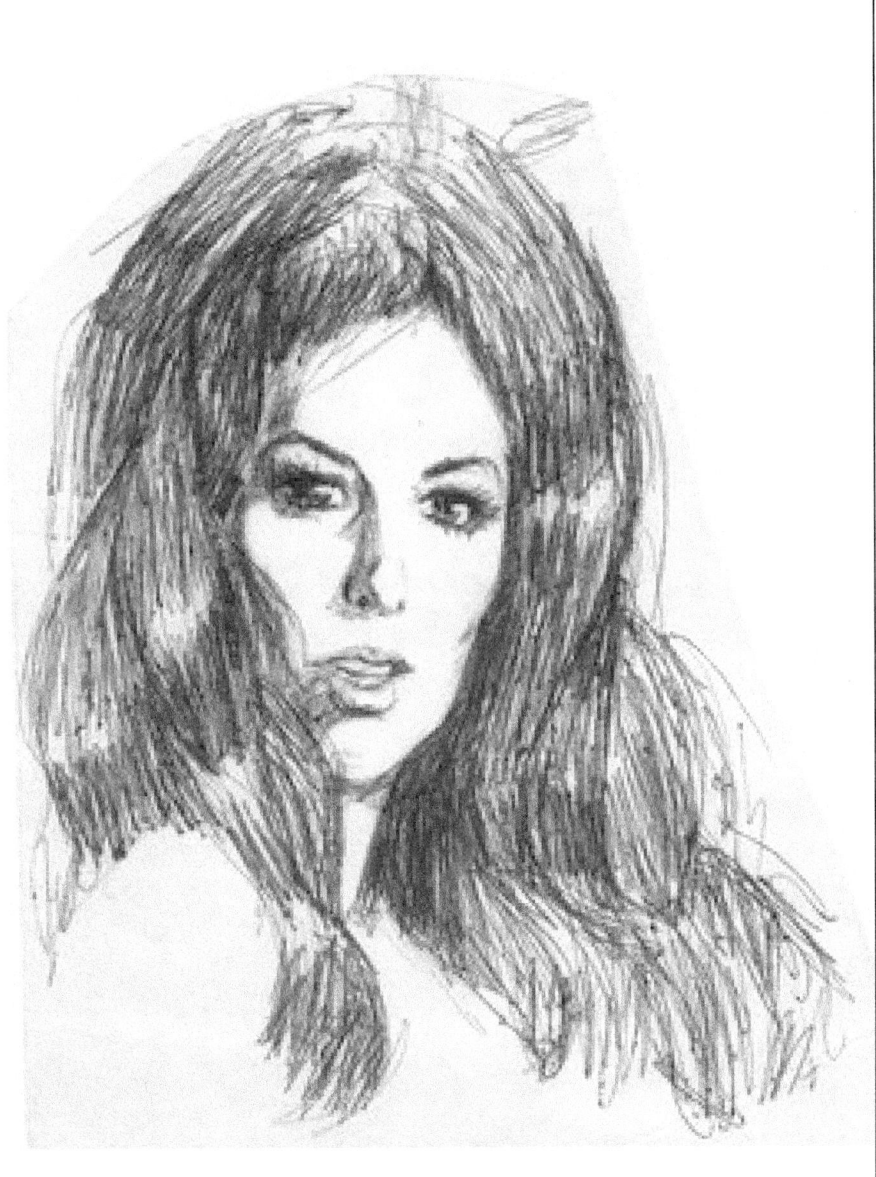

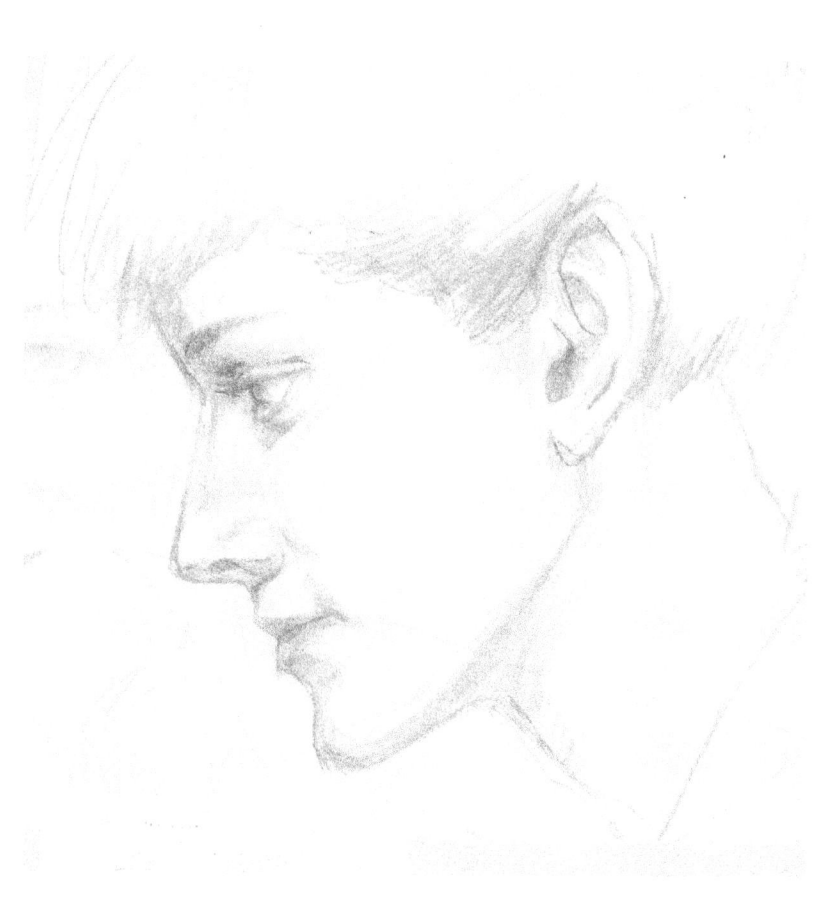

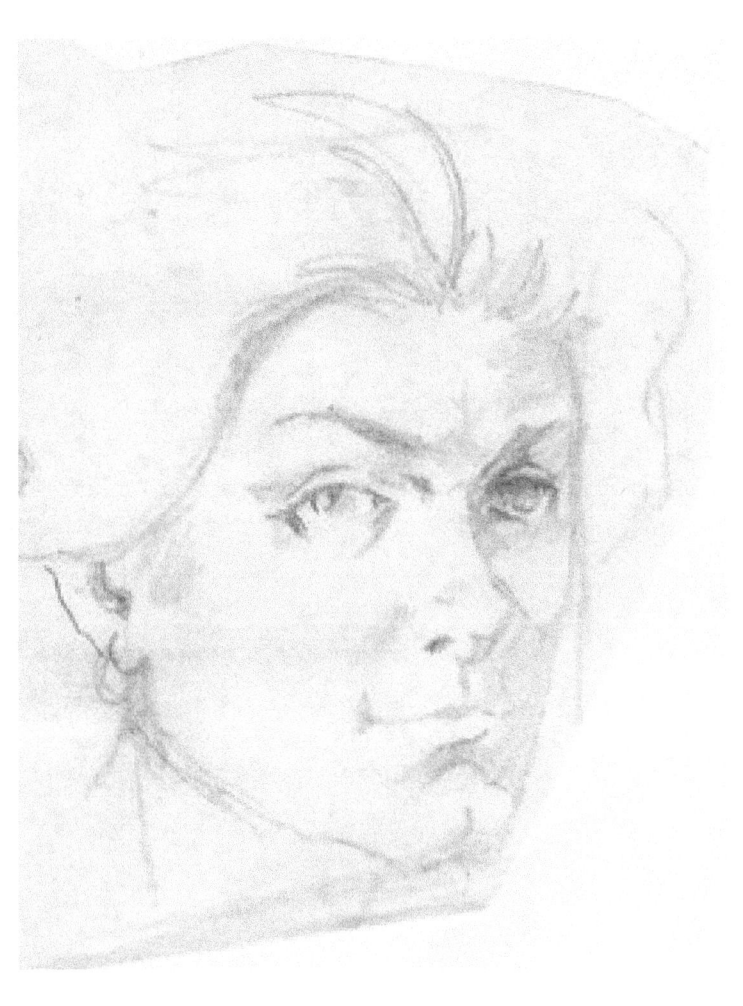

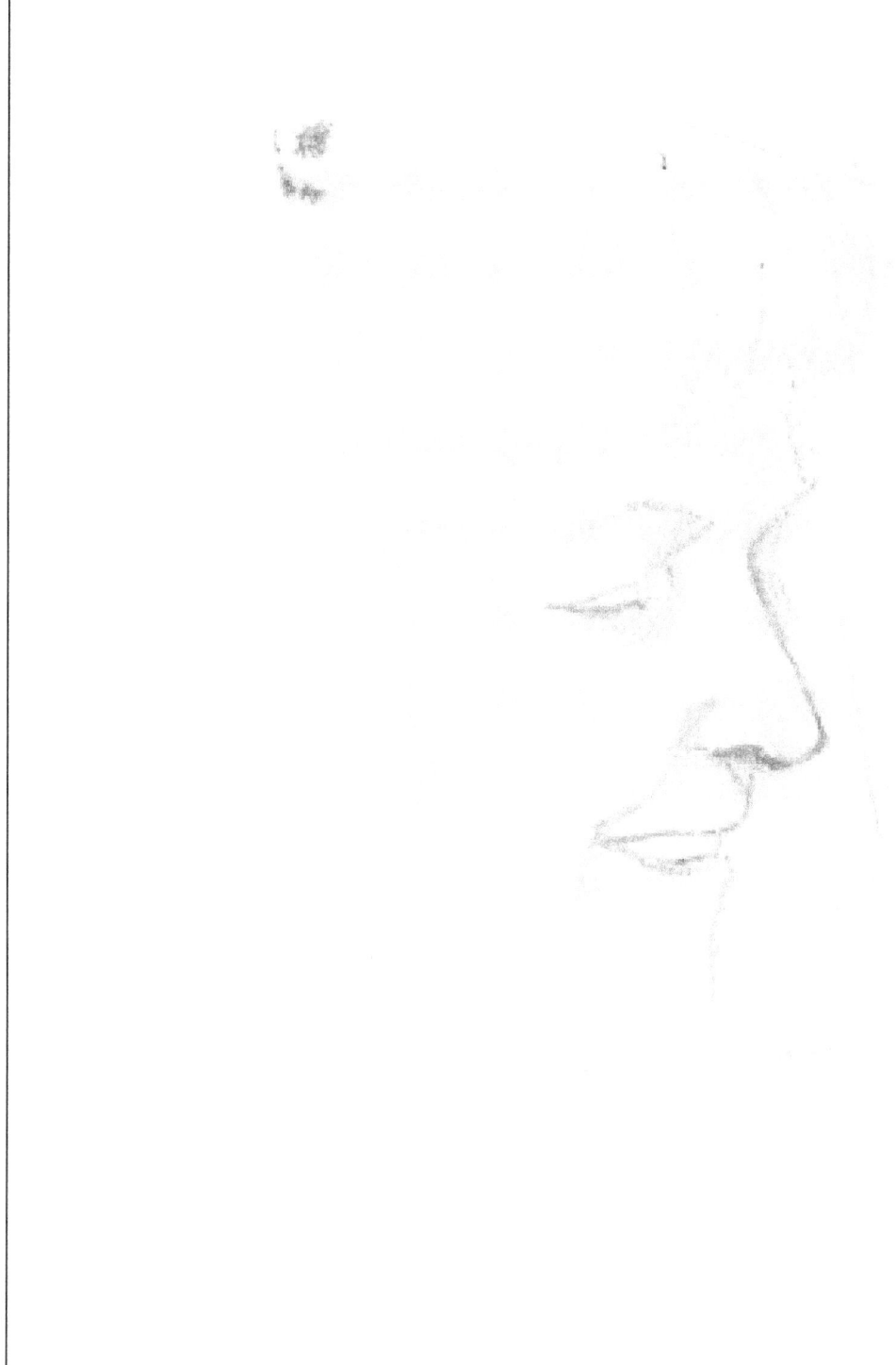

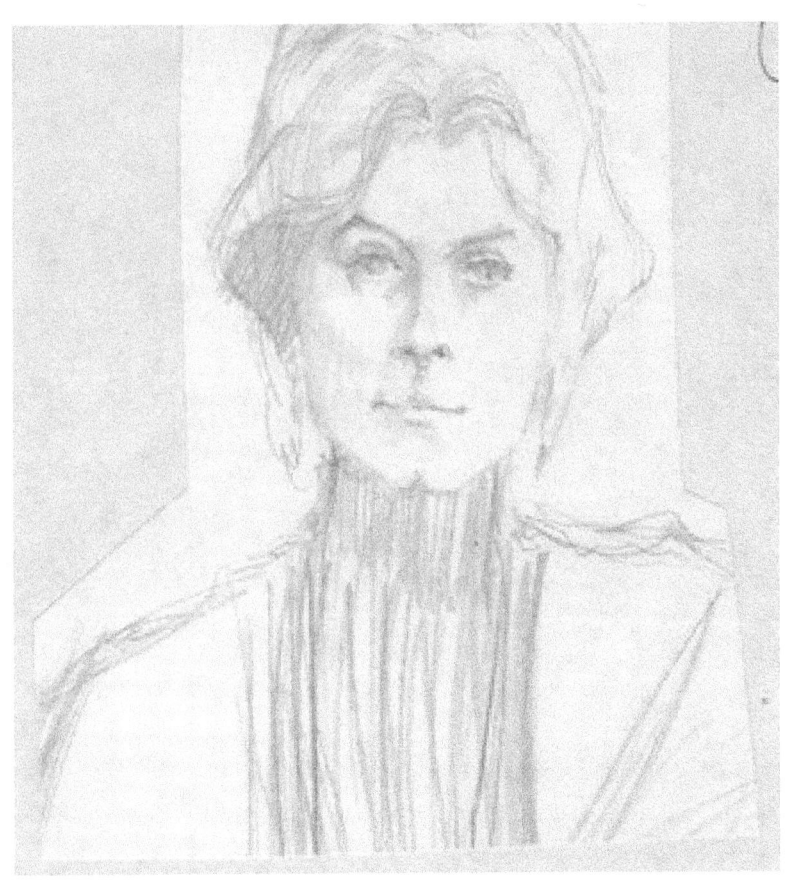

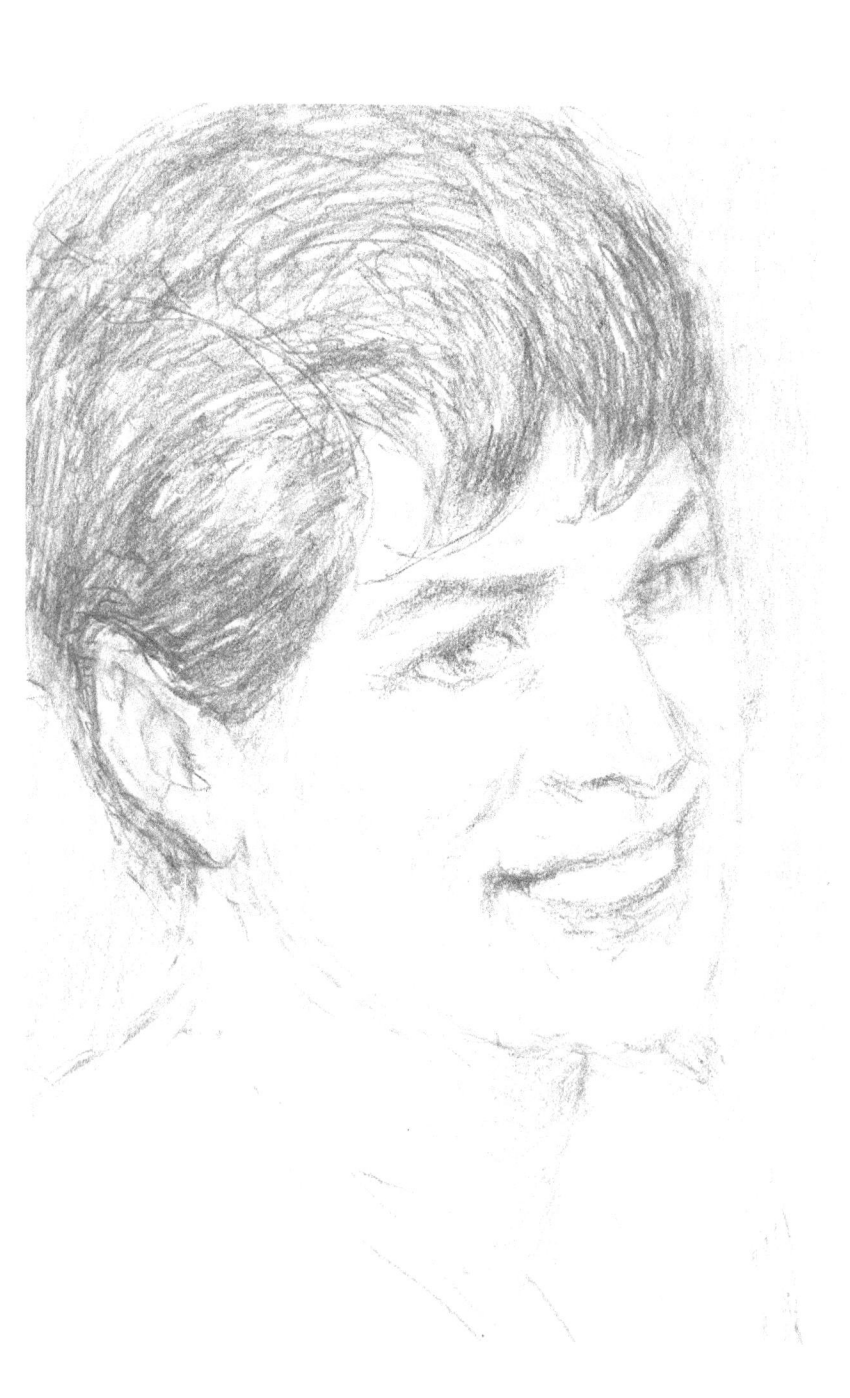

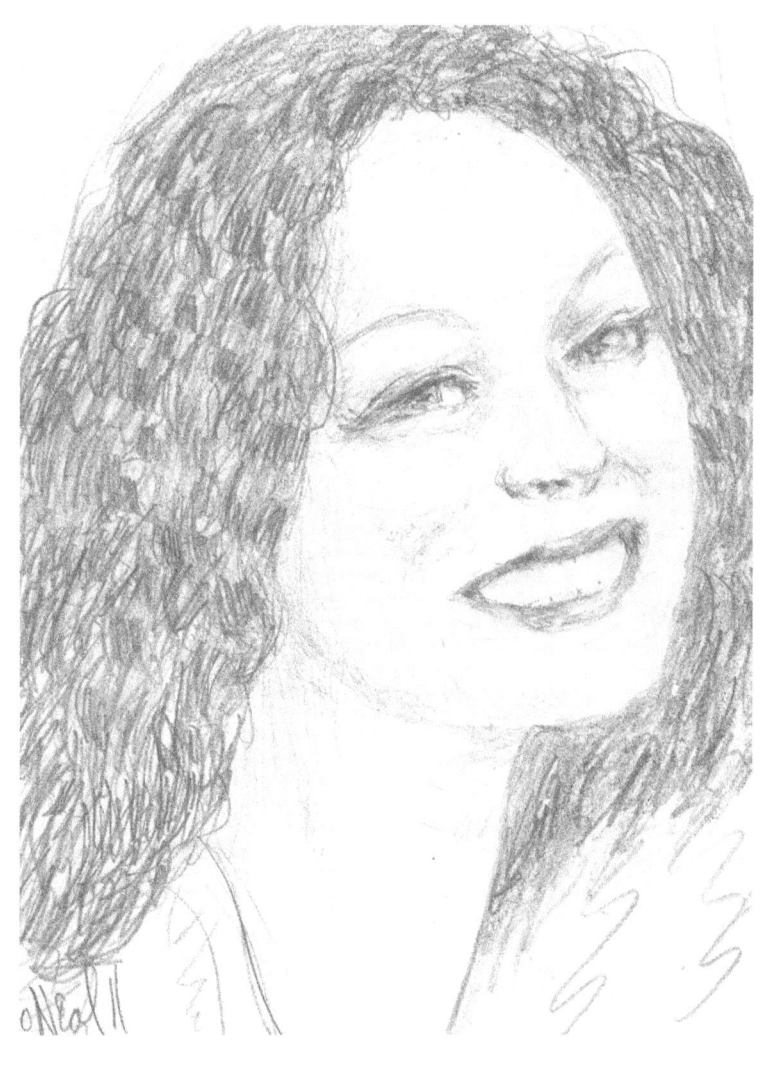

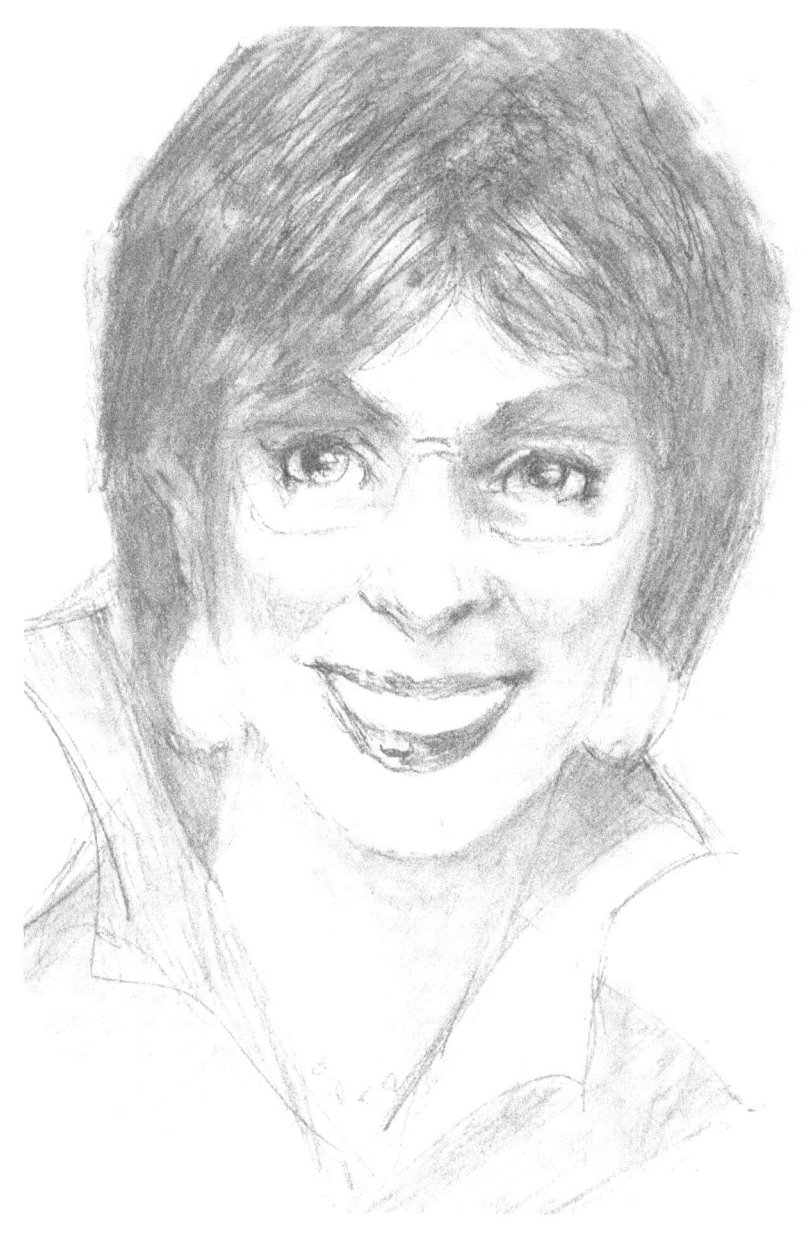

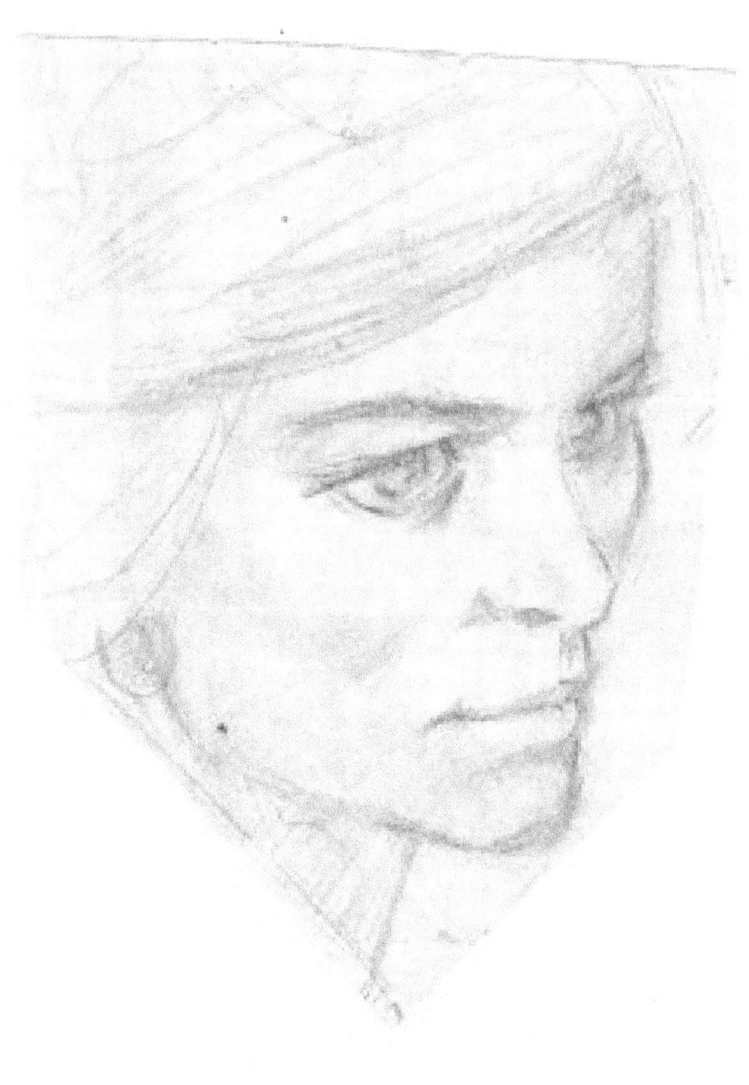

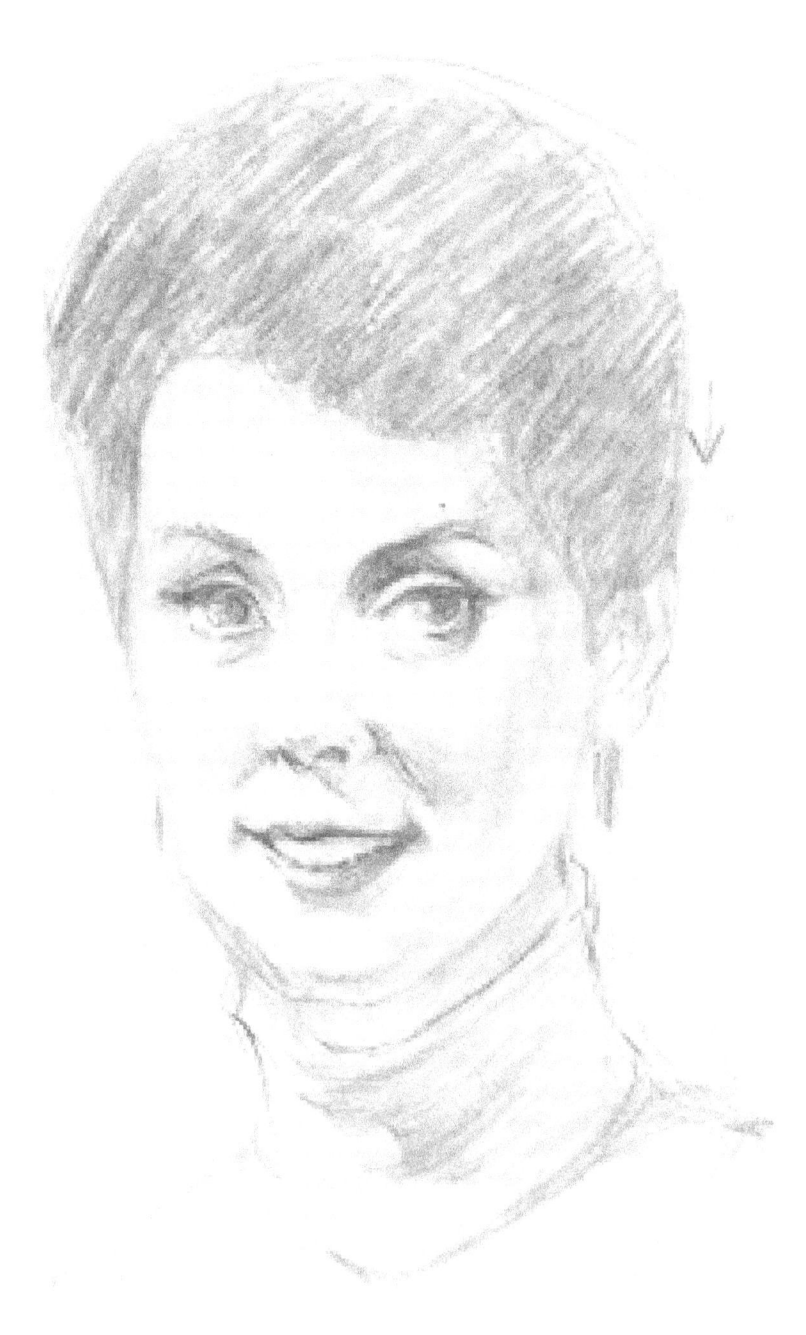

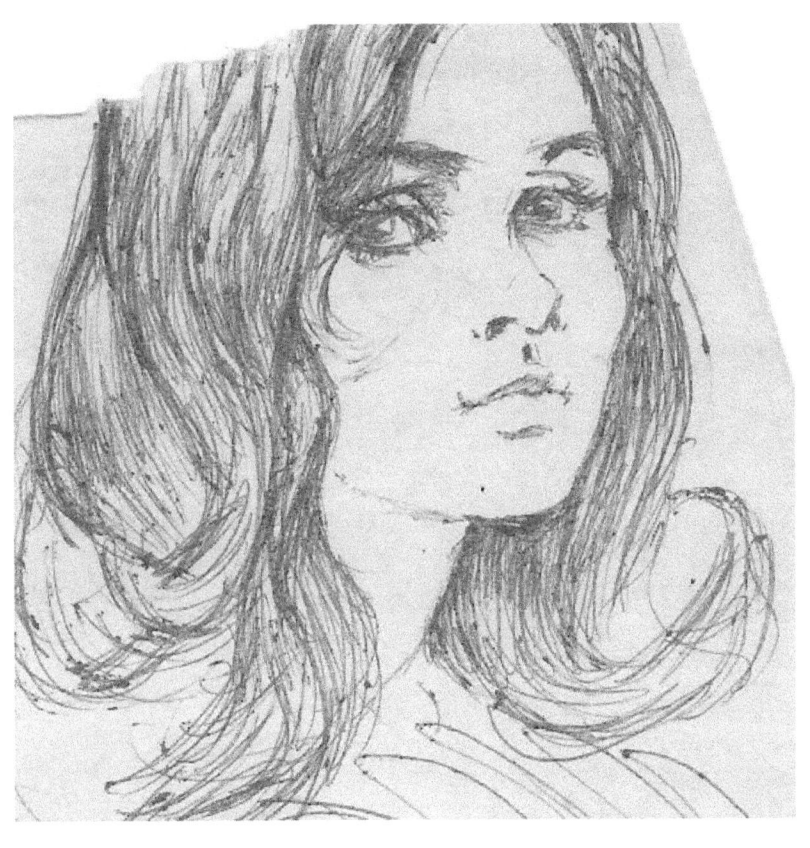

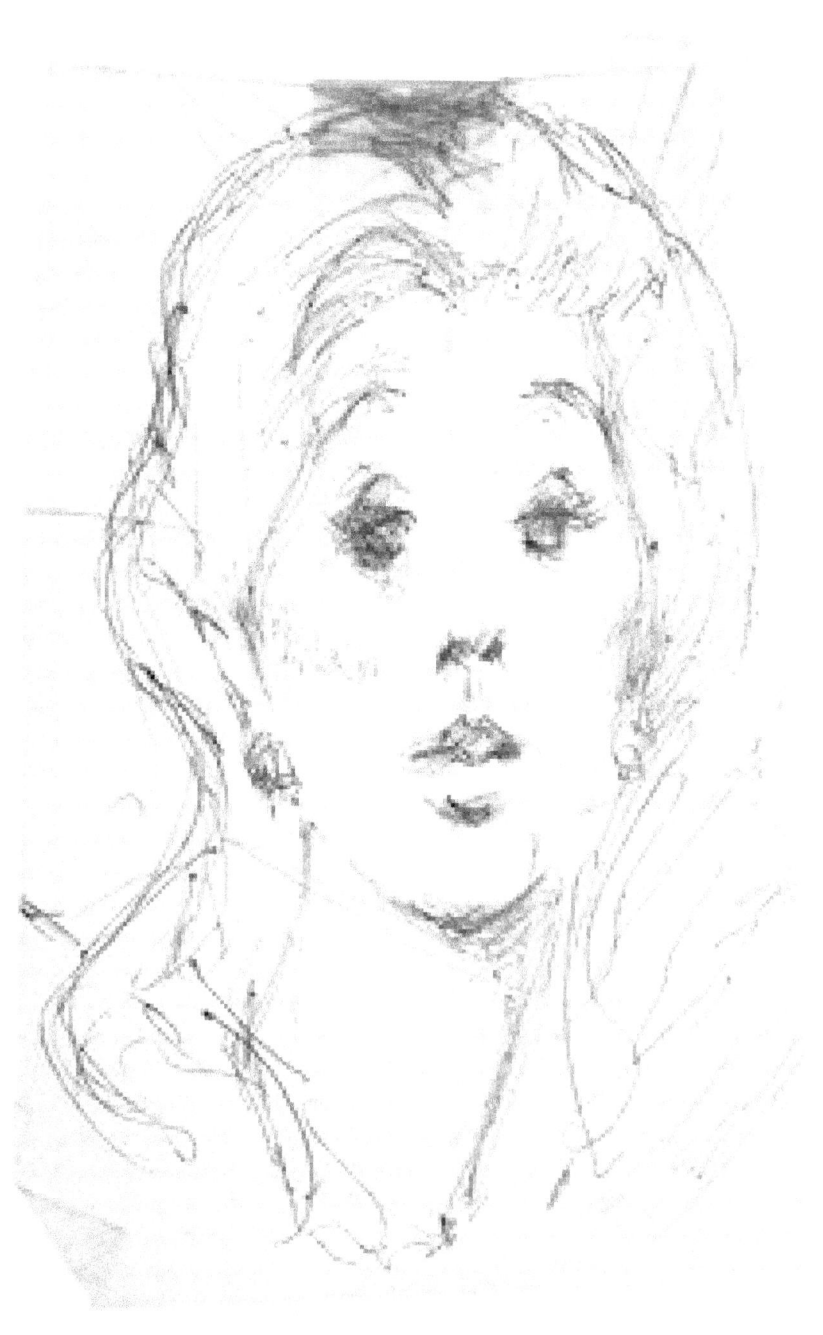

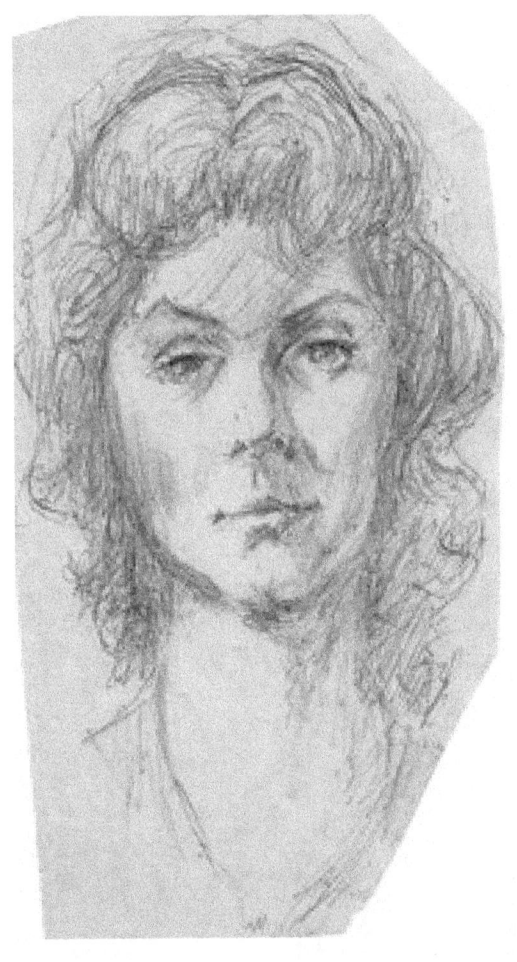

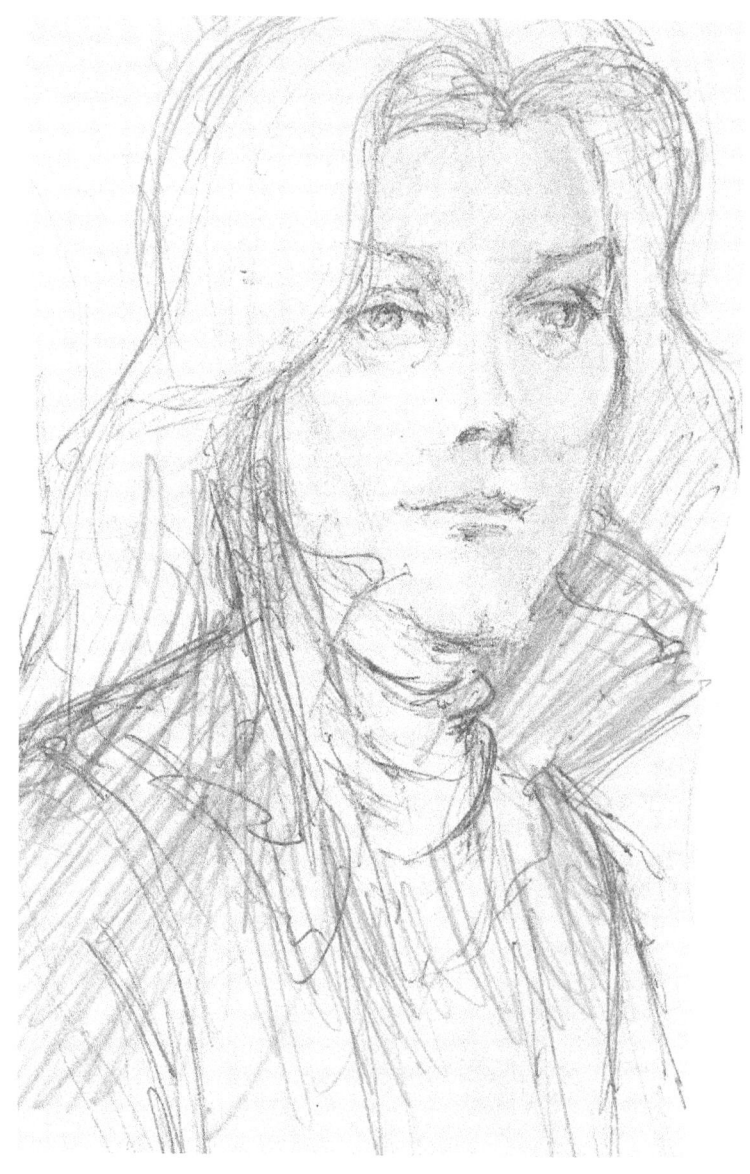

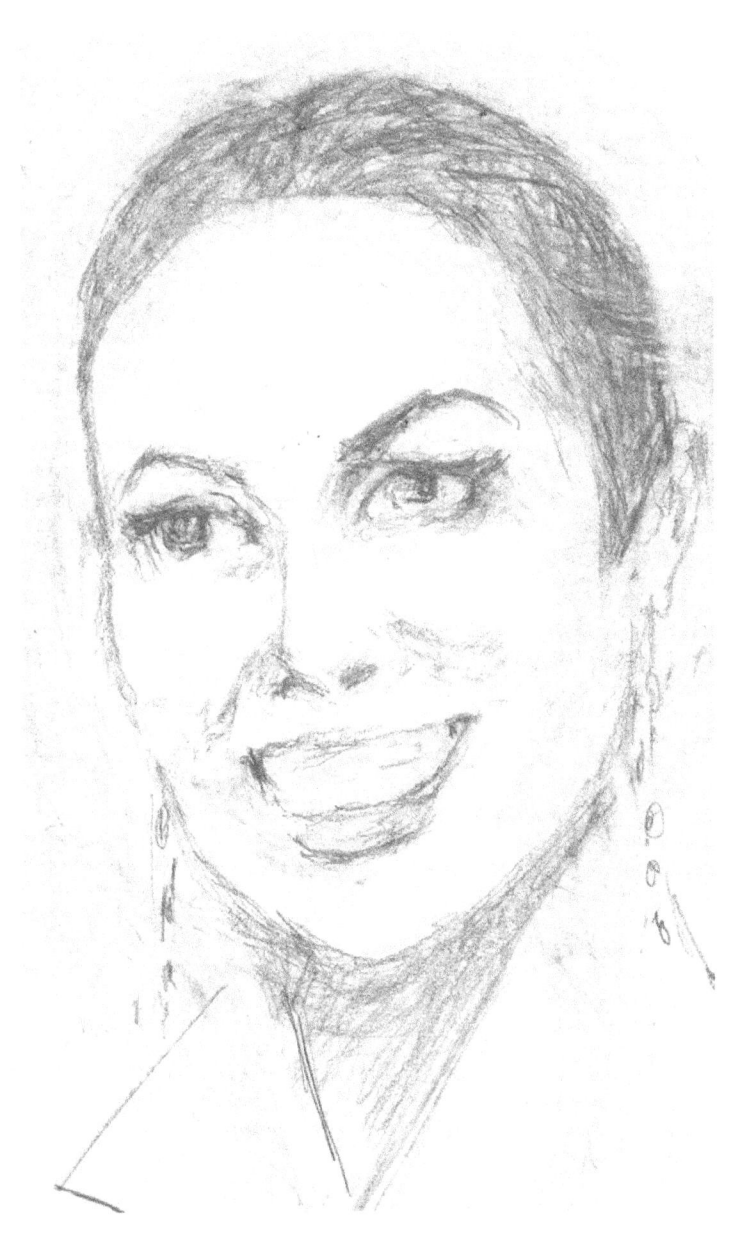

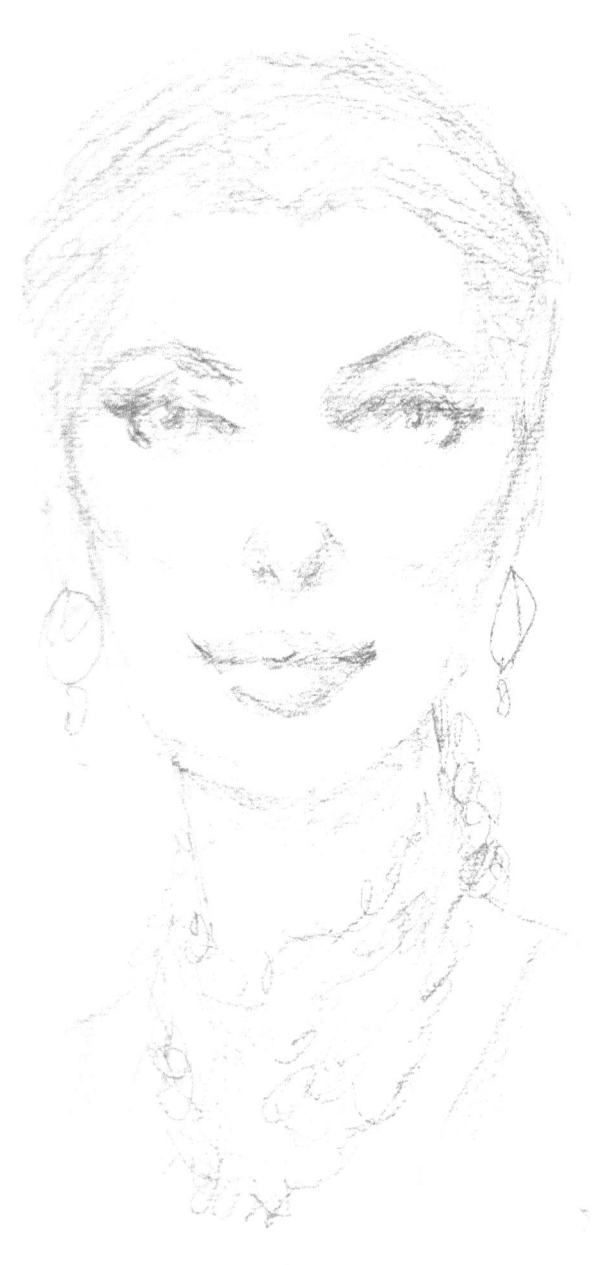

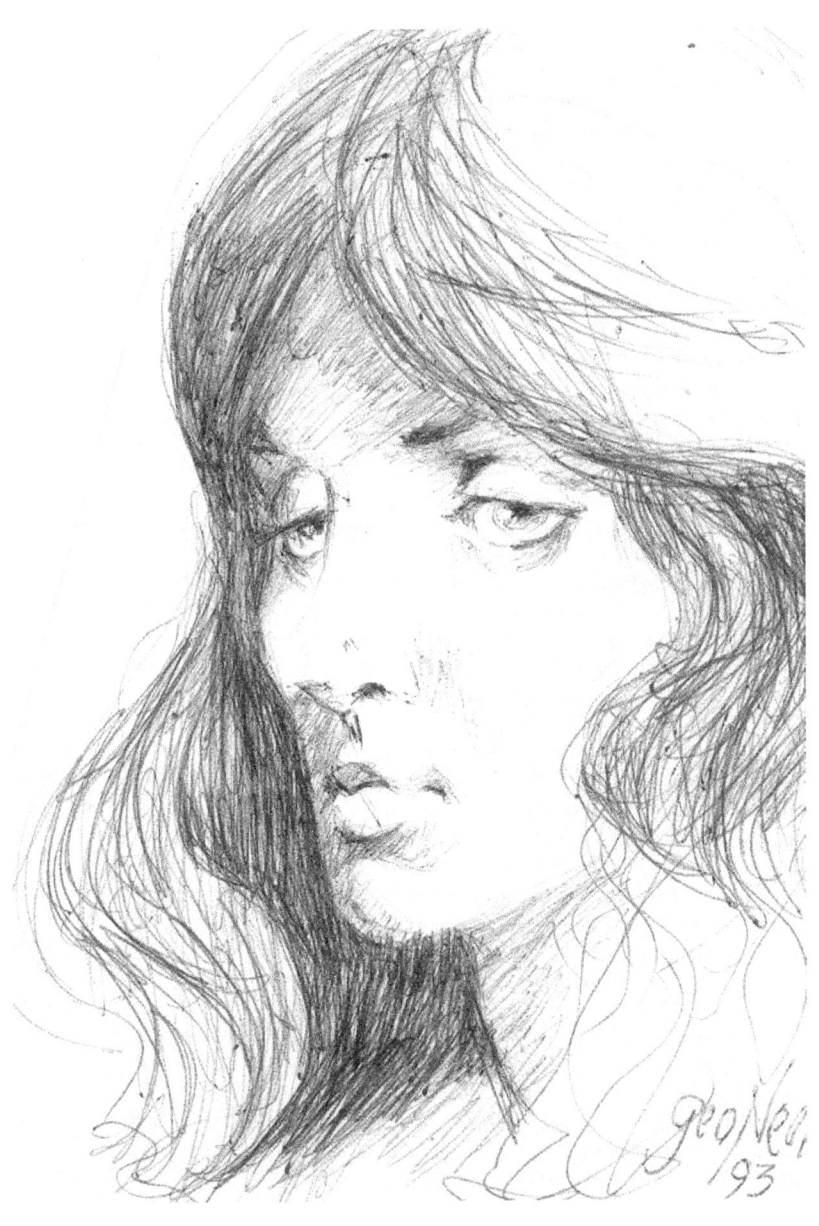

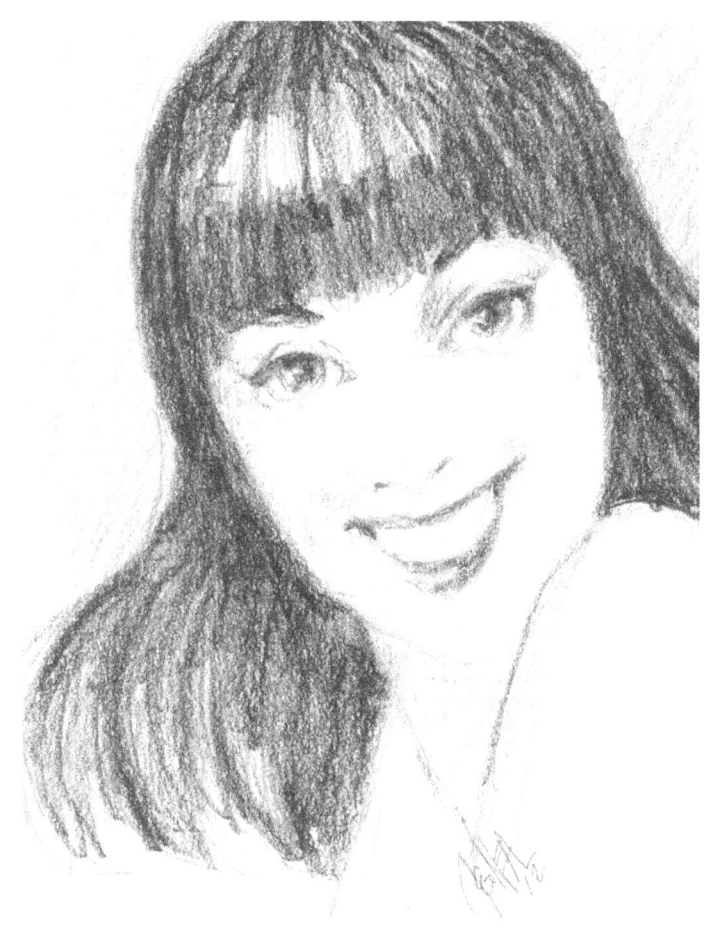

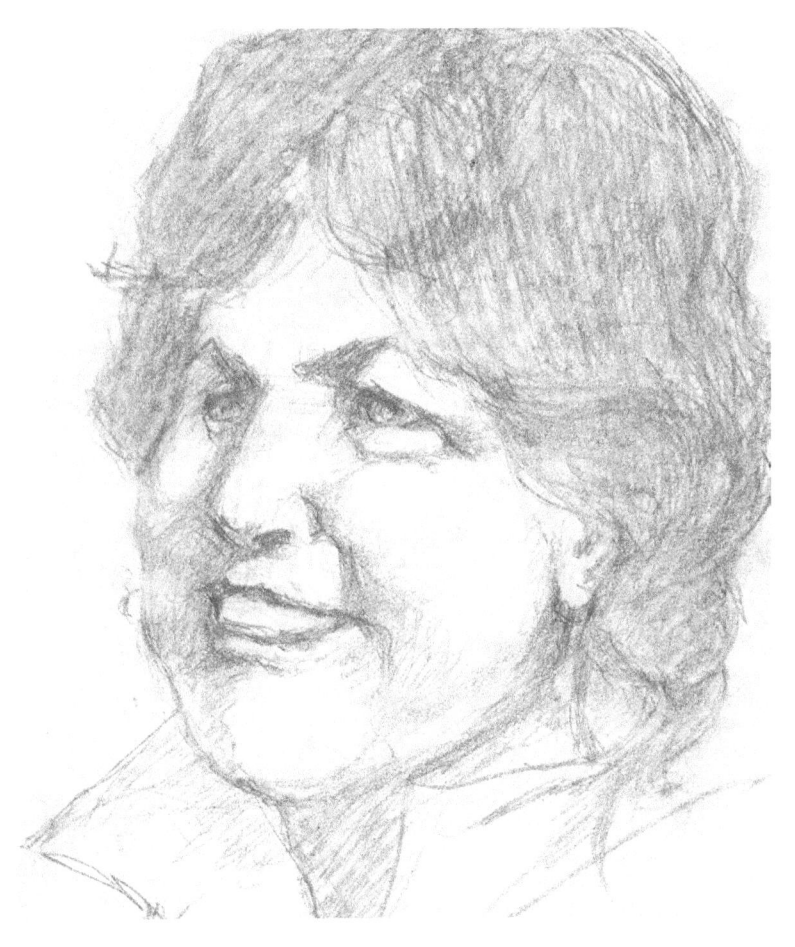

101

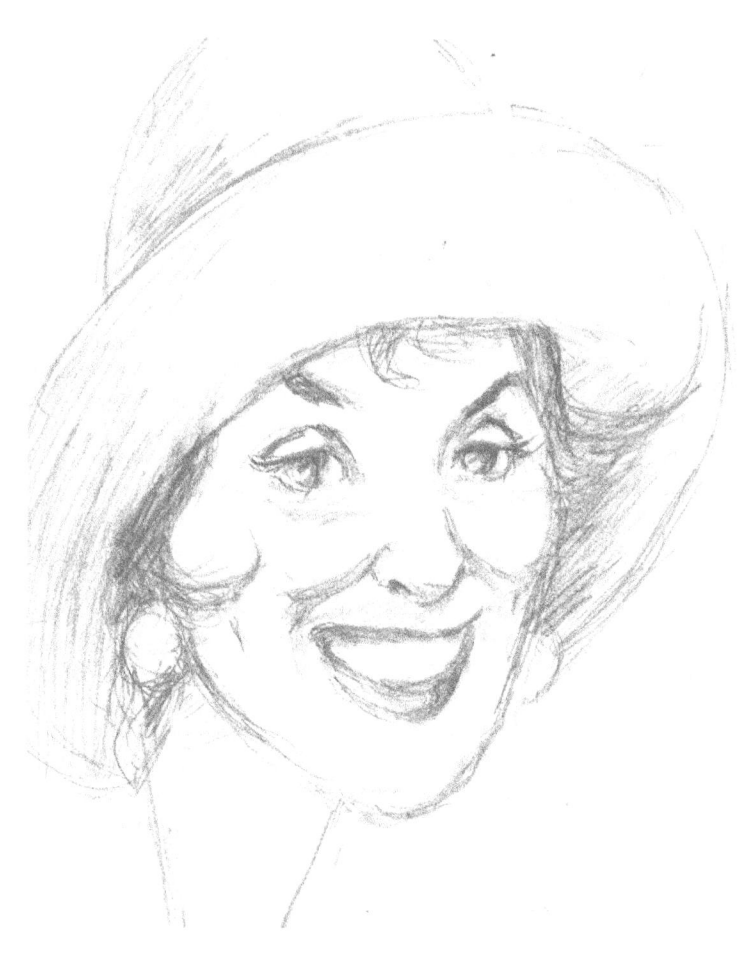

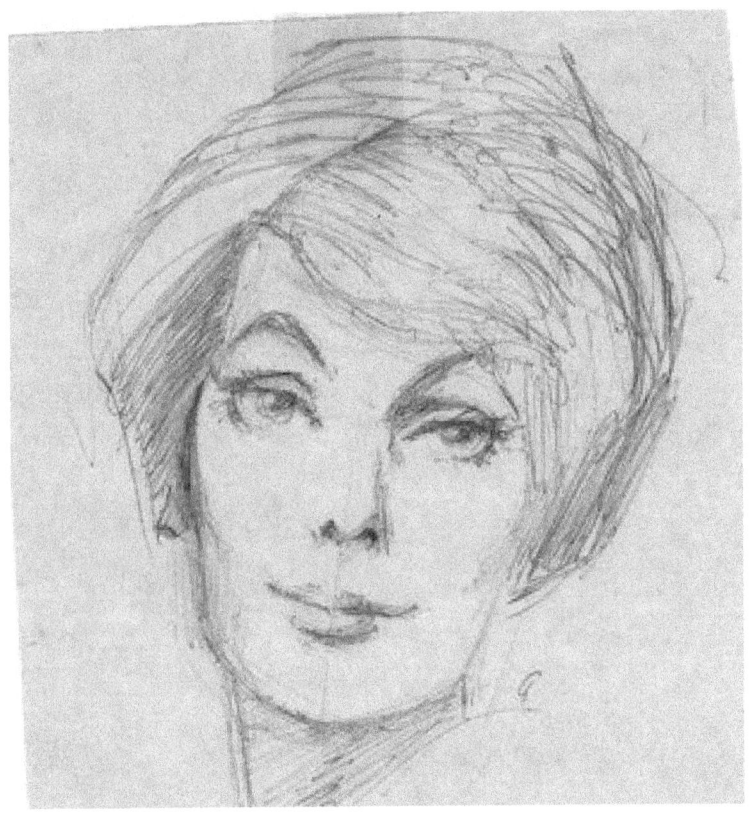

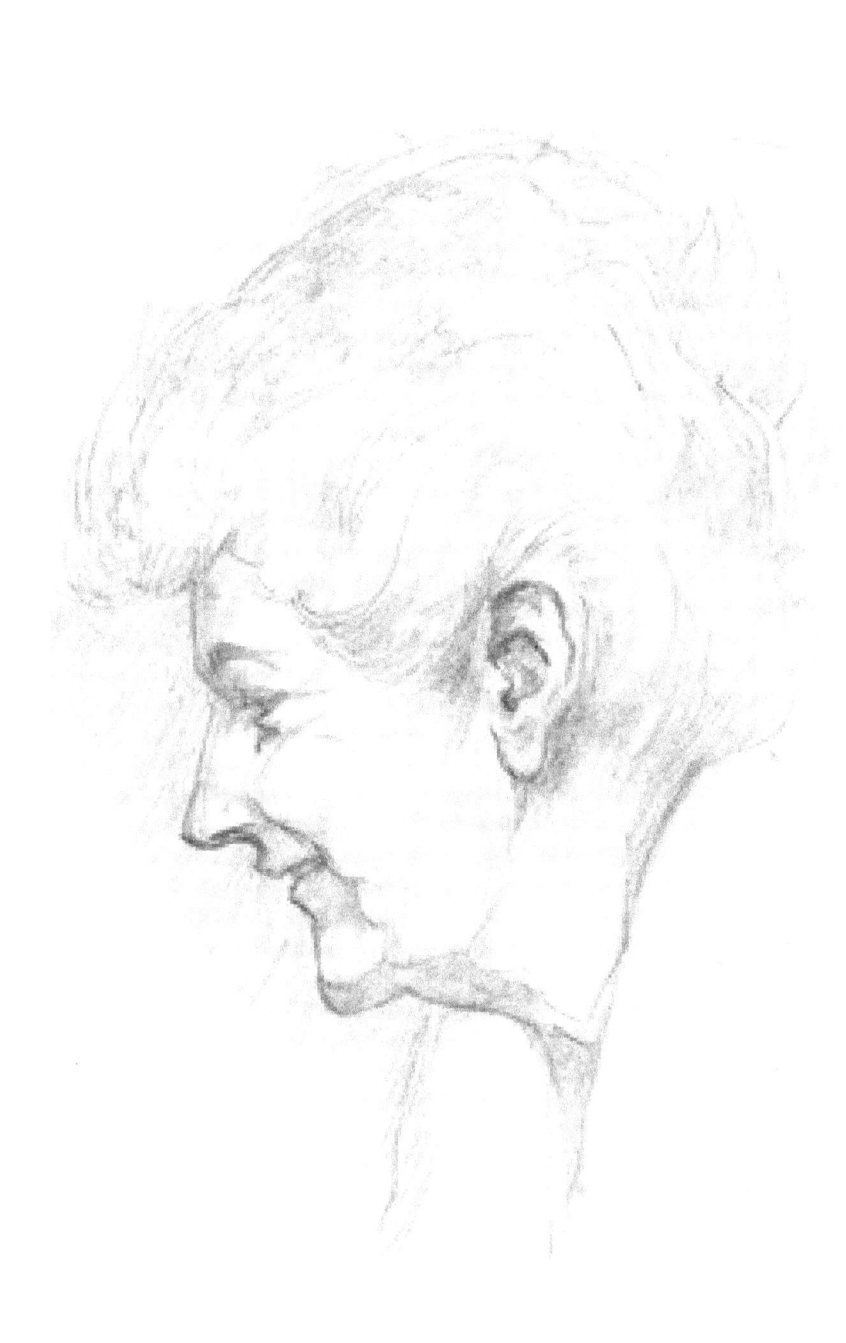

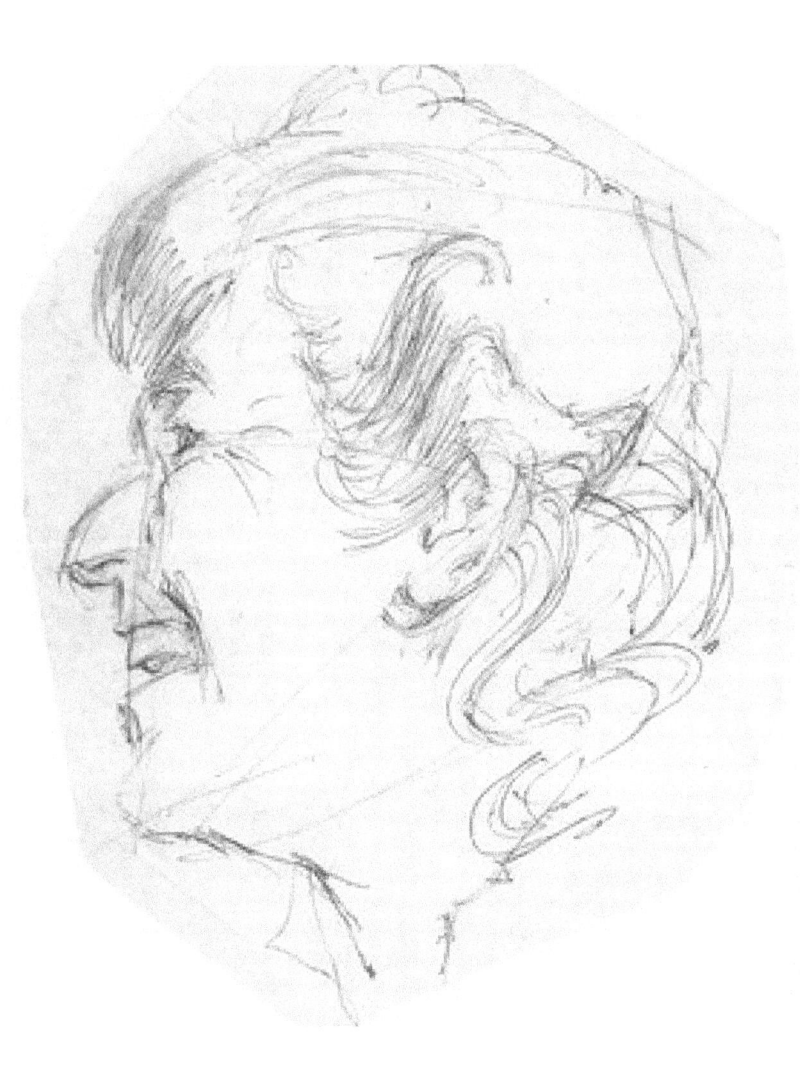

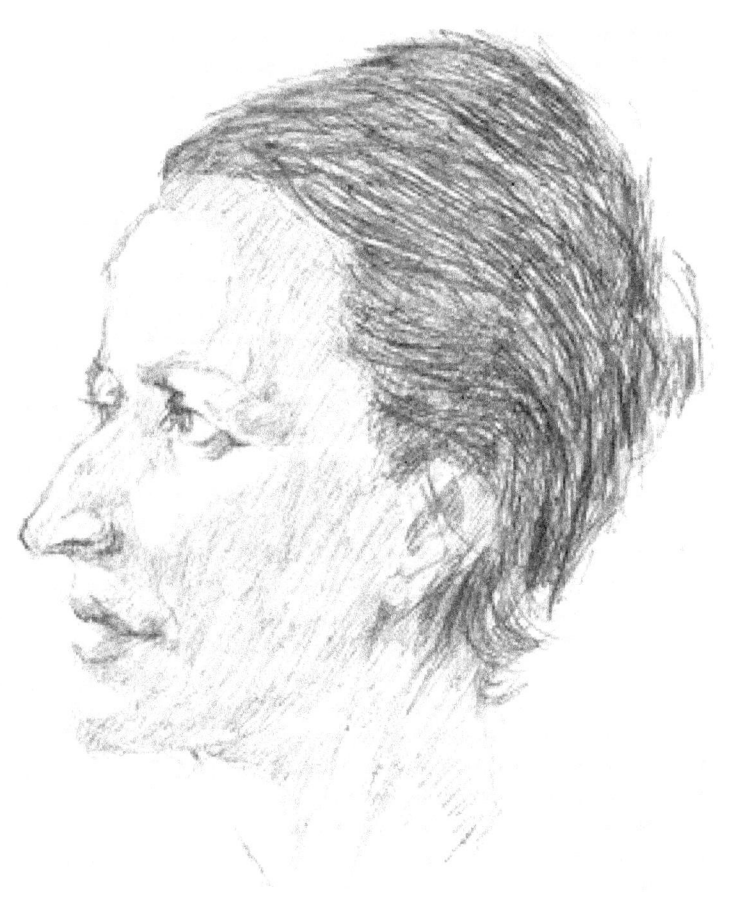

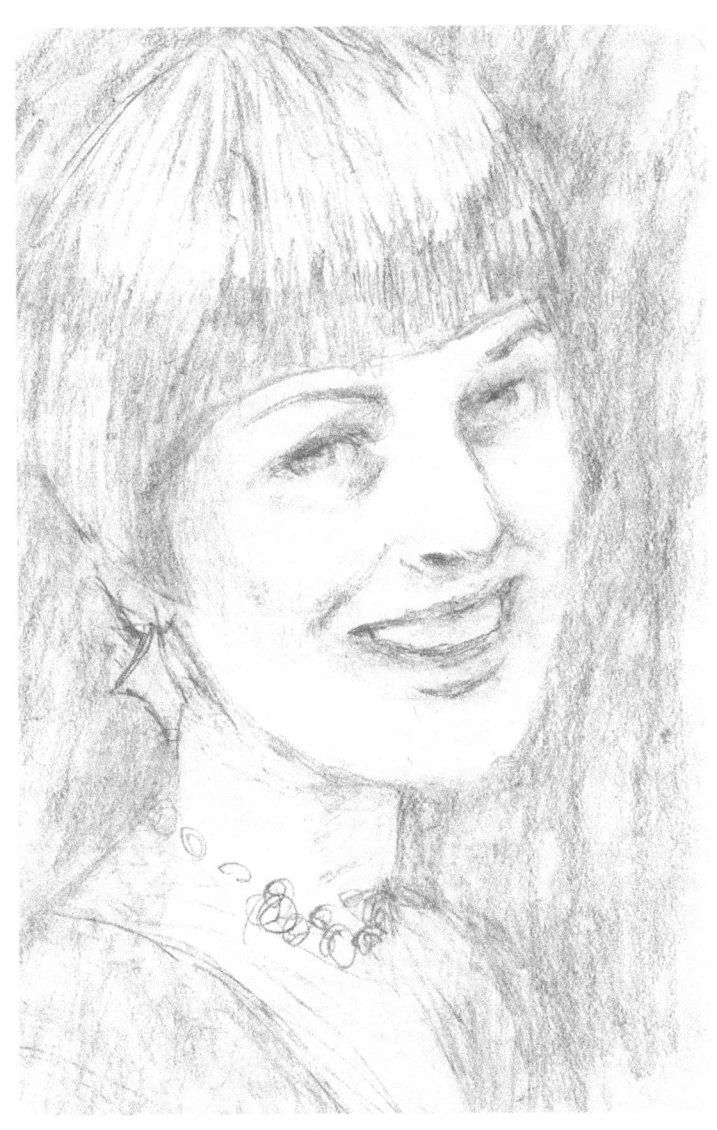

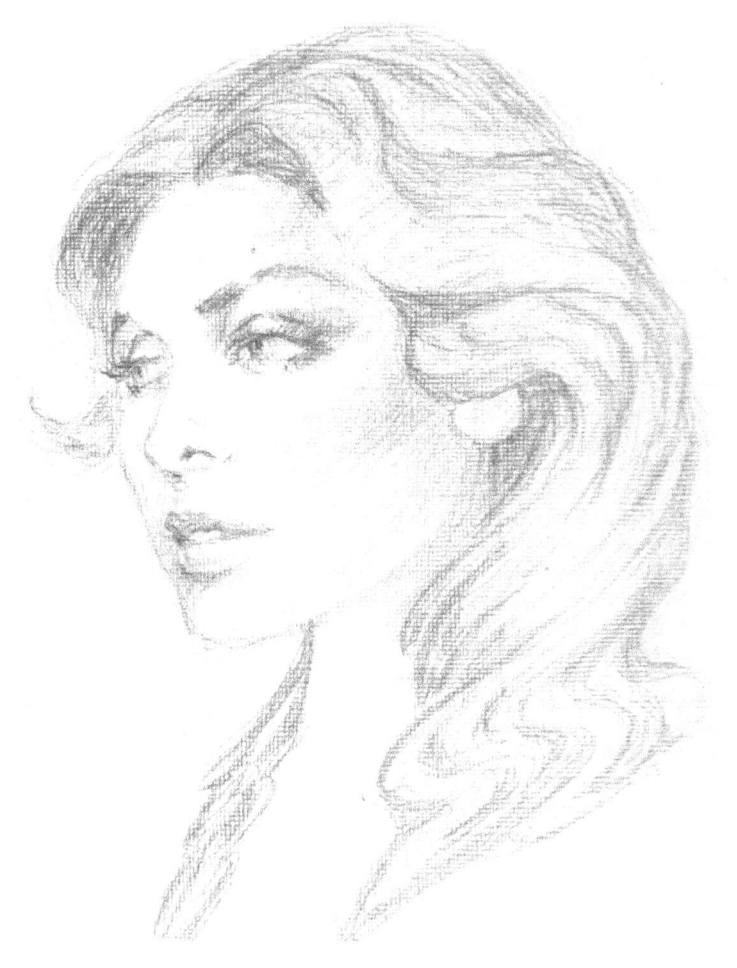

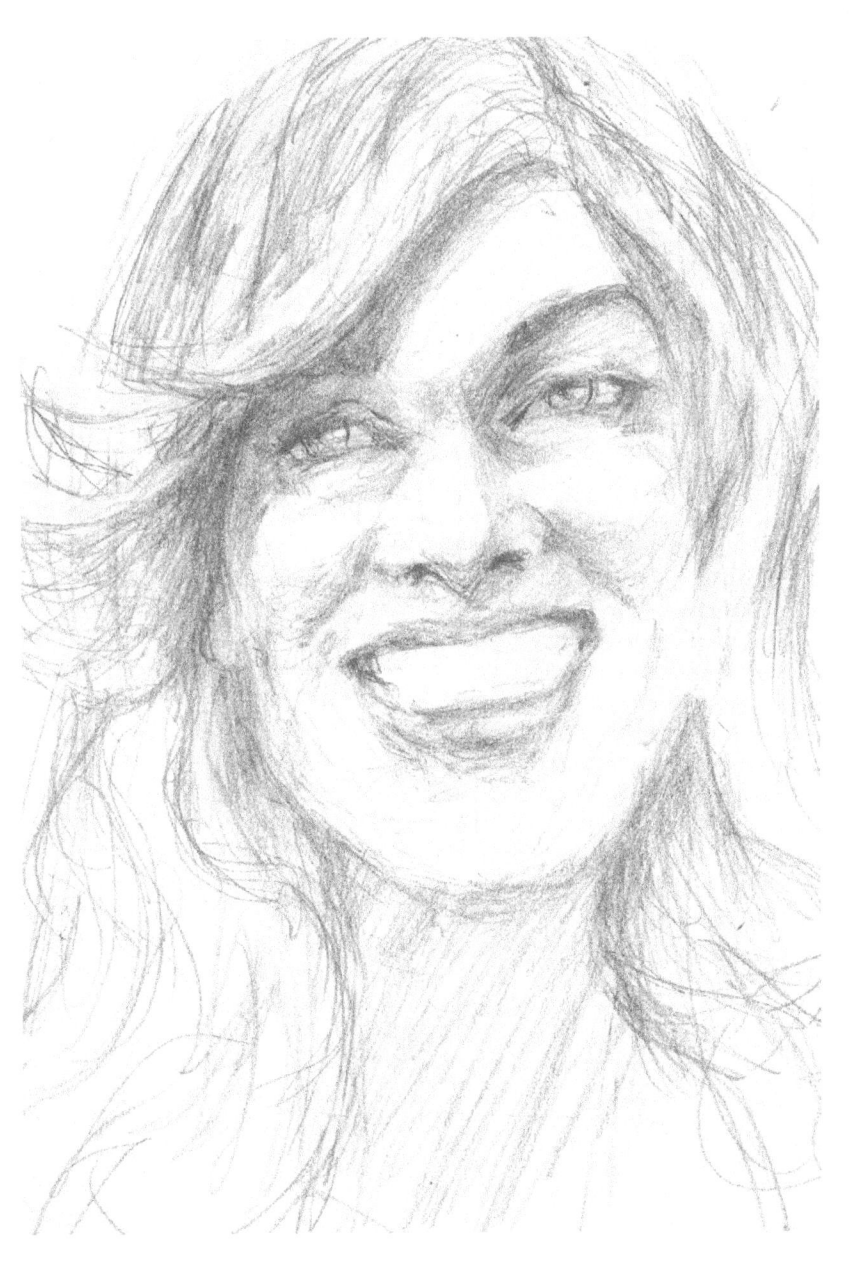

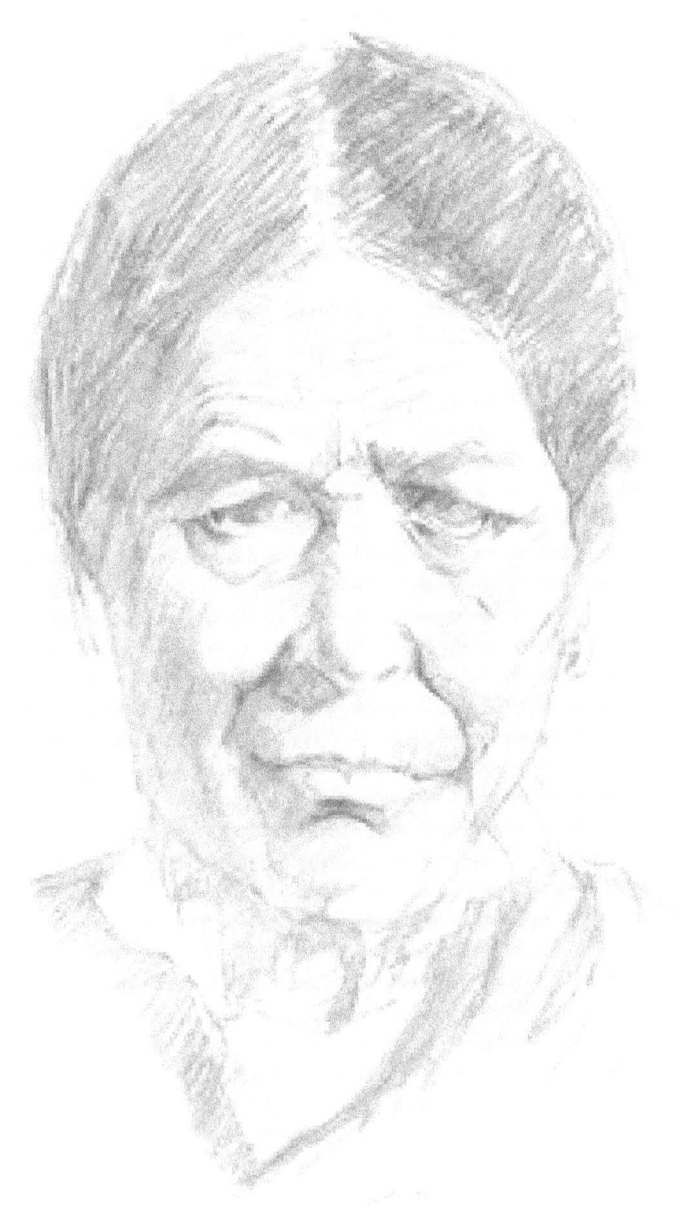

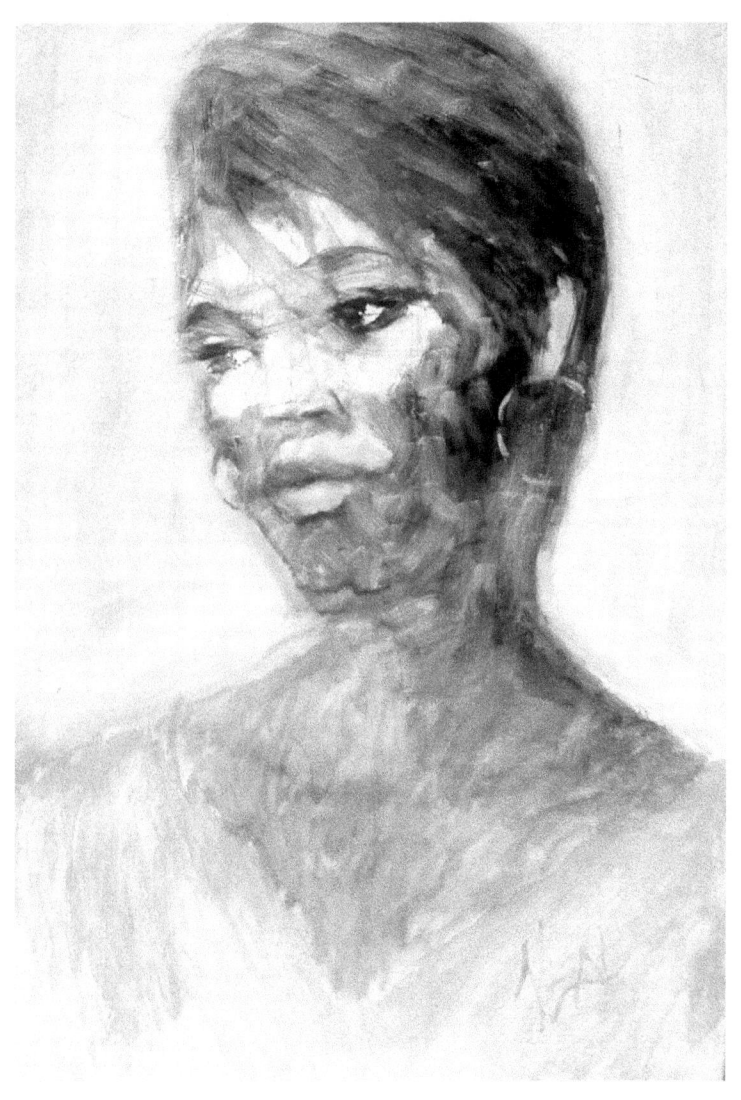

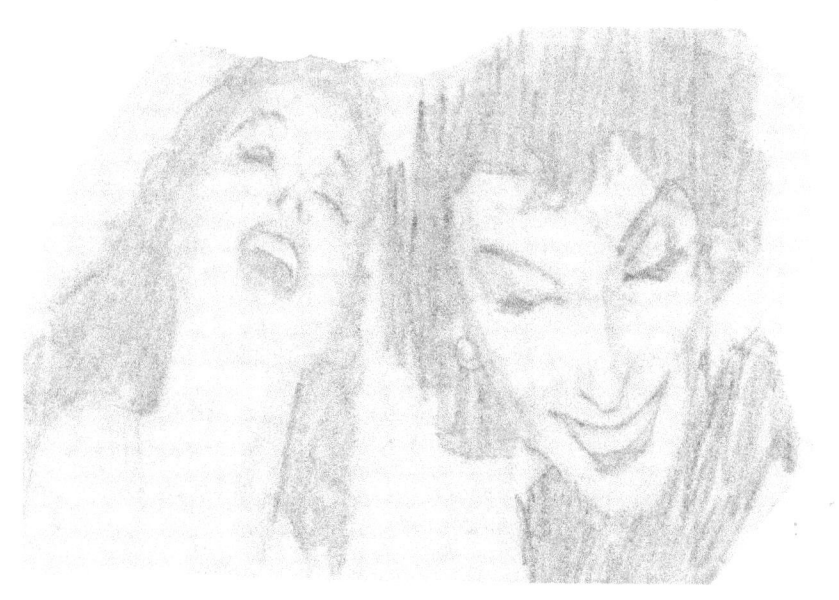

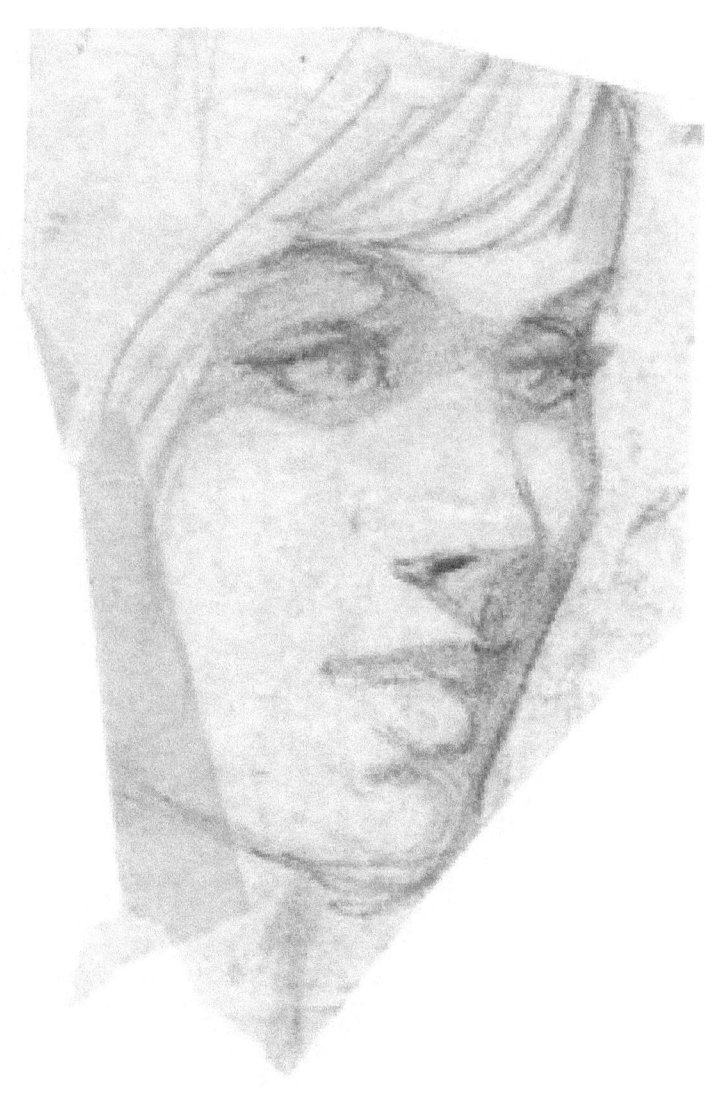

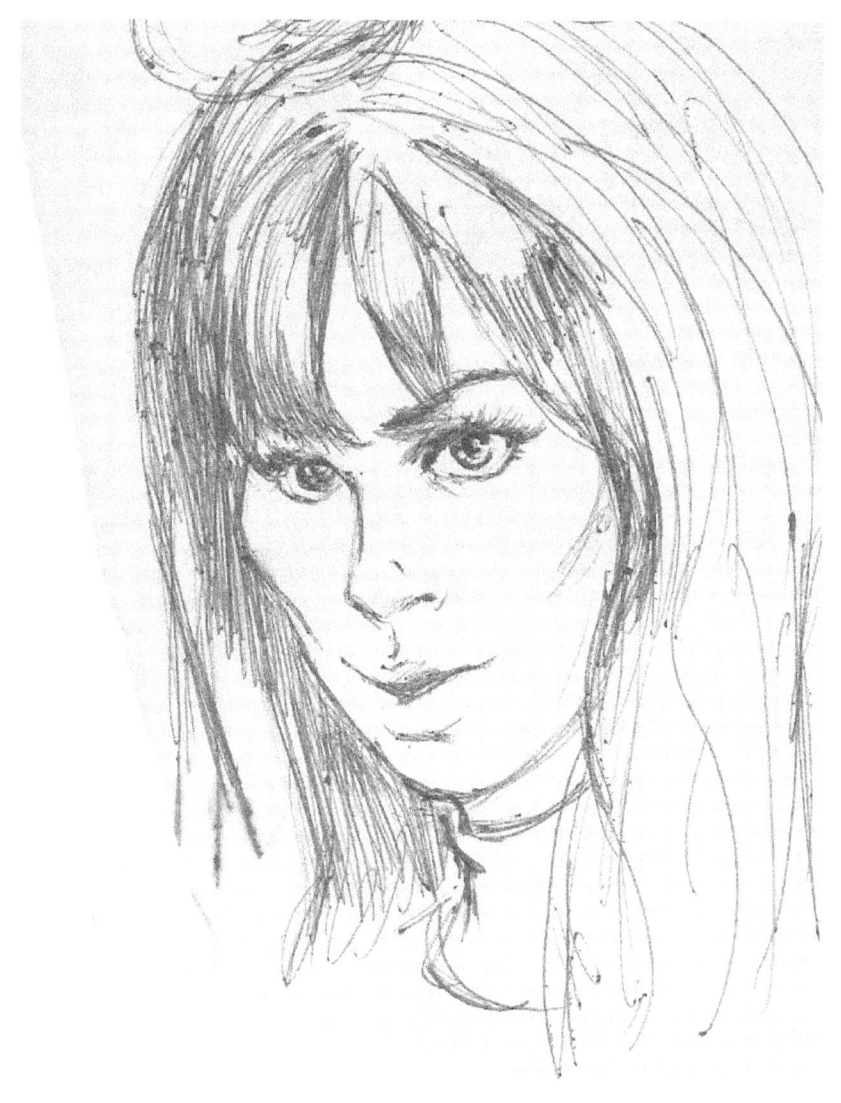

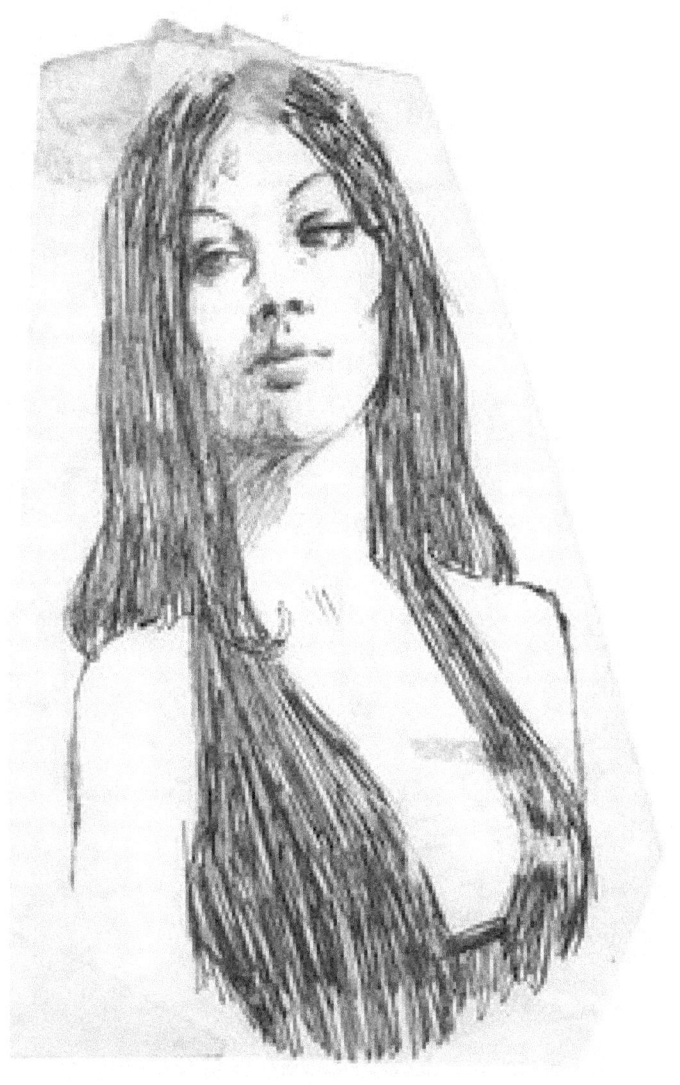

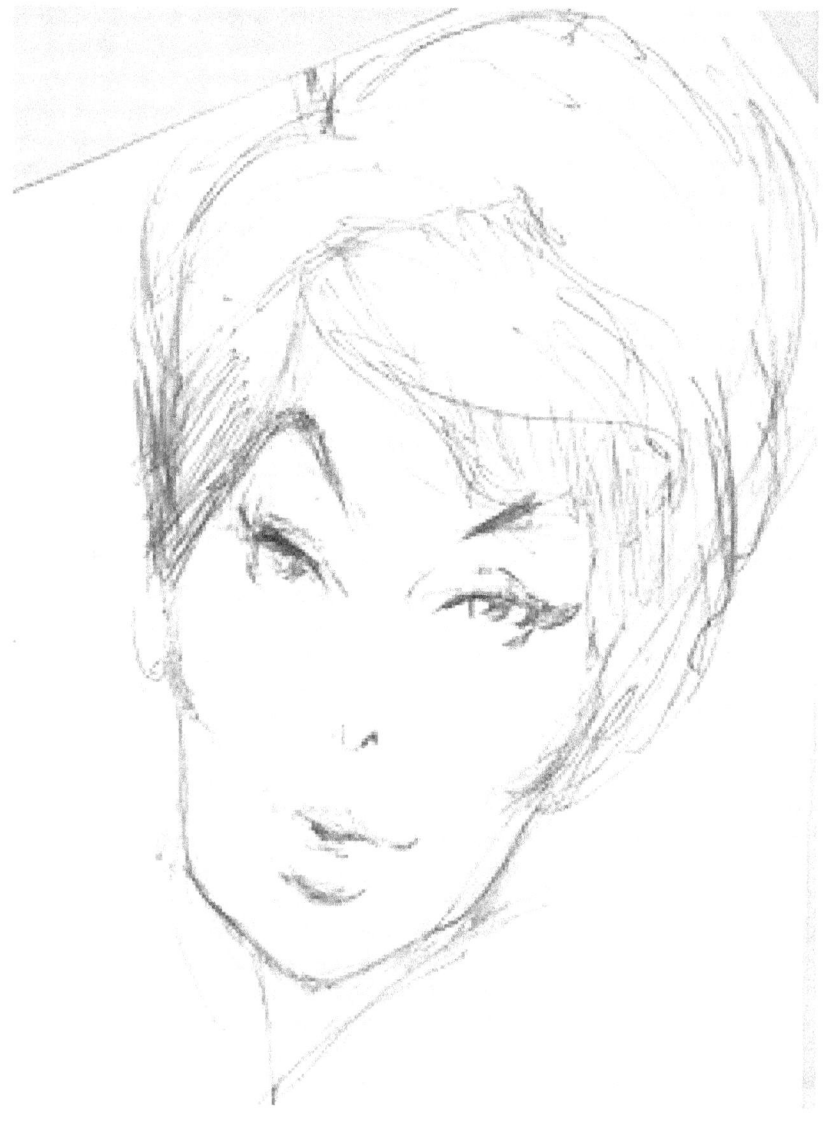

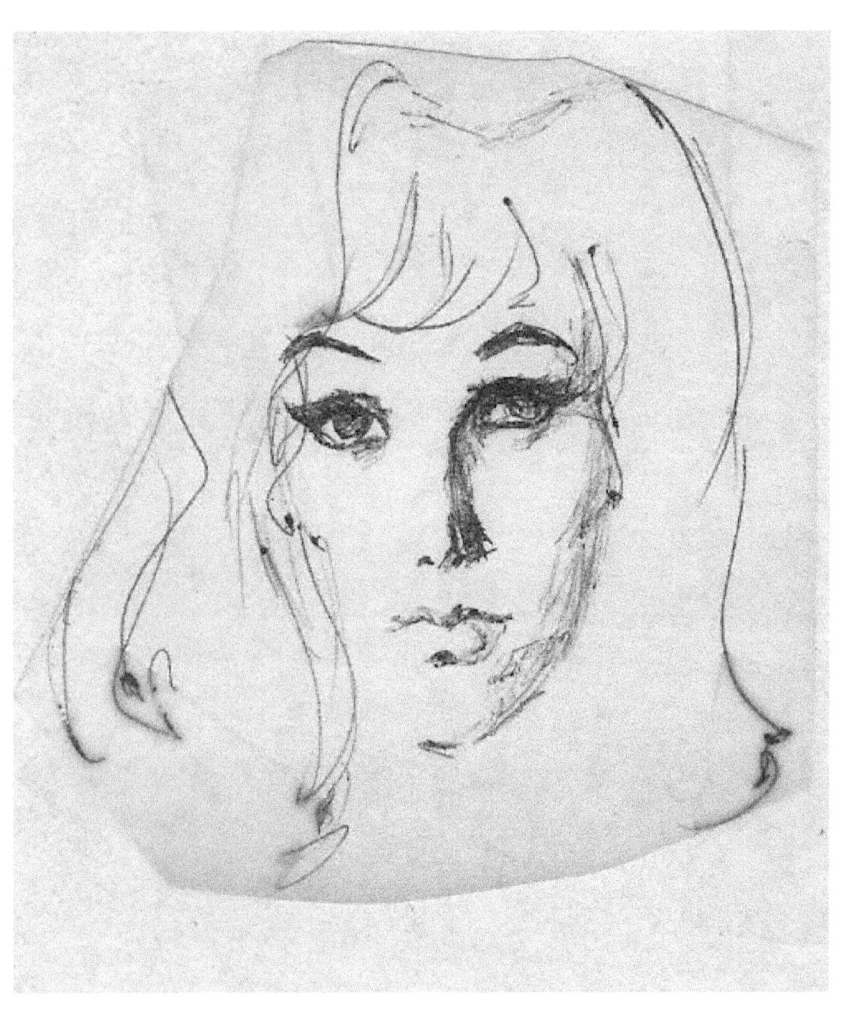

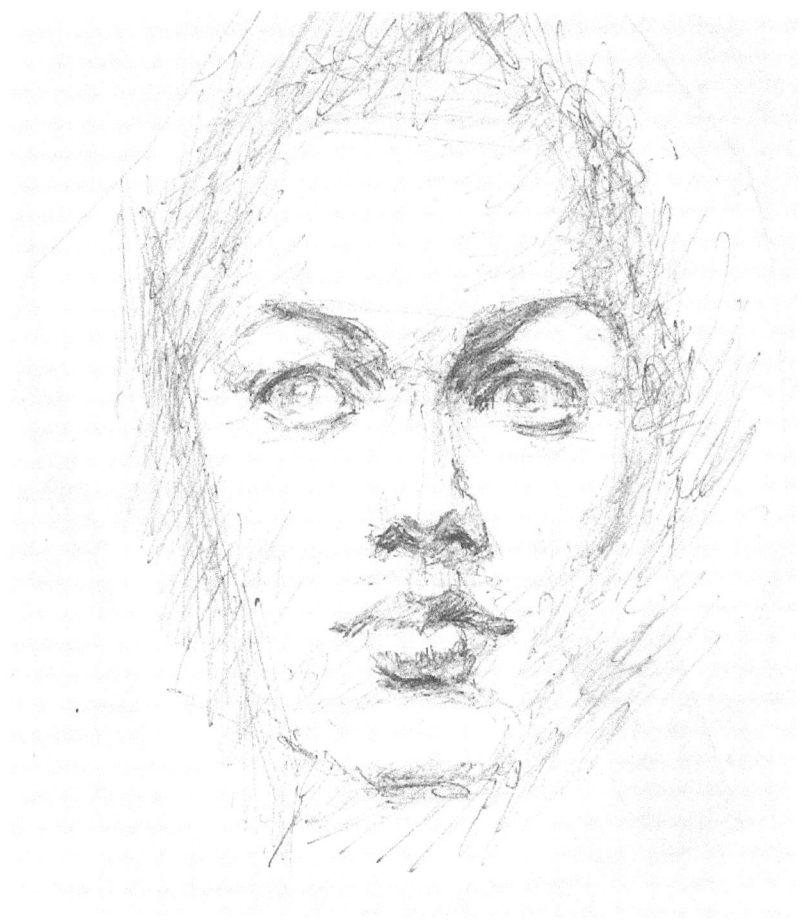

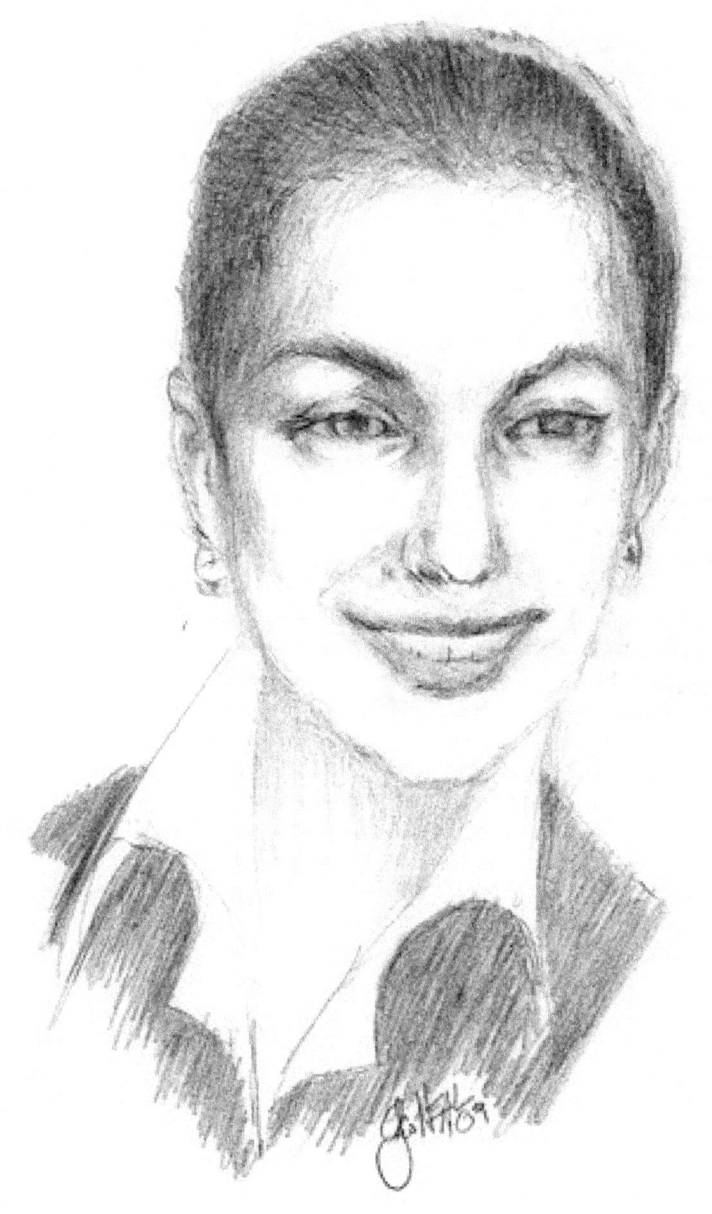

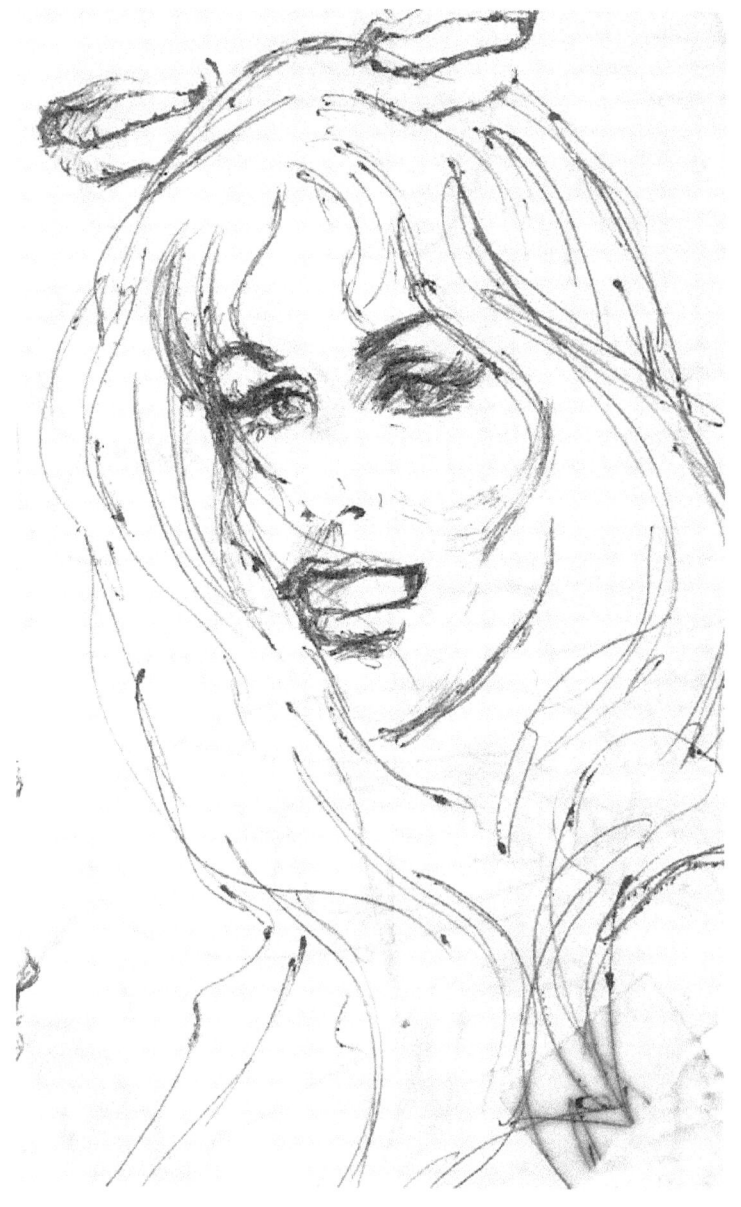

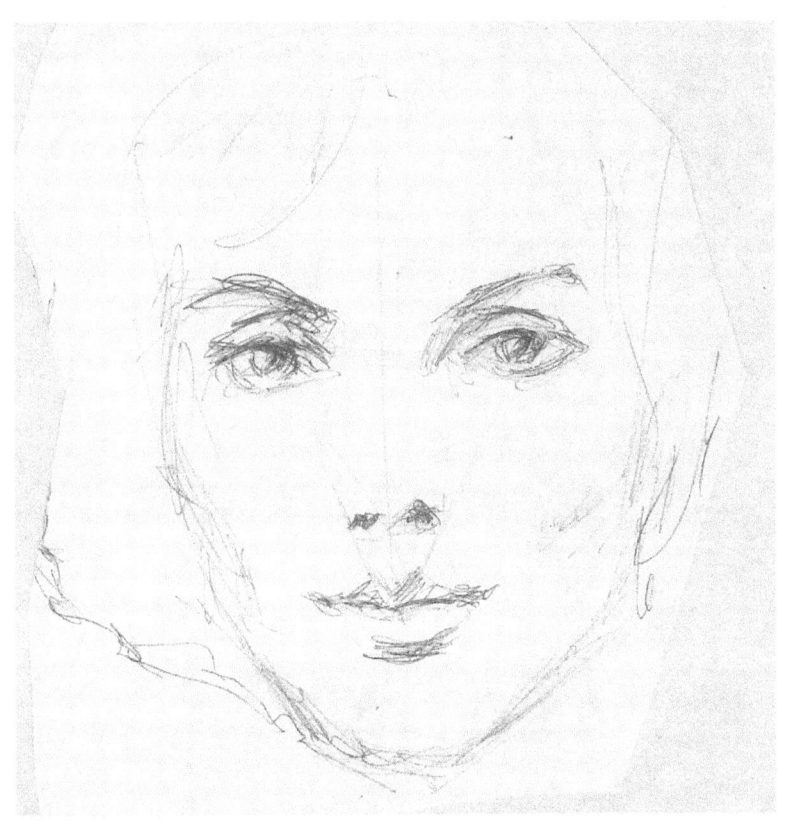

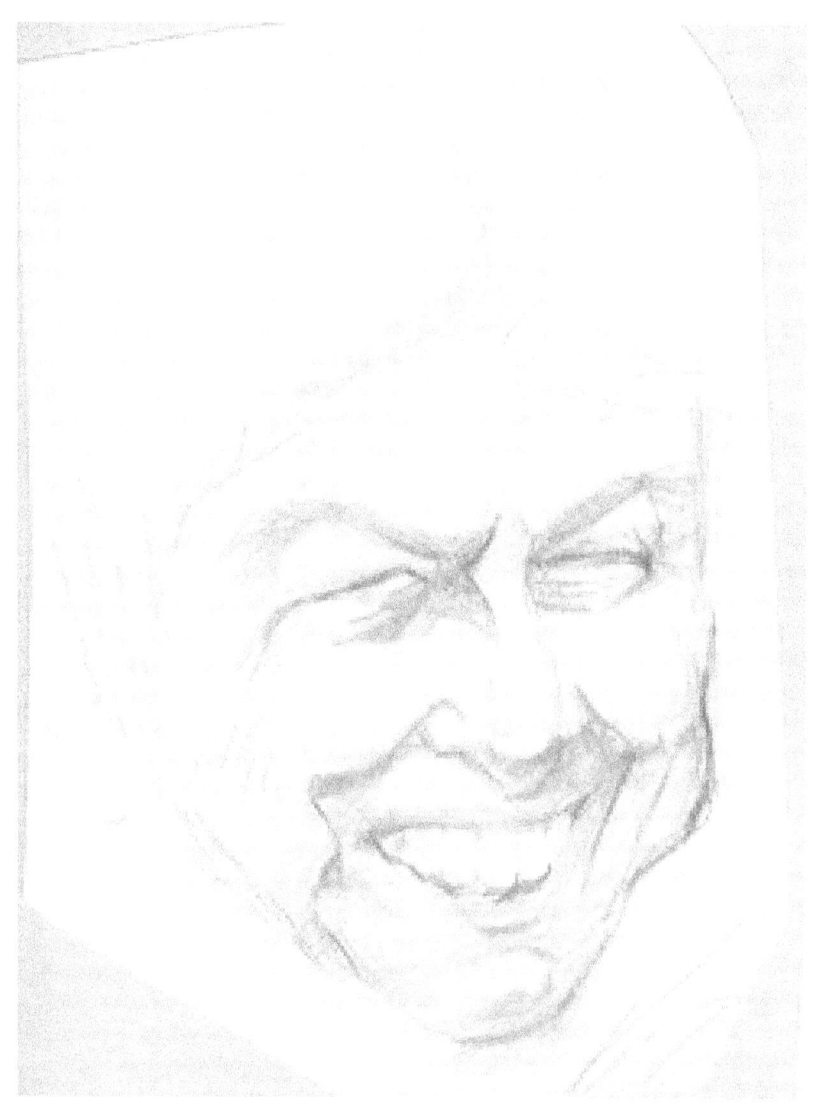

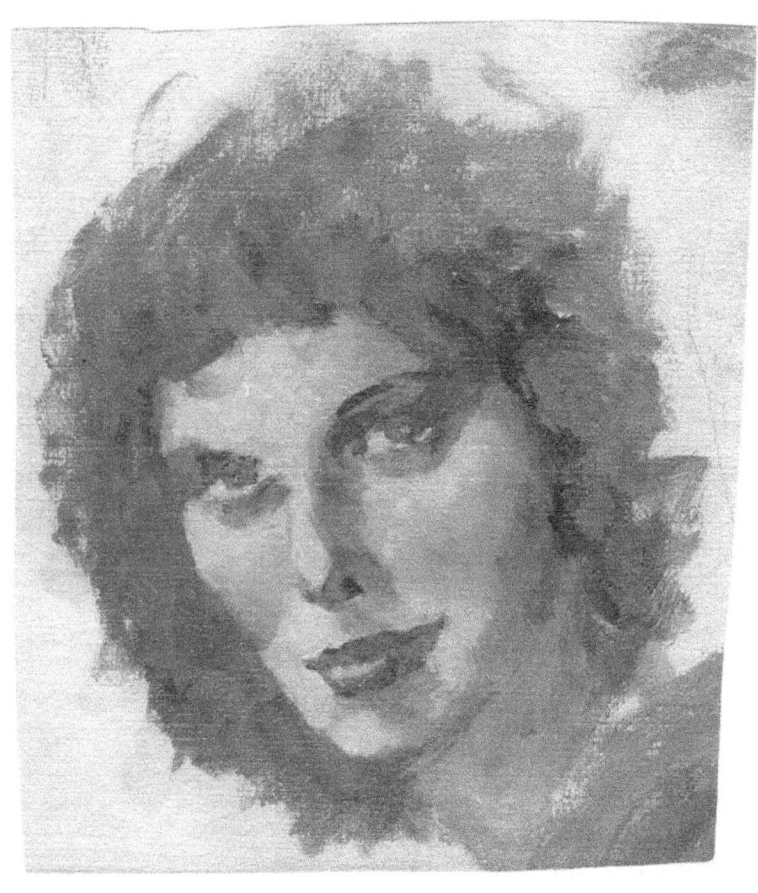

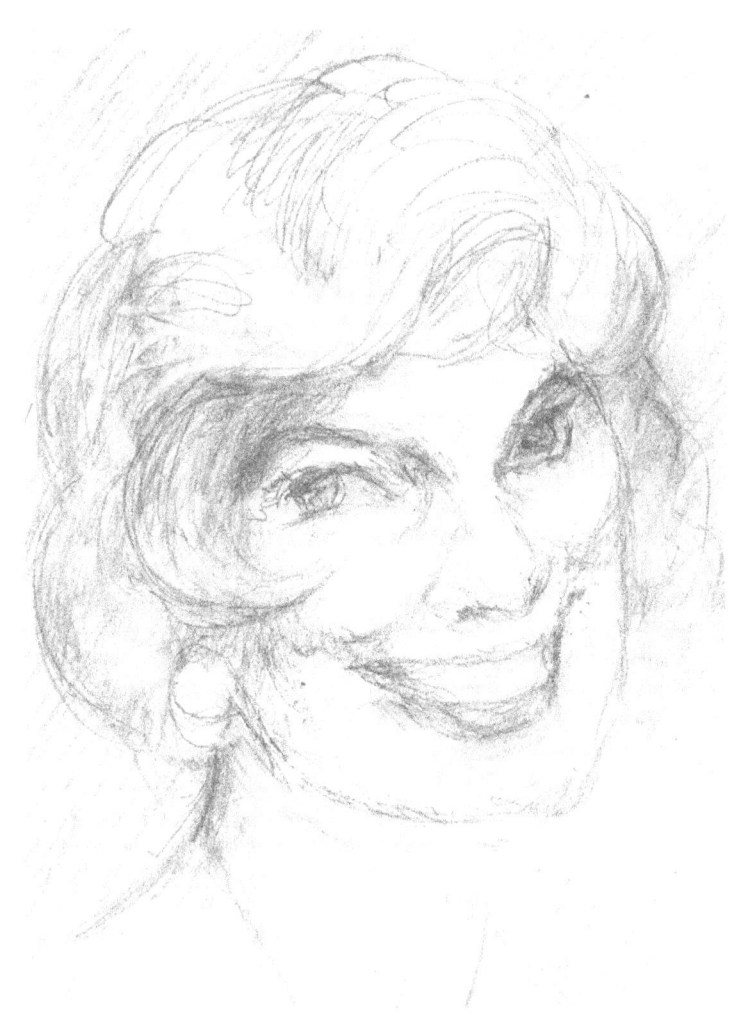

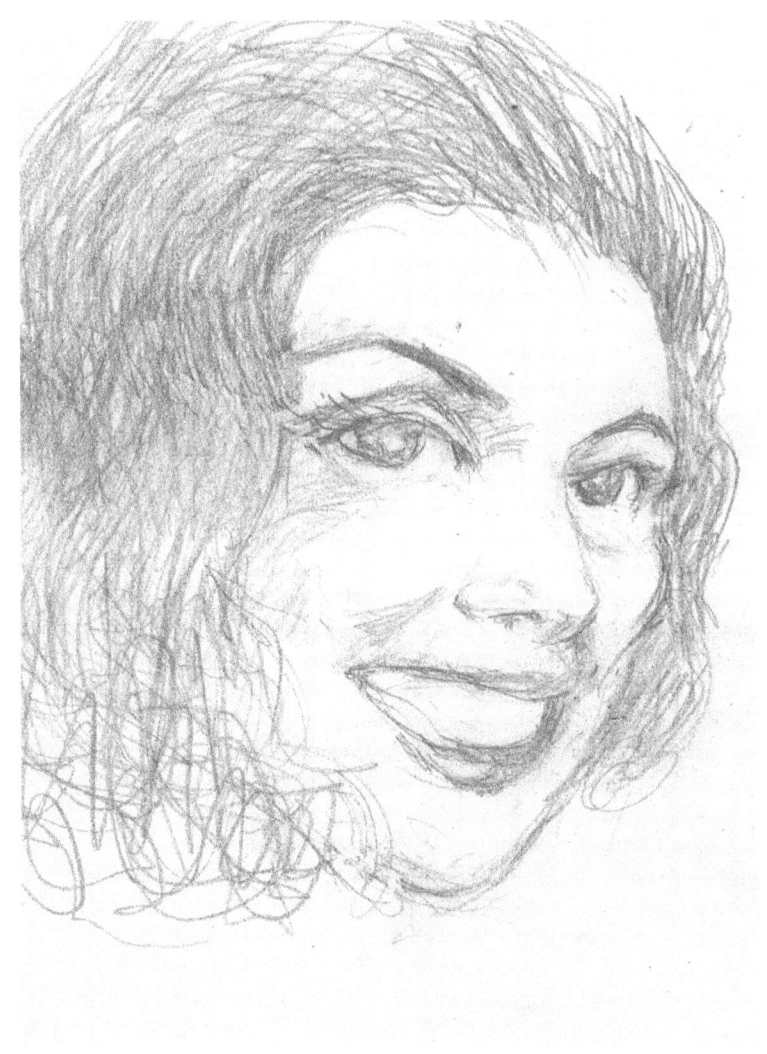

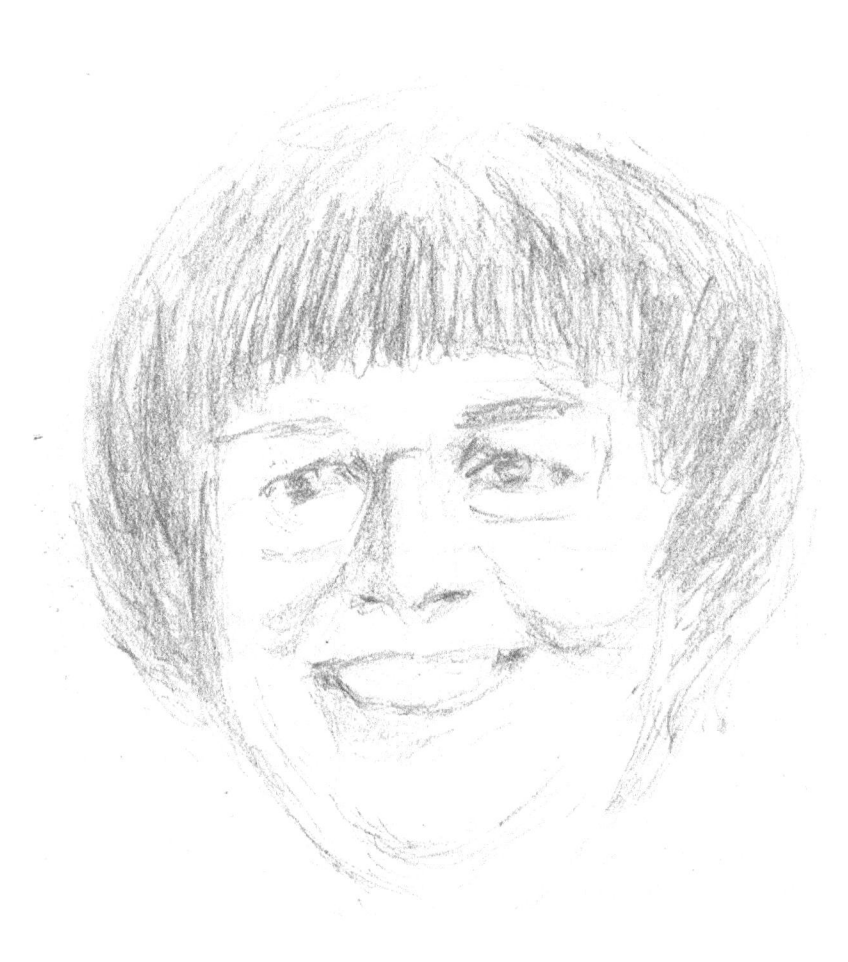

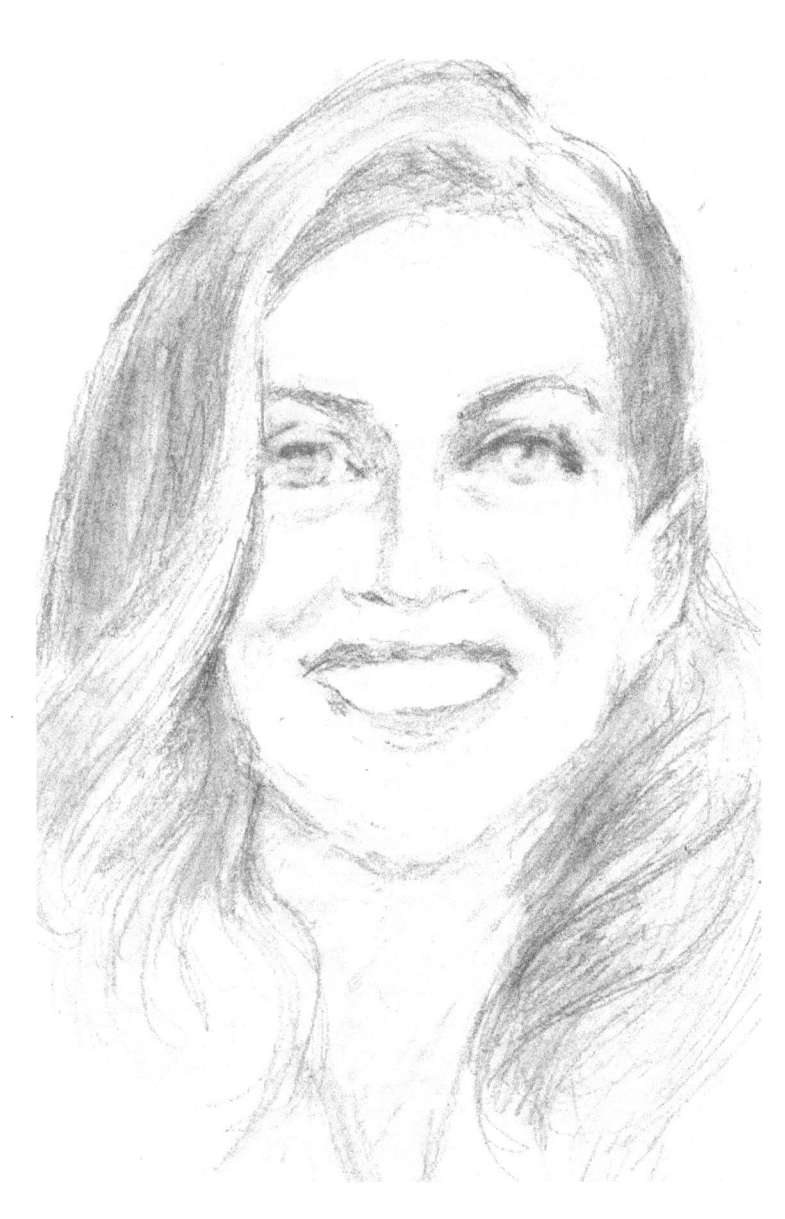

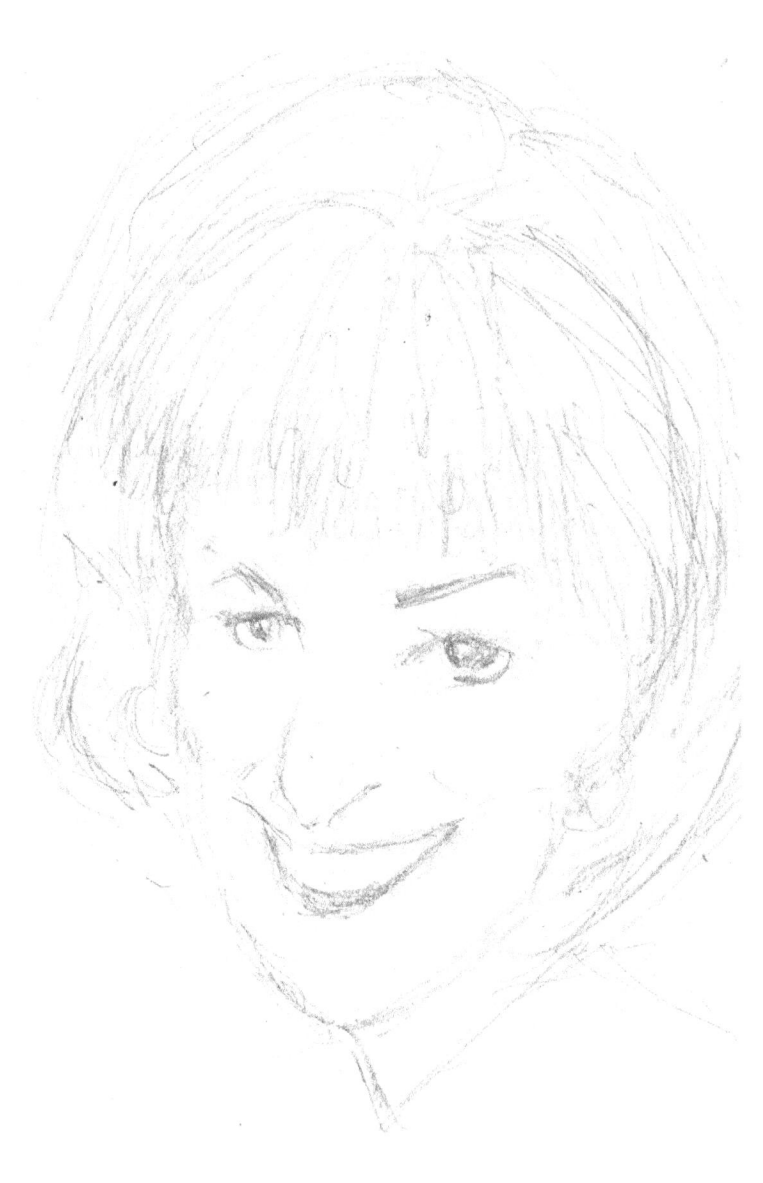

128

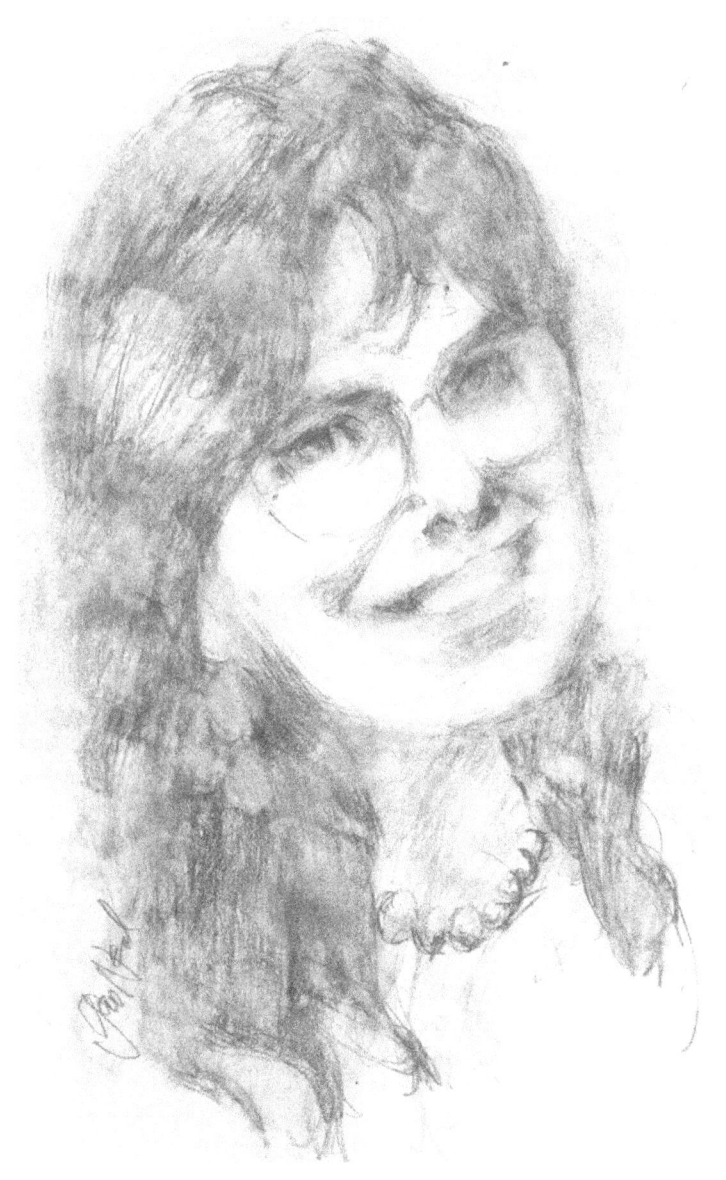

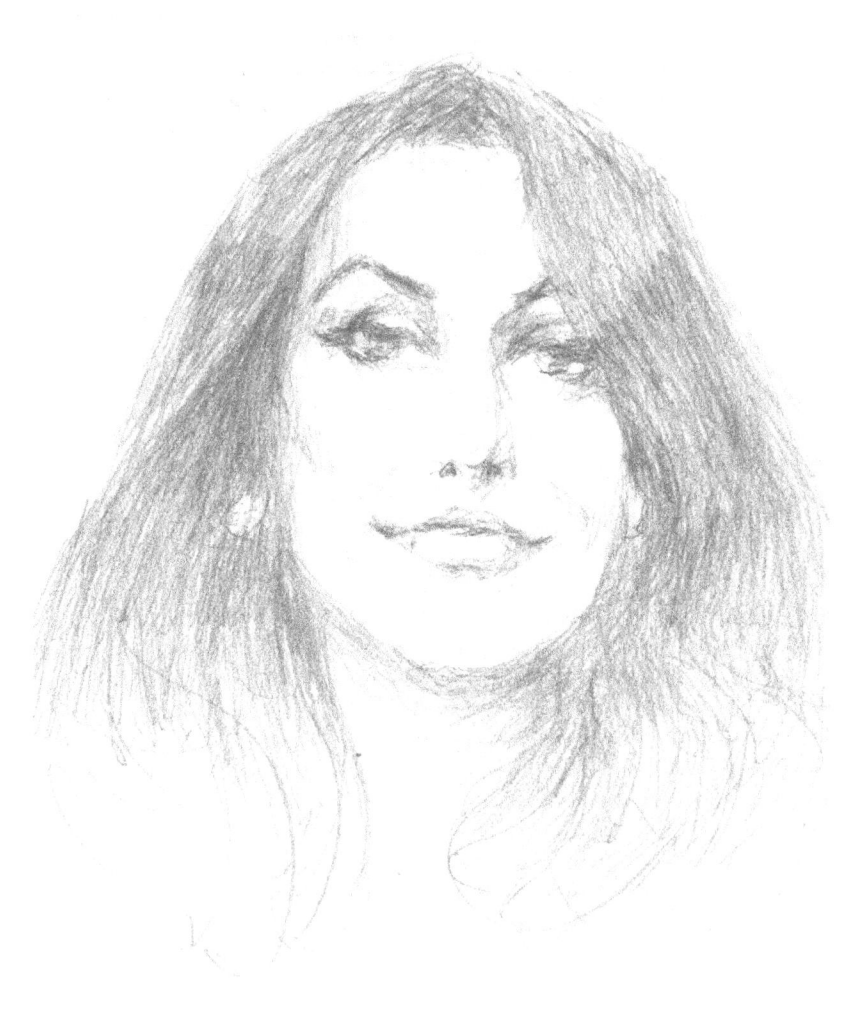

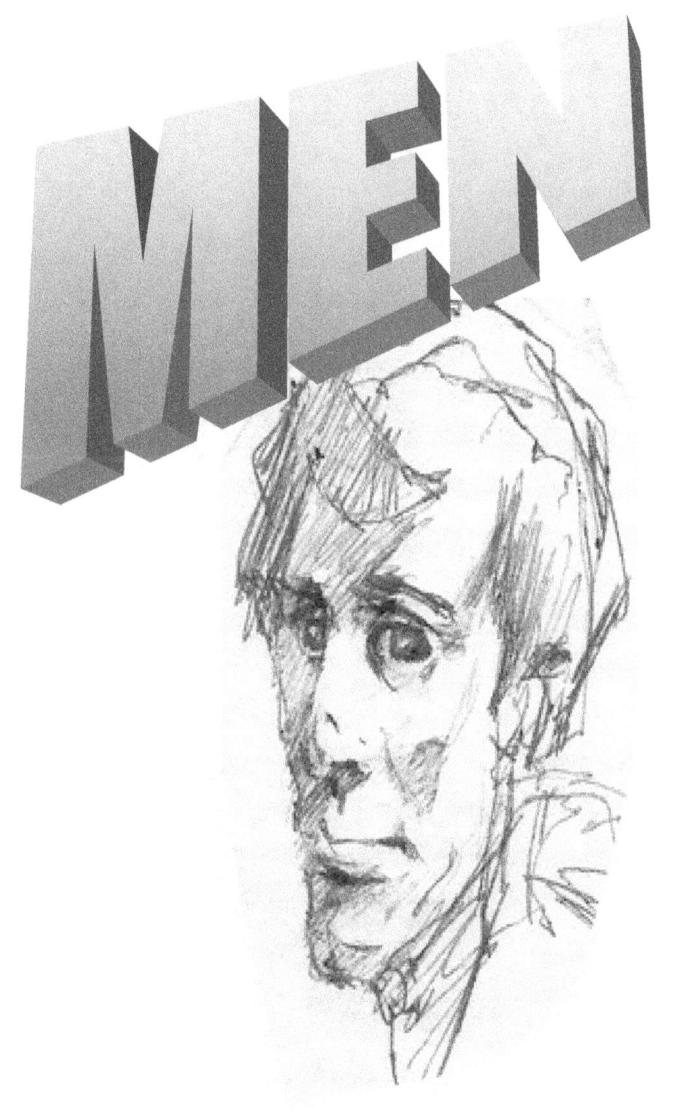

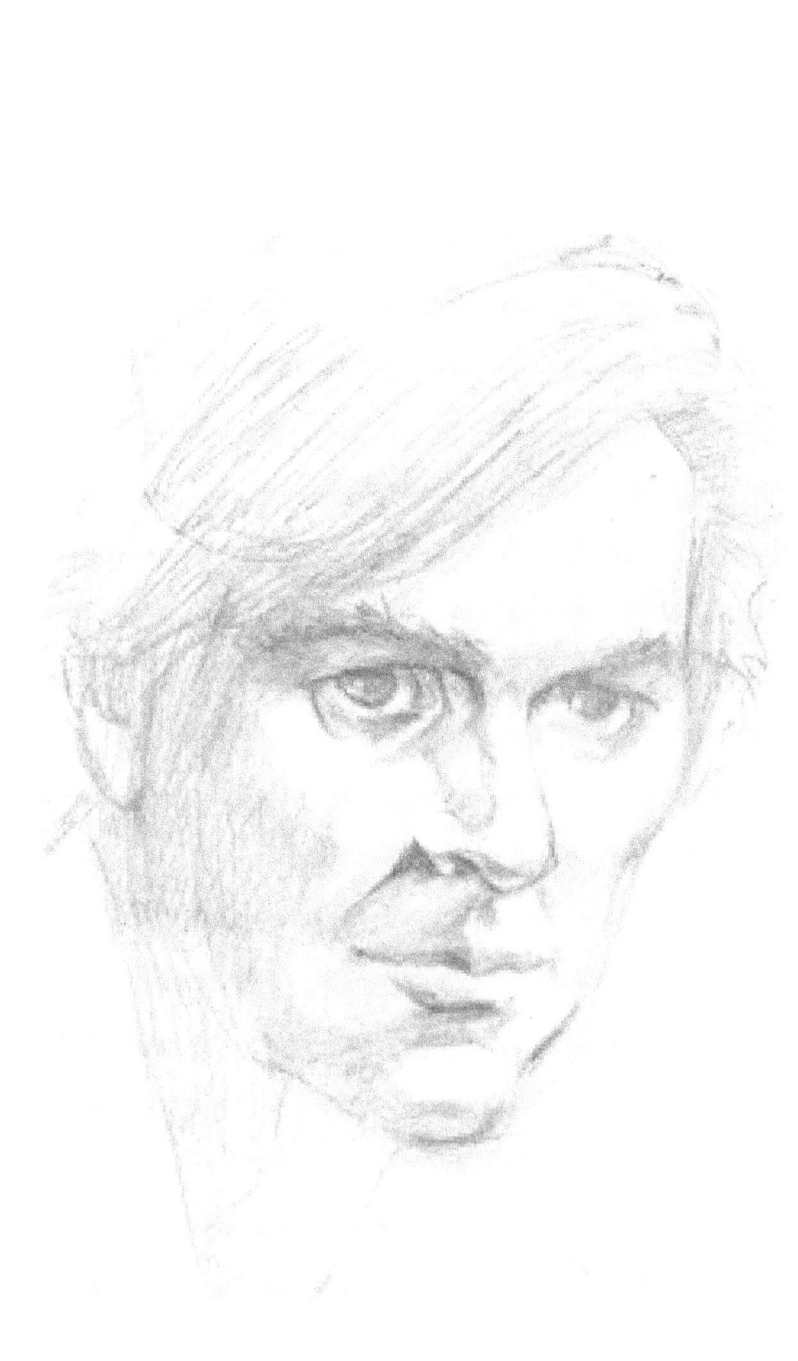

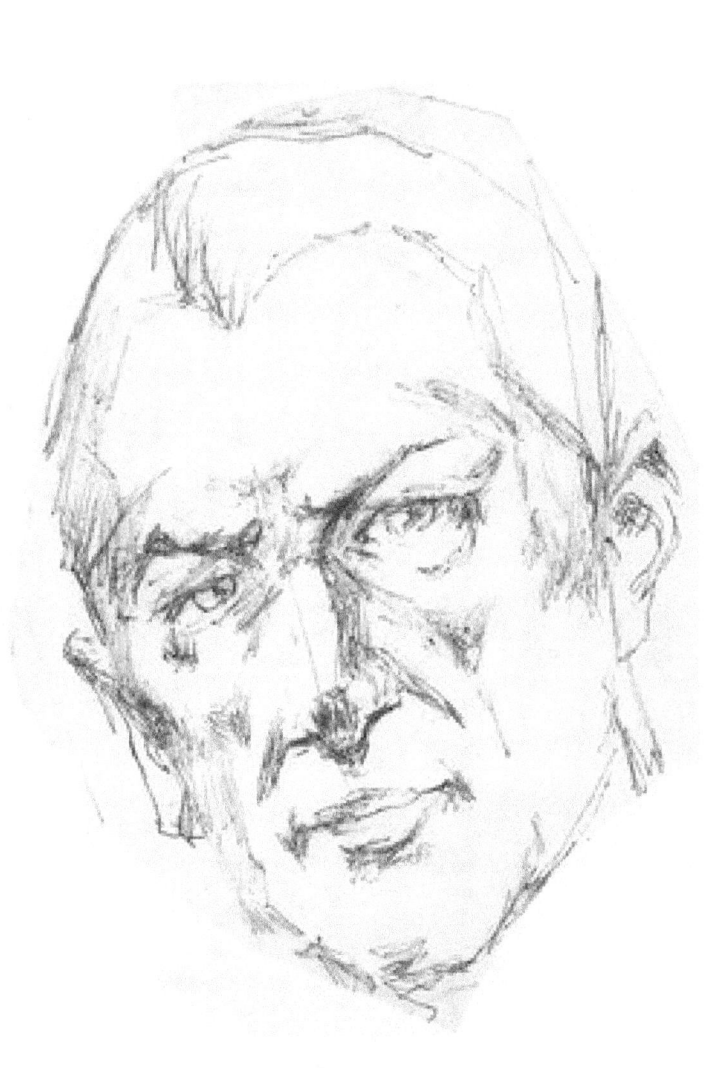

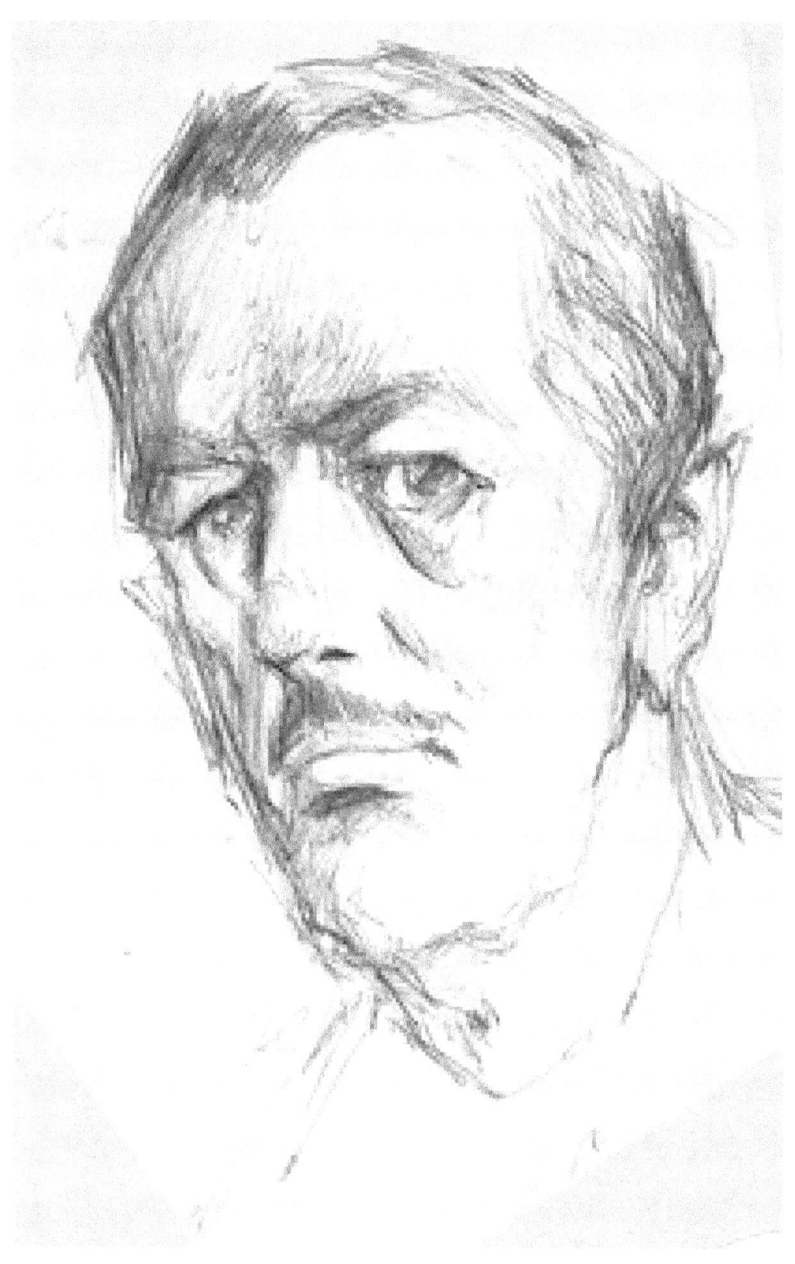

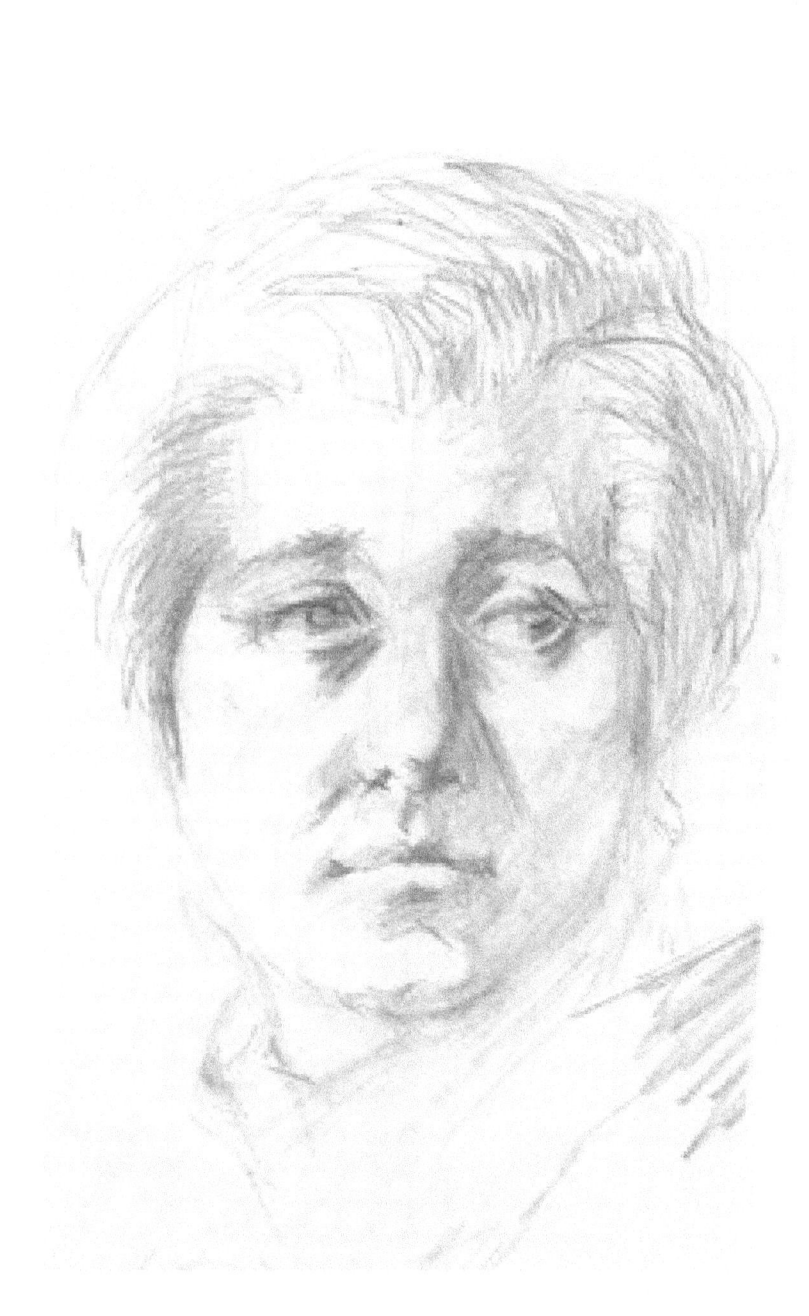

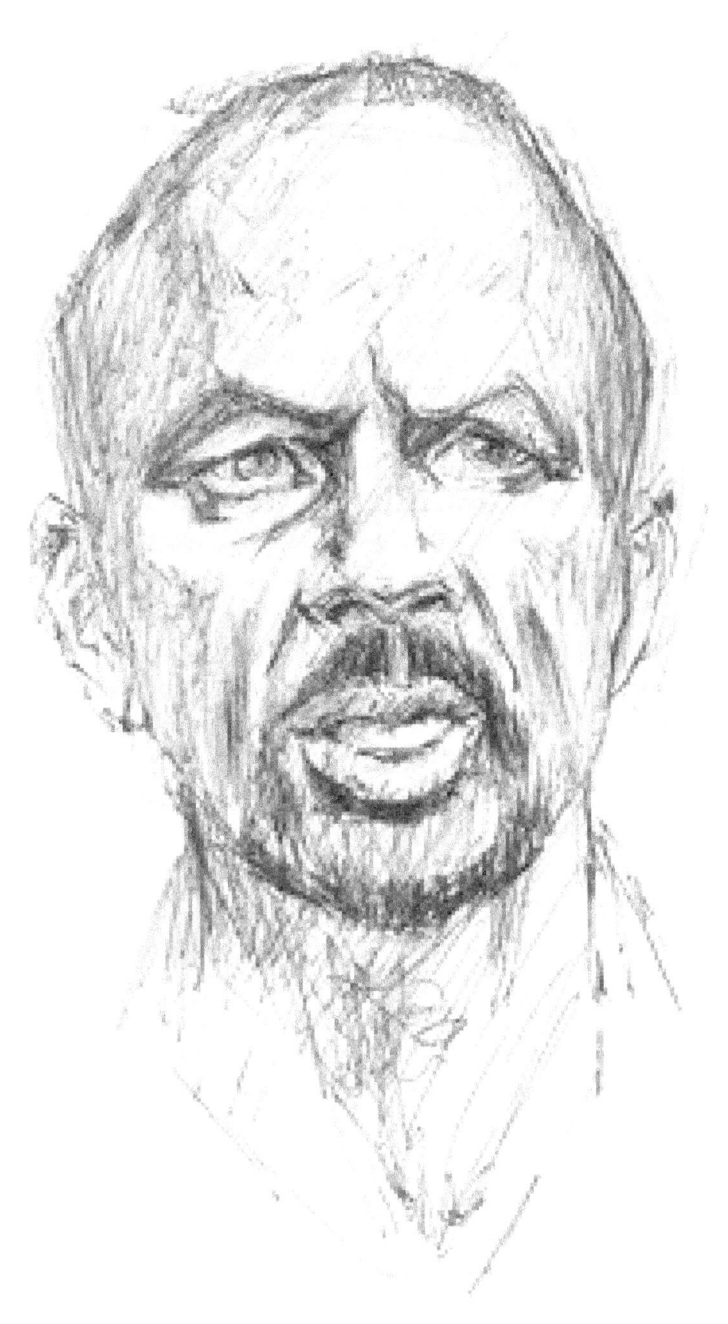

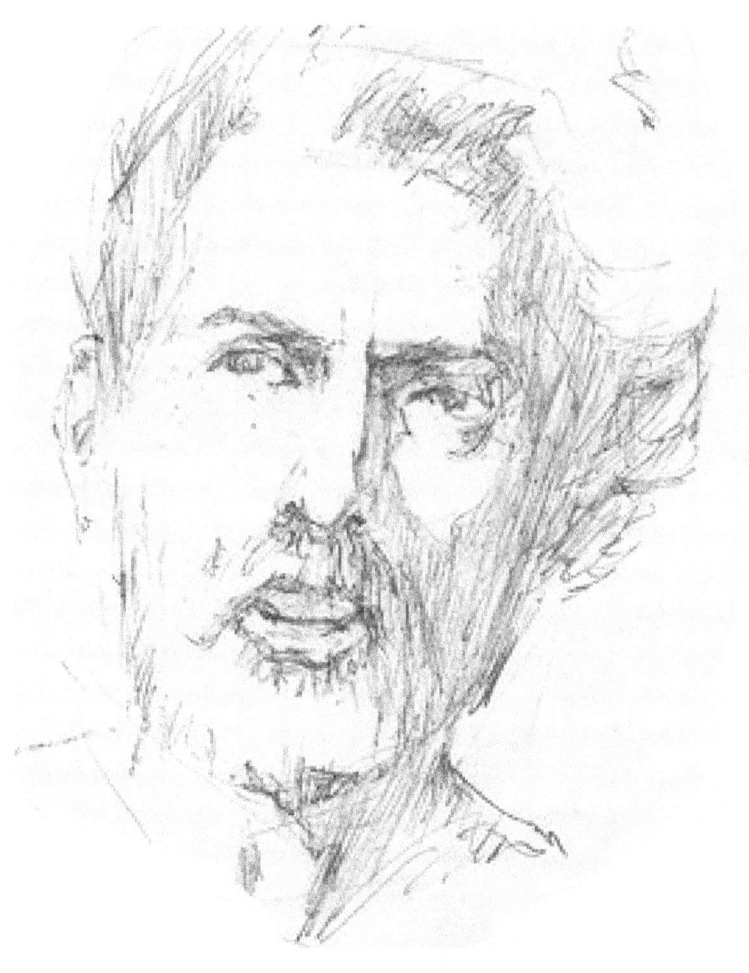

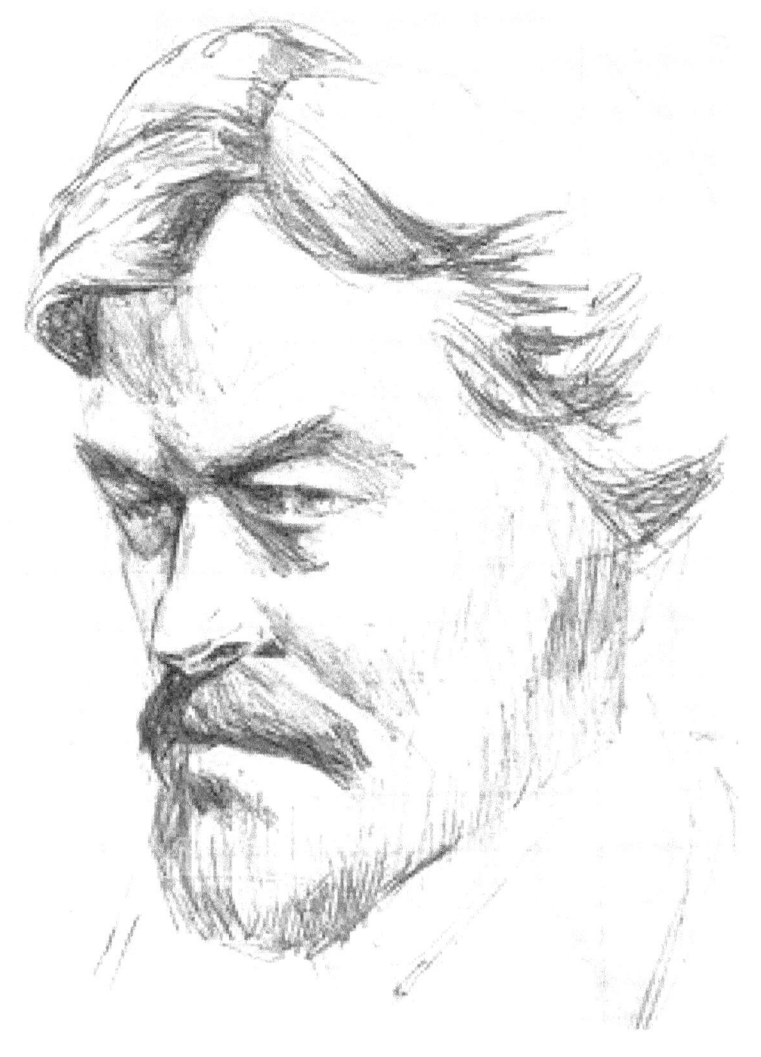

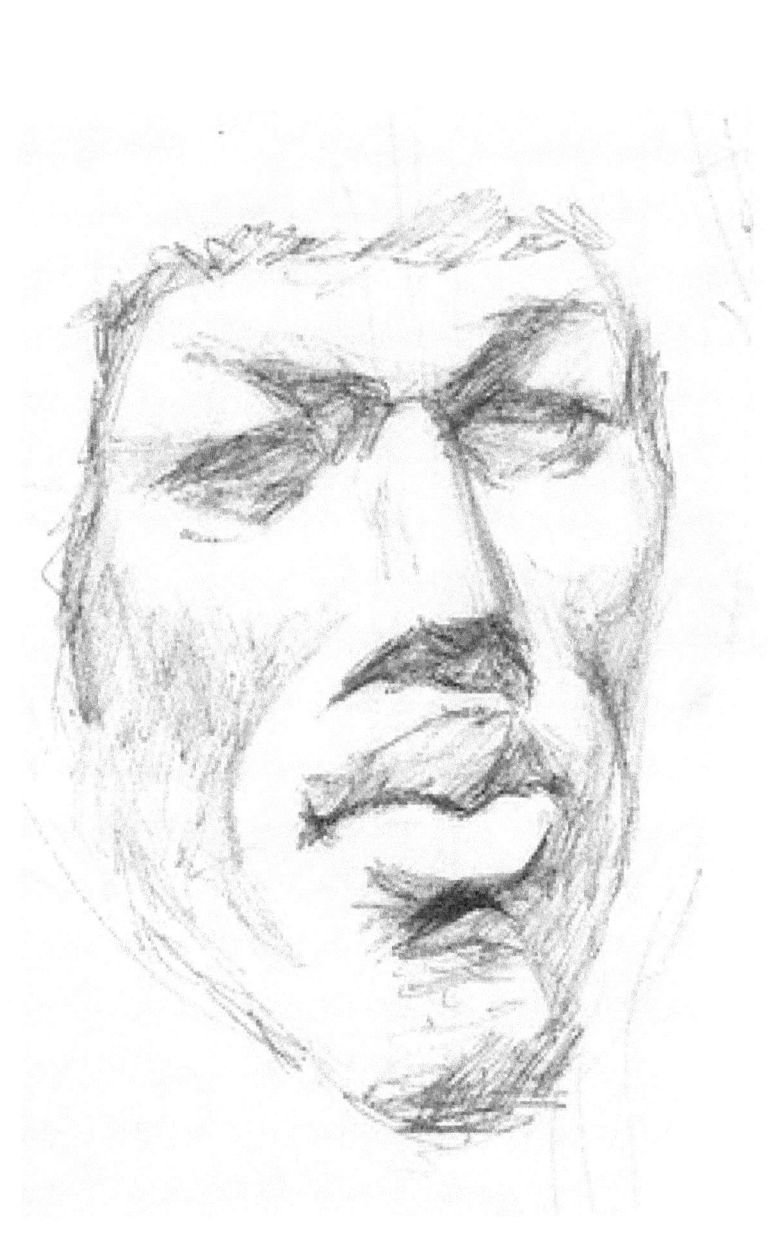

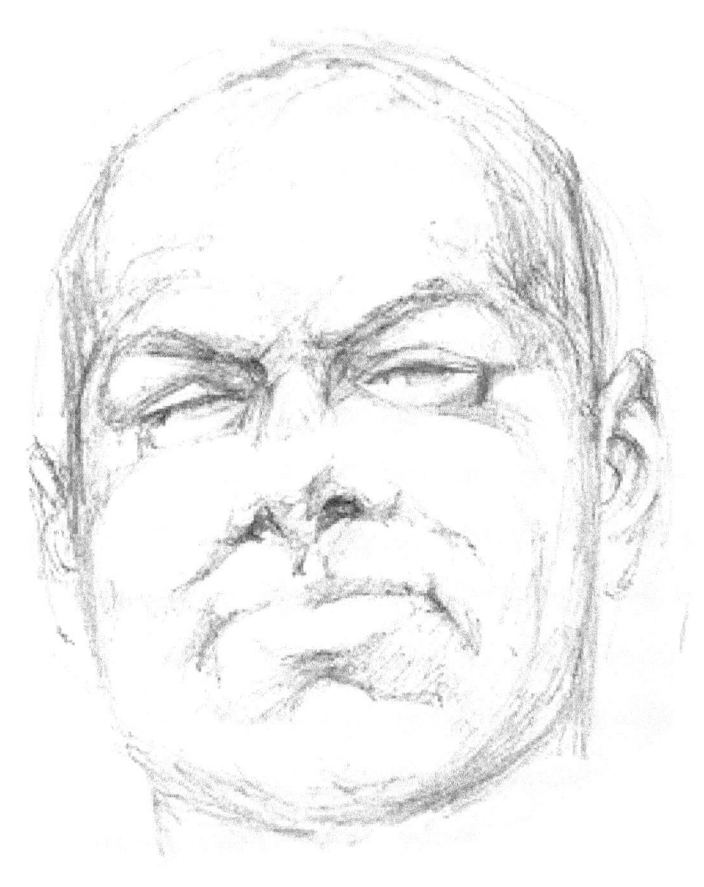

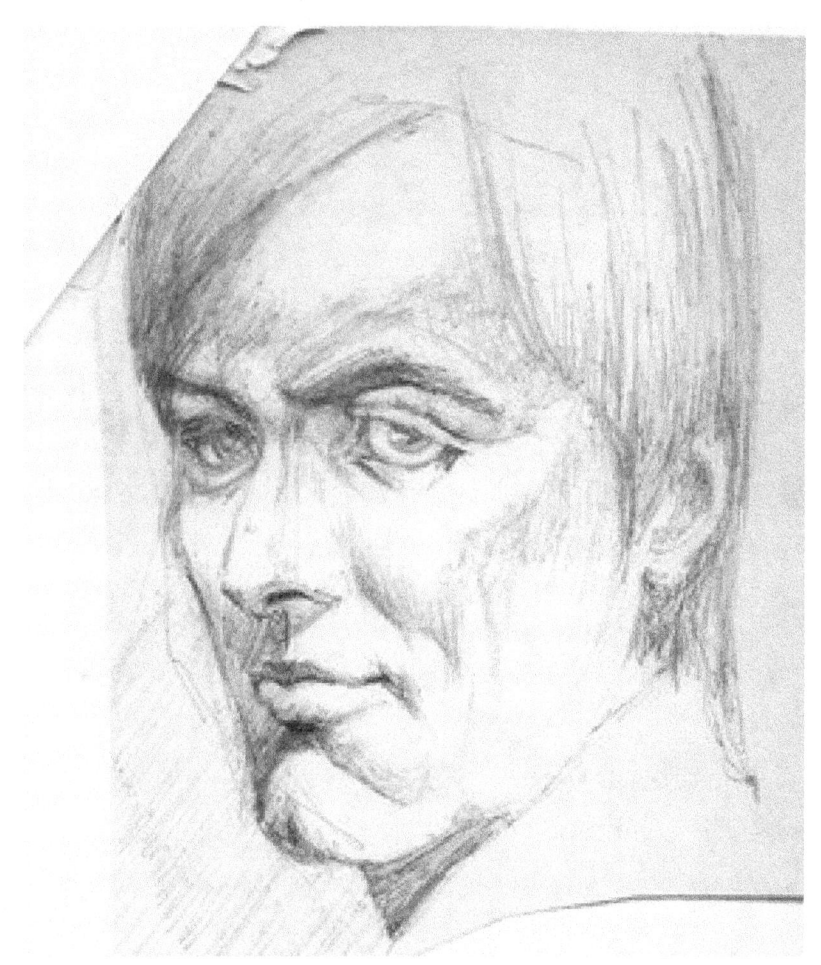

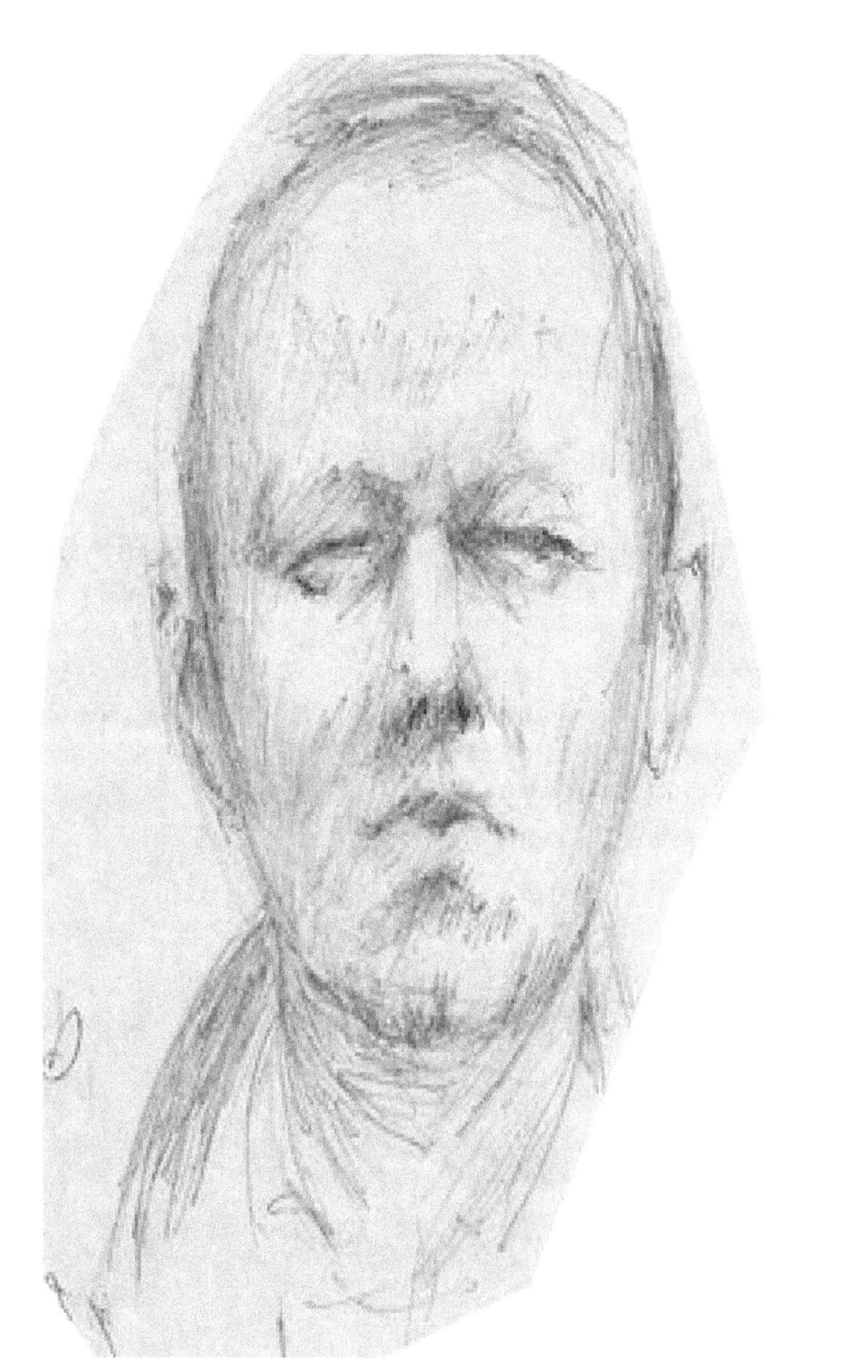

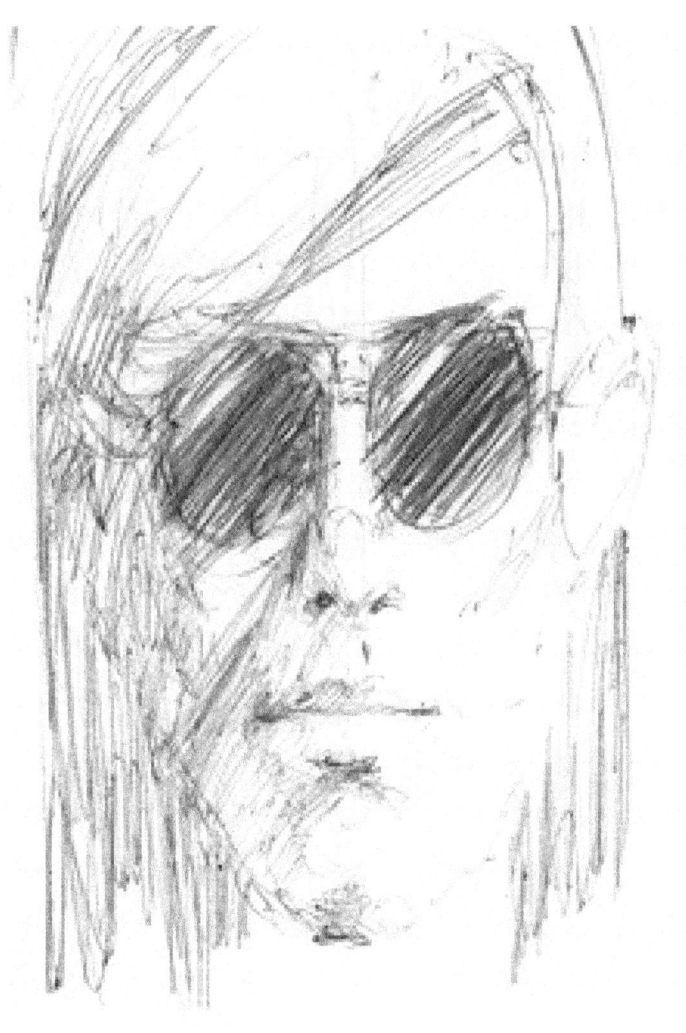

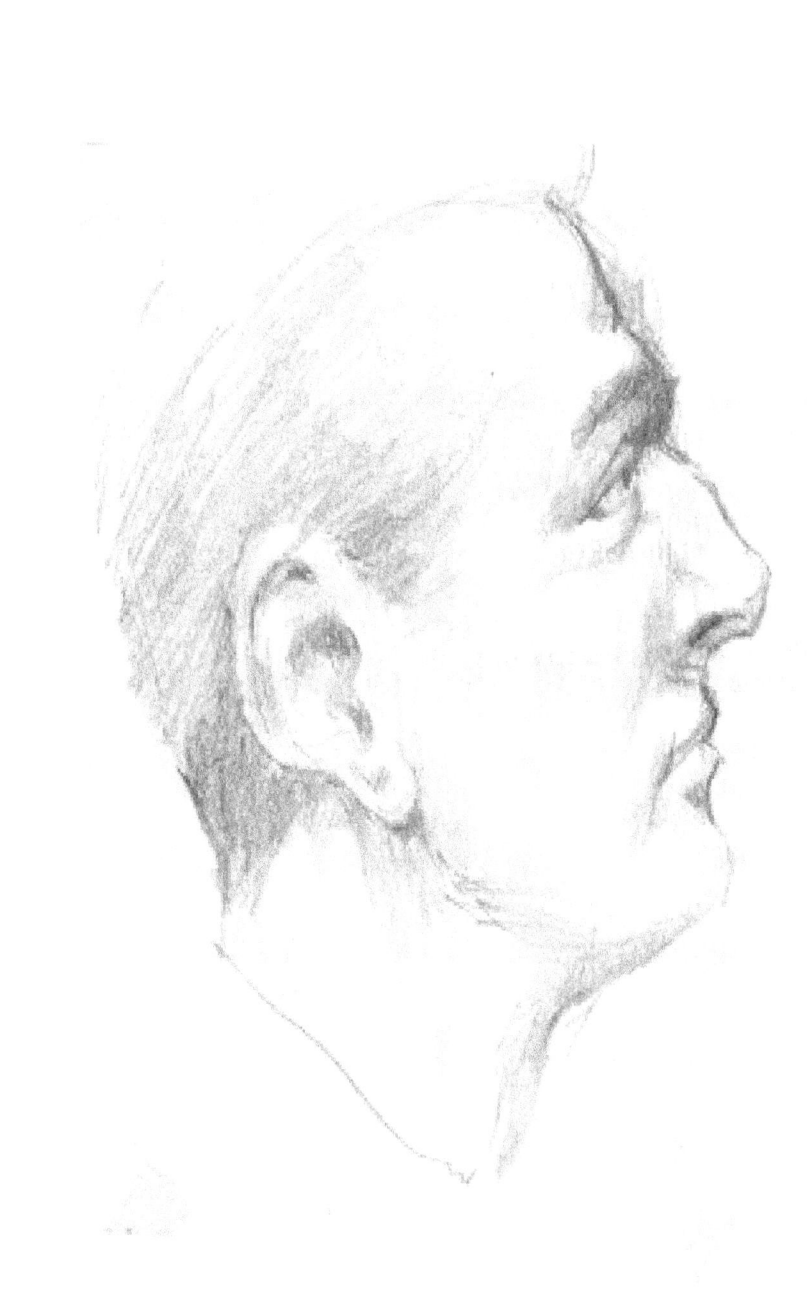

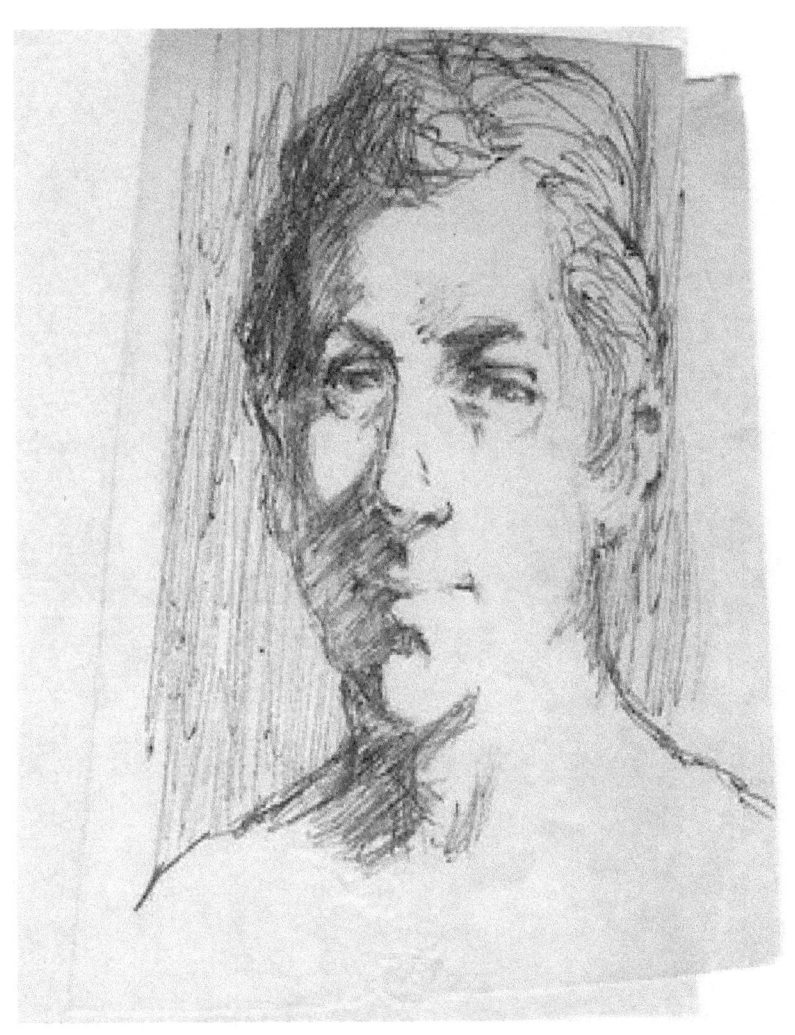

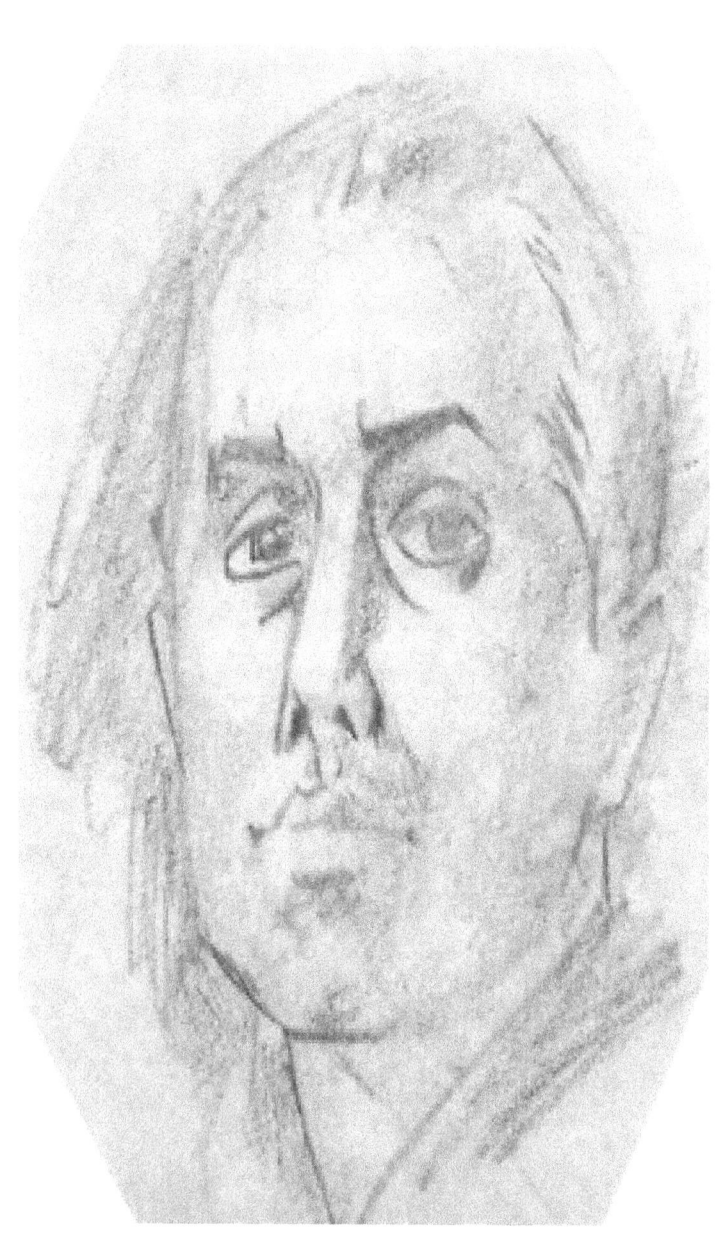

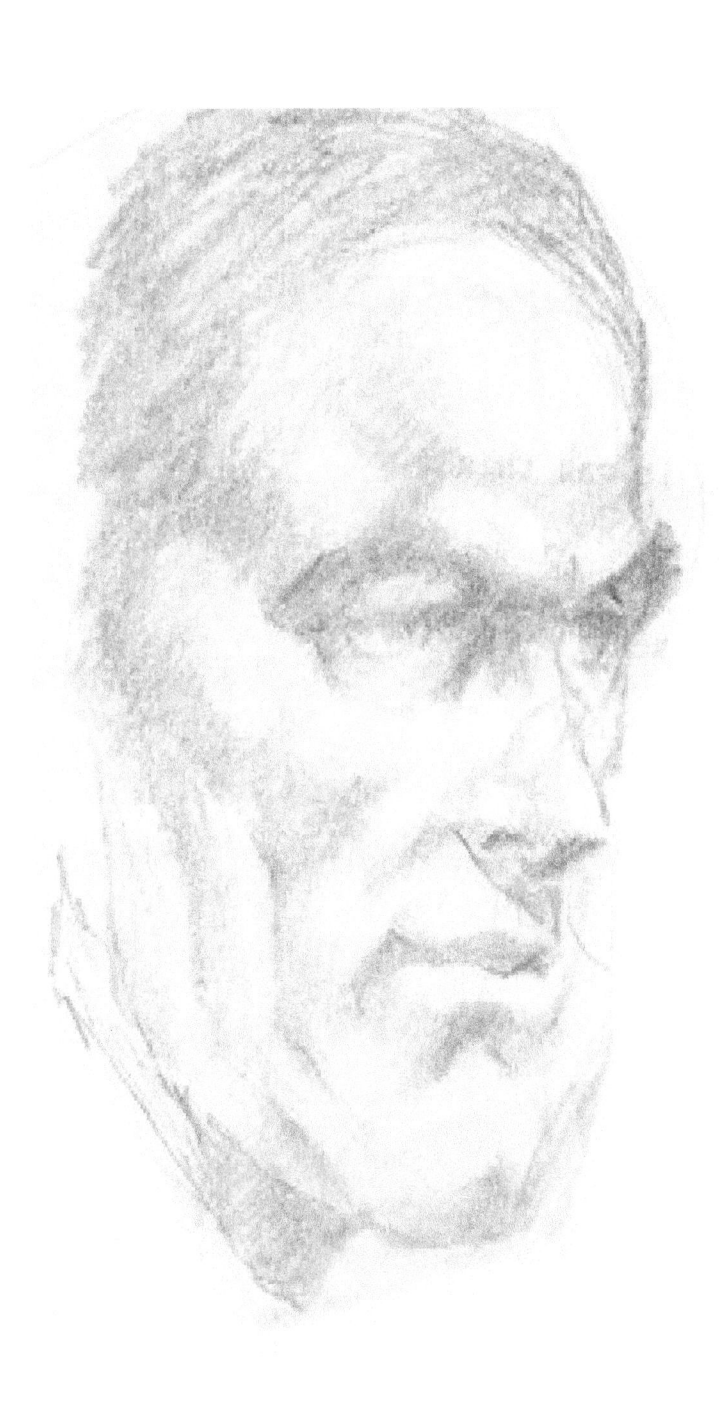

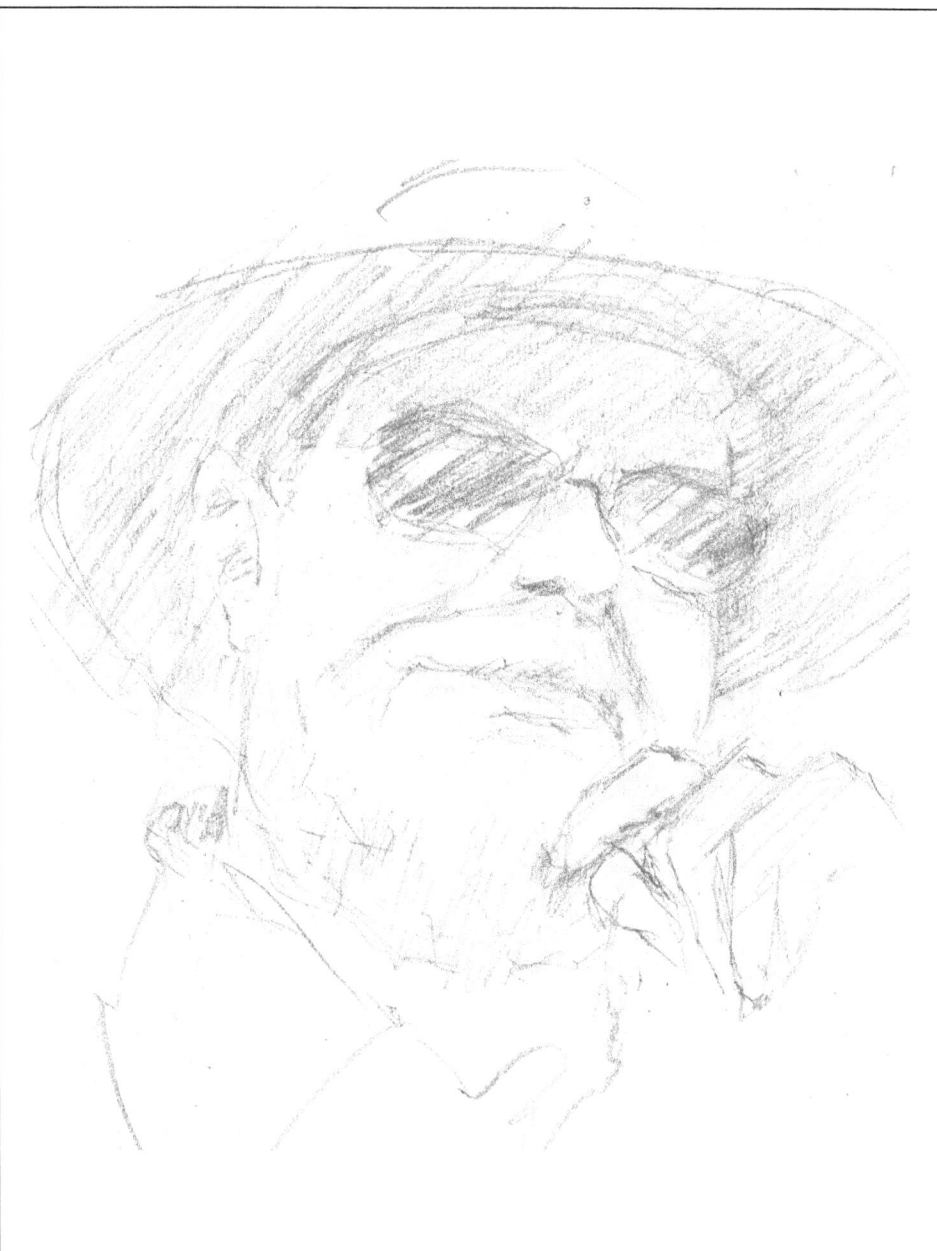

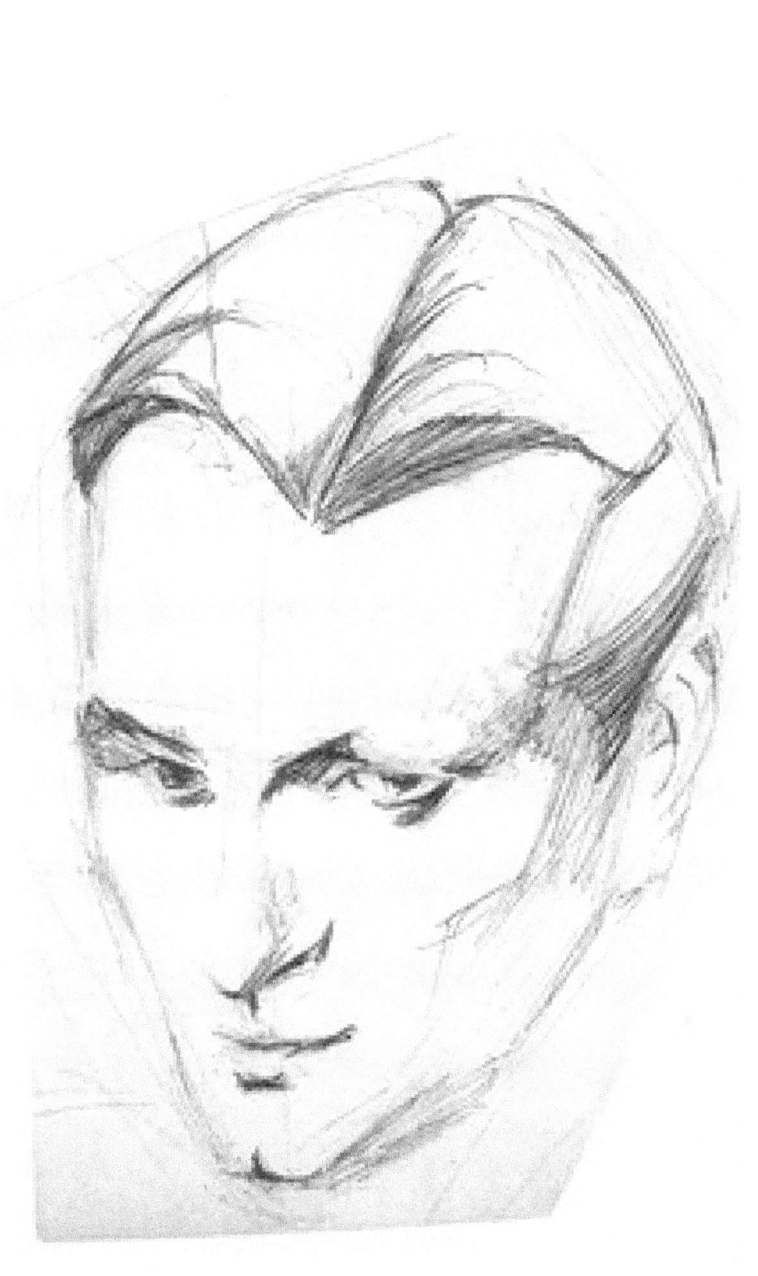

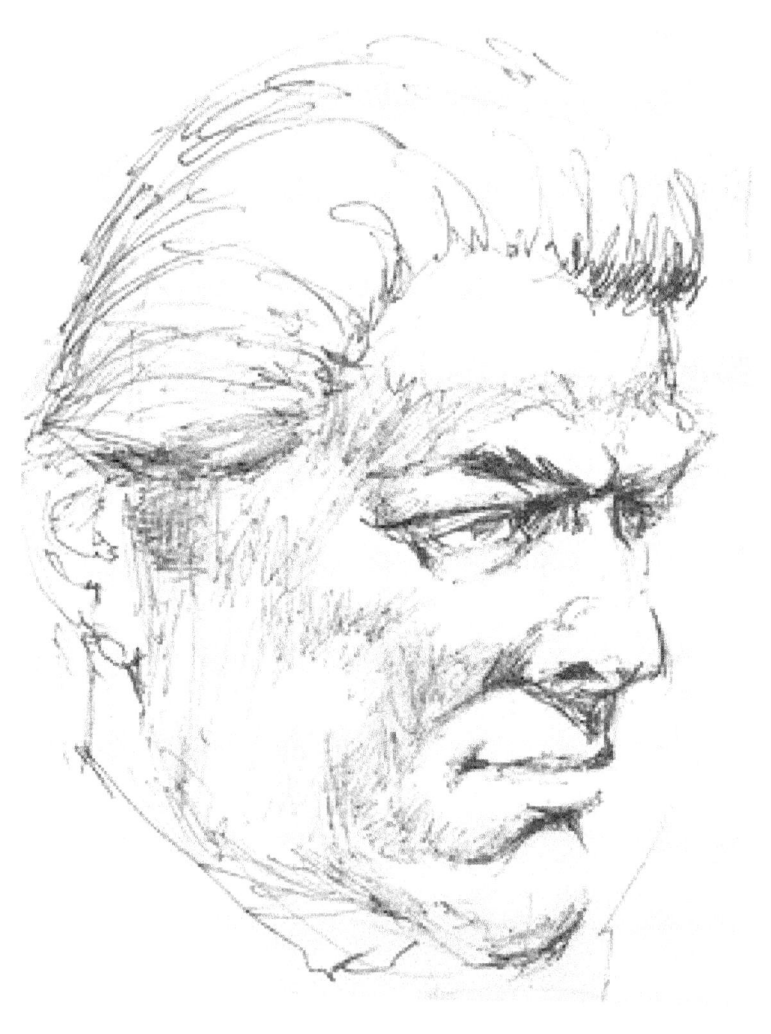

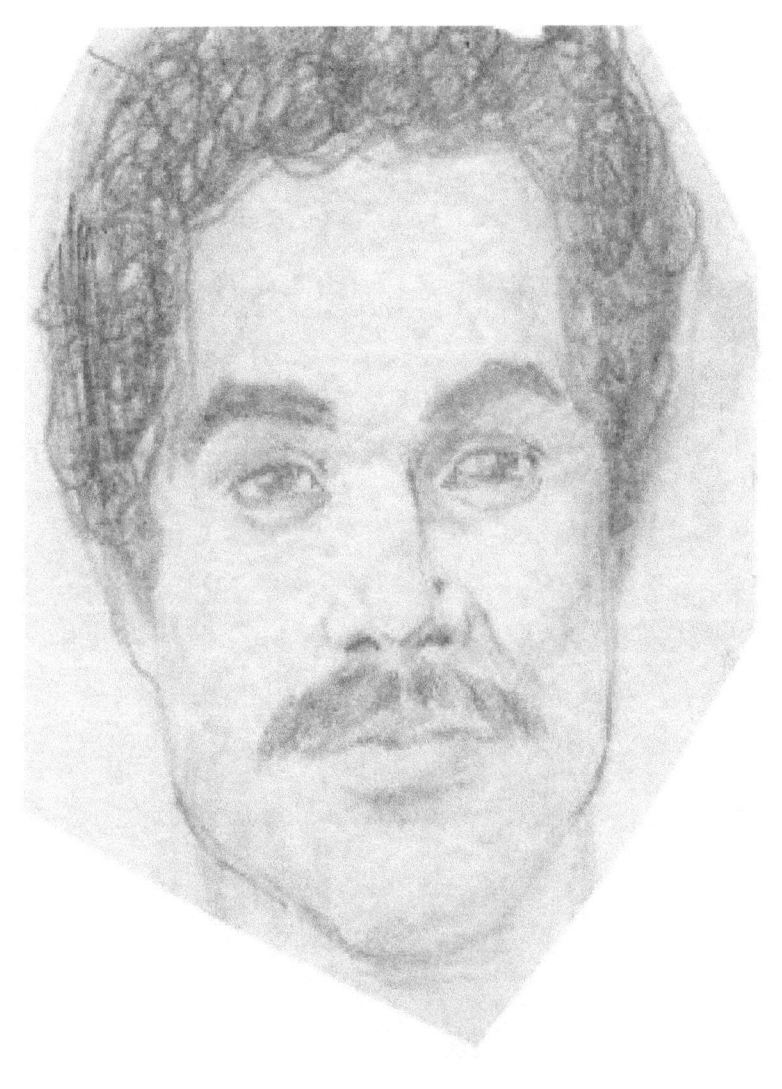

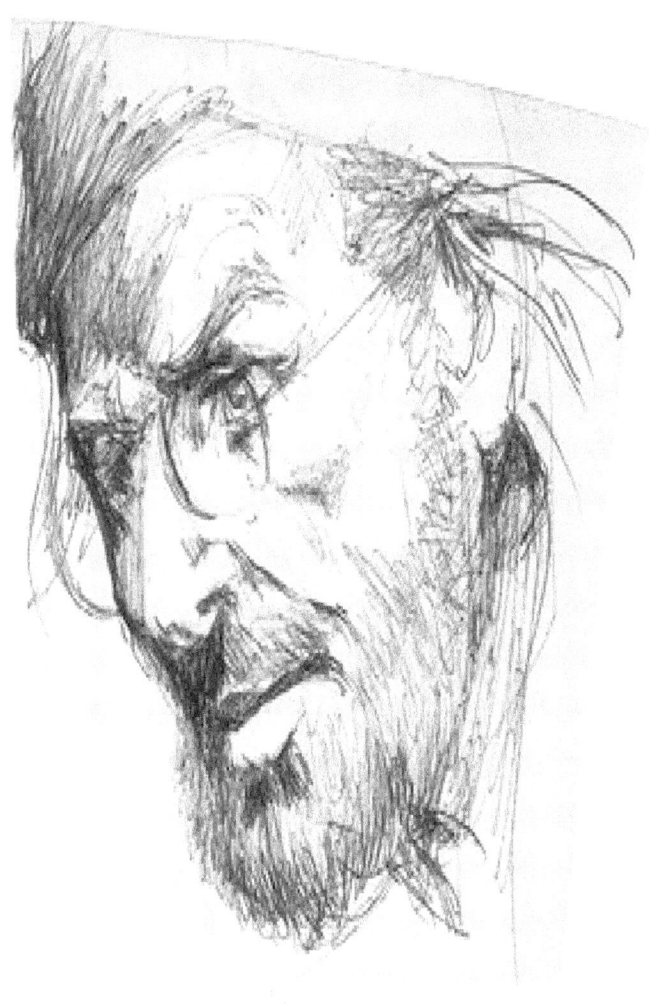

152

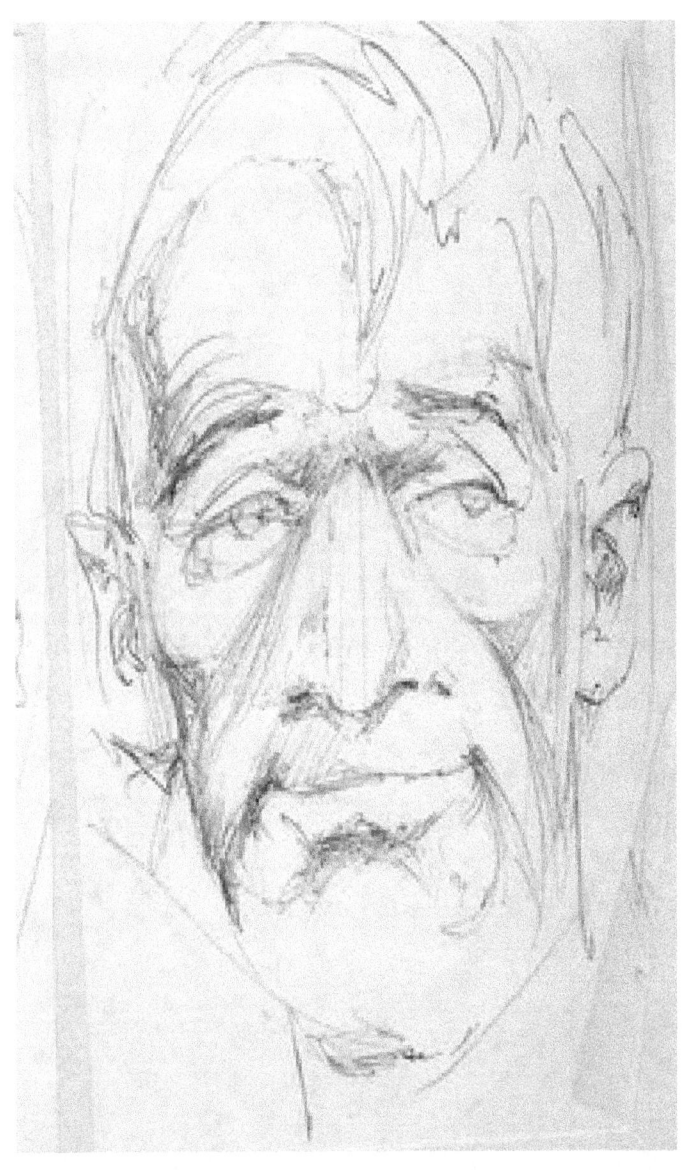

153

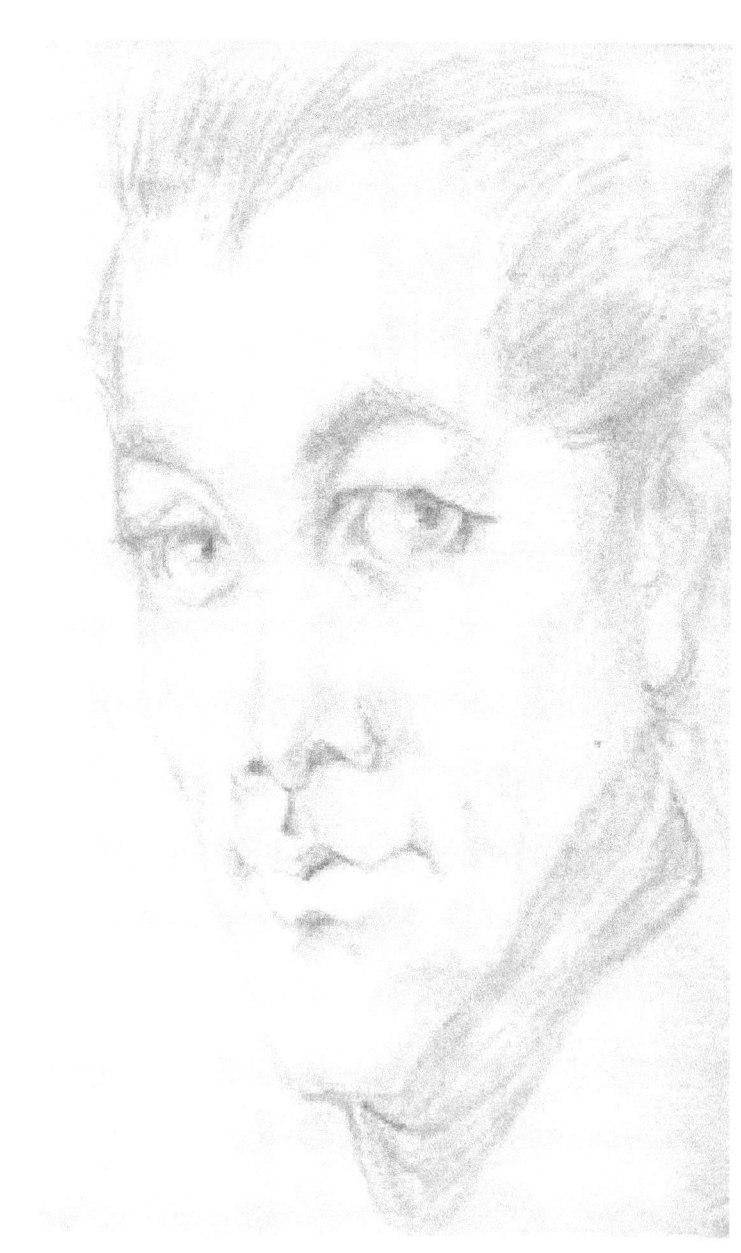

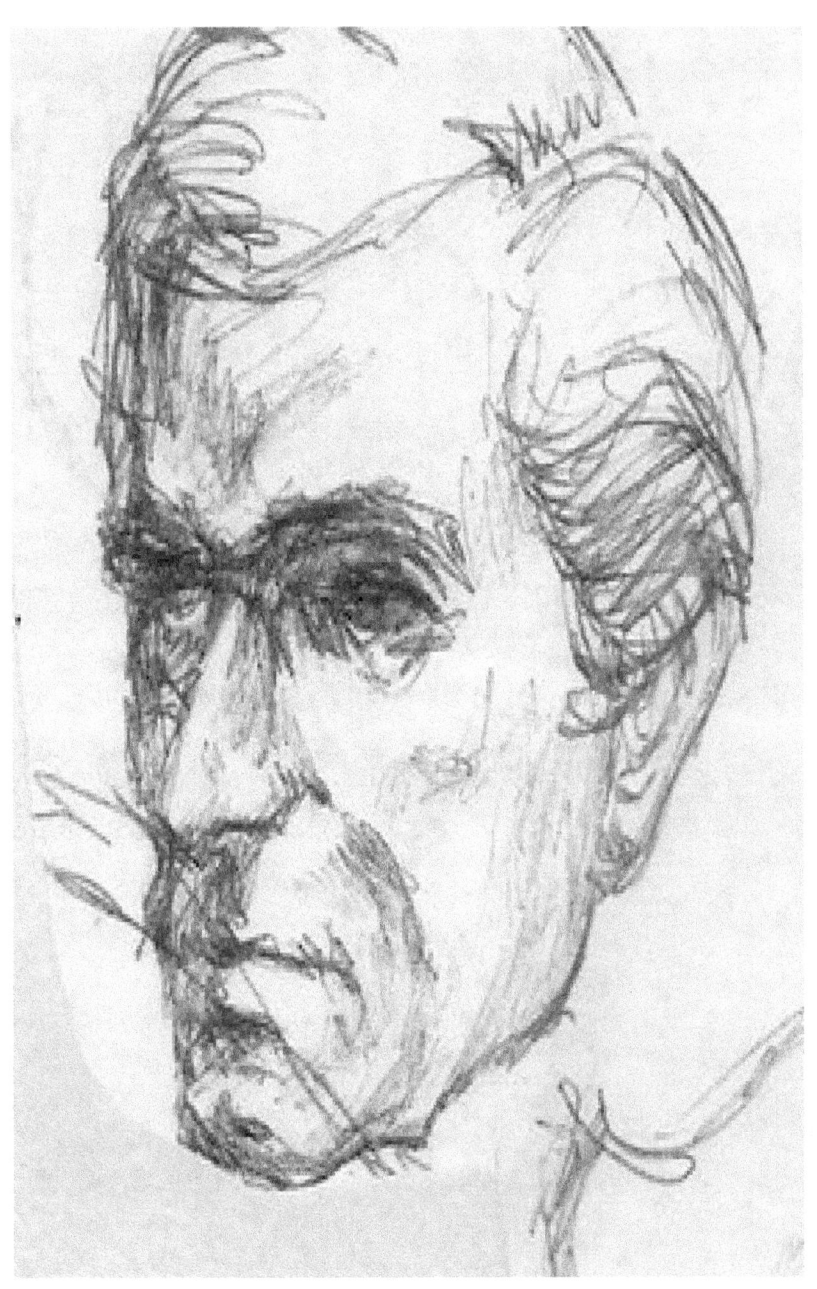

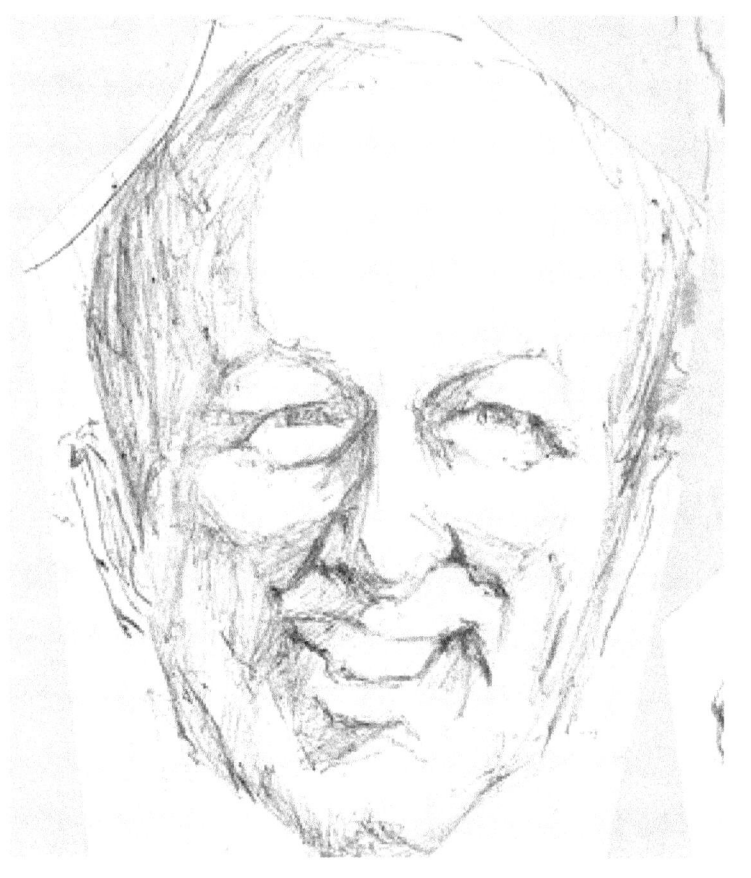

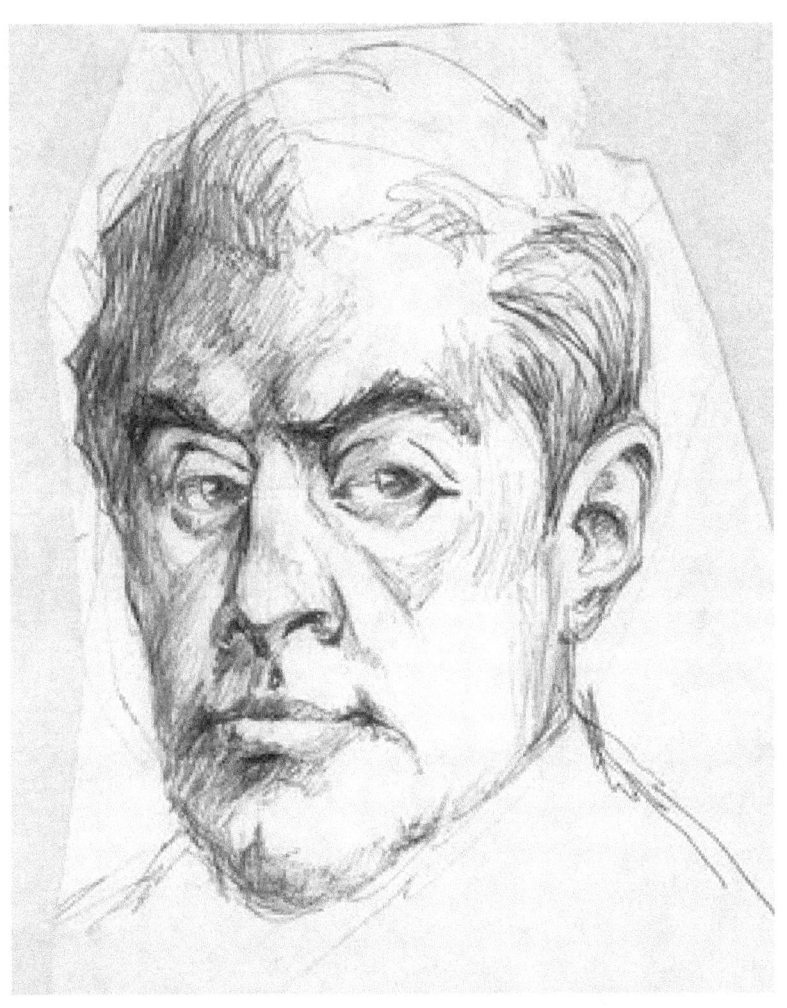

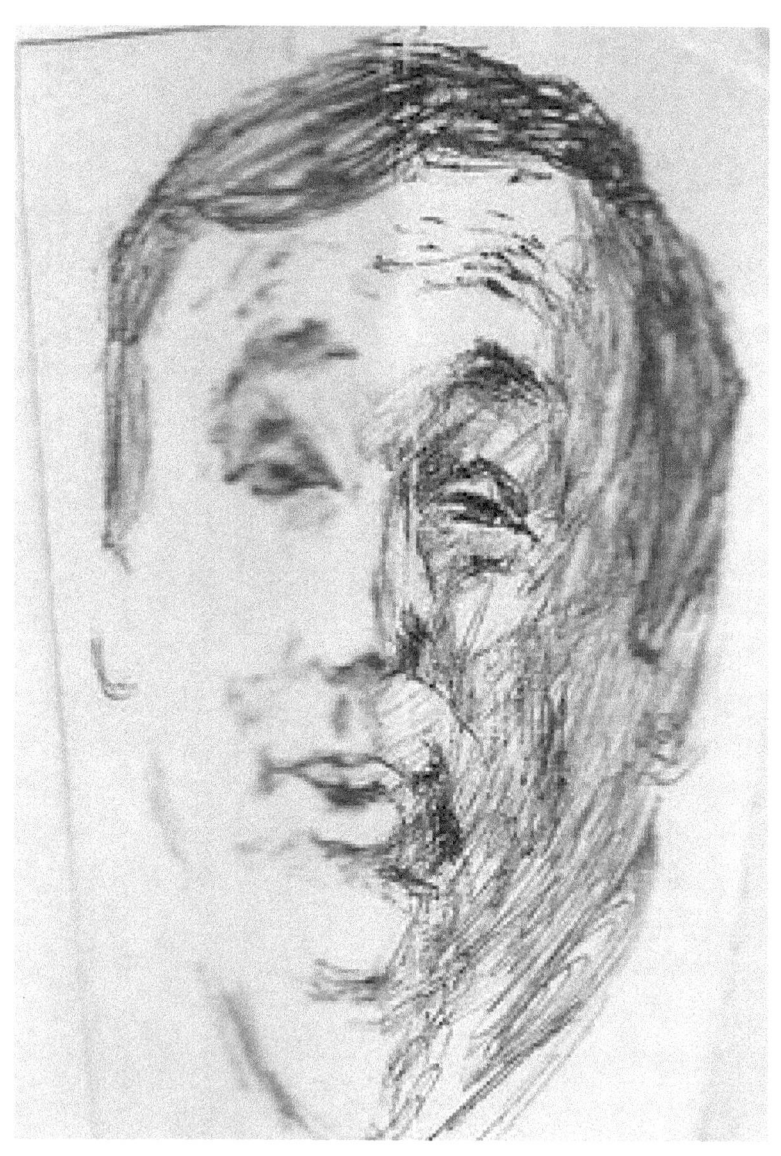

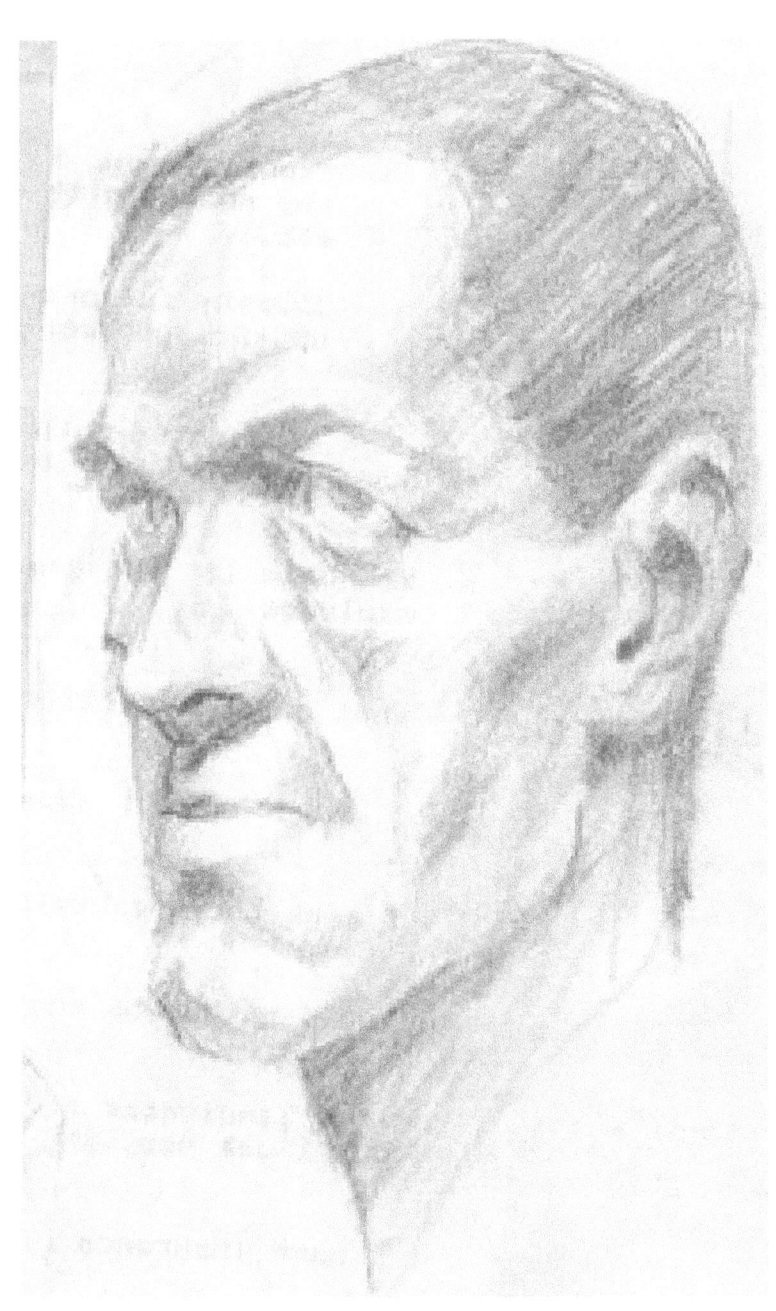

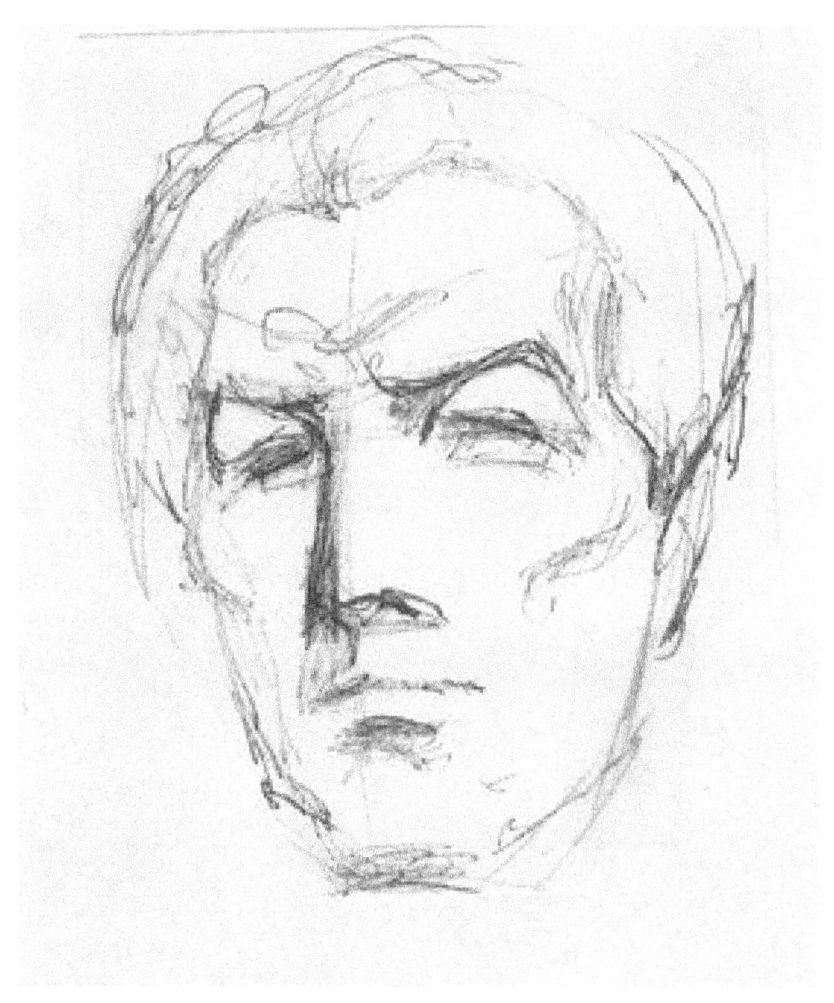

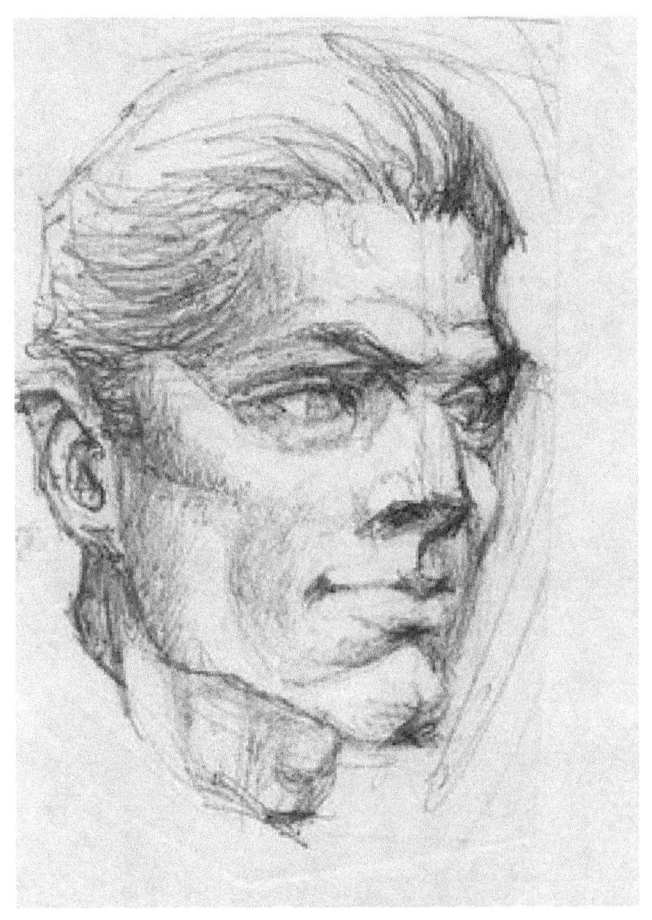

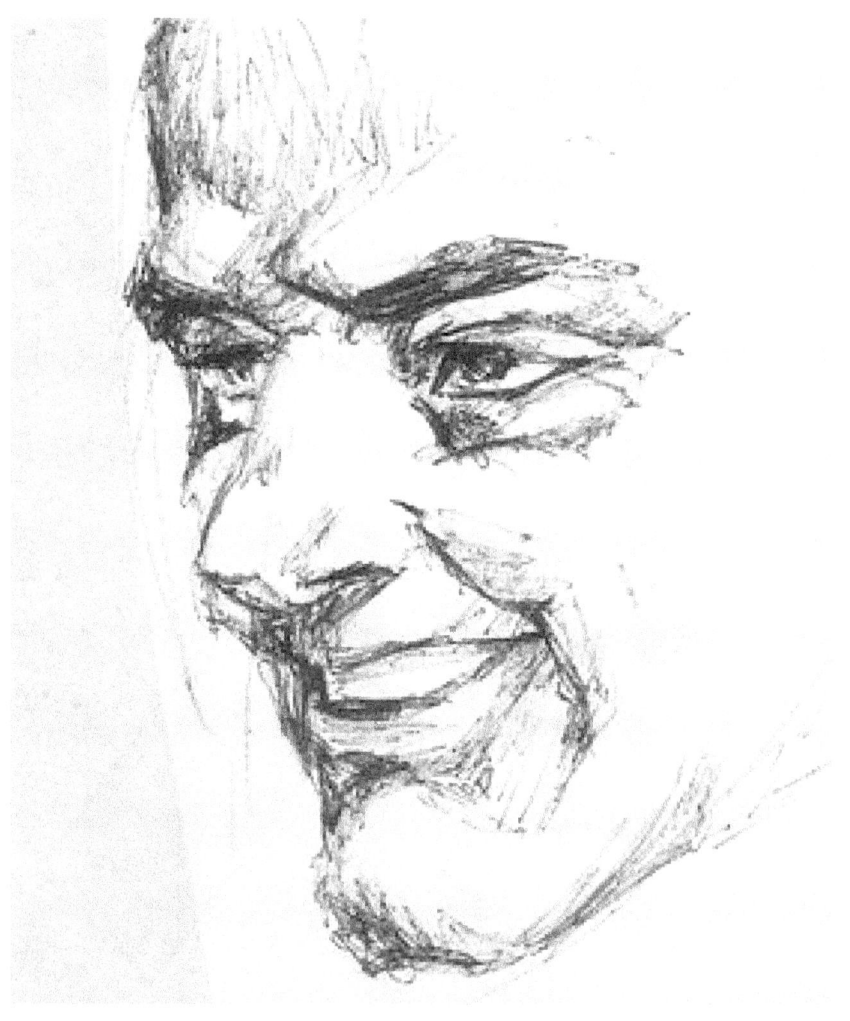

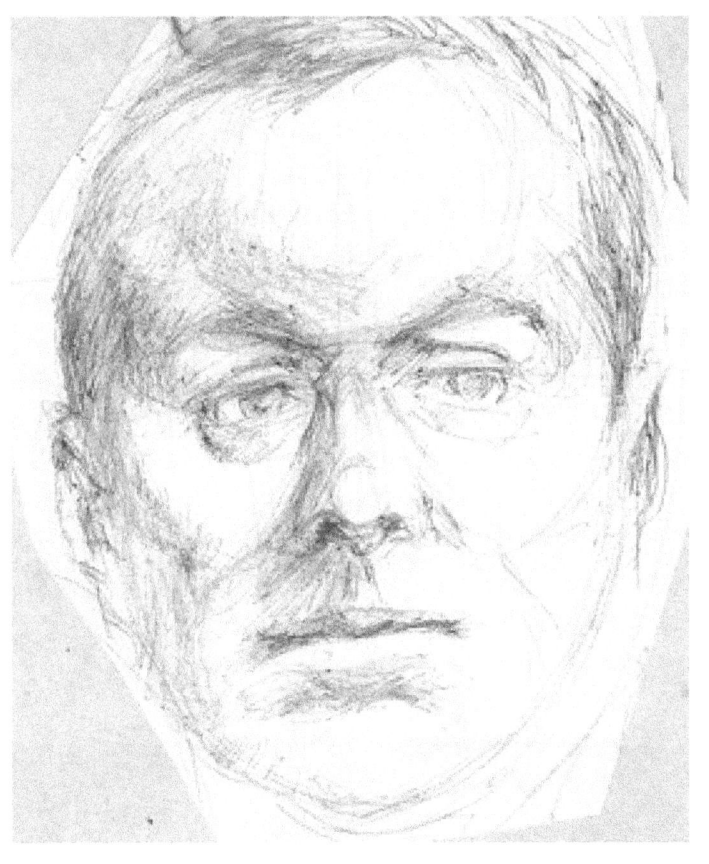

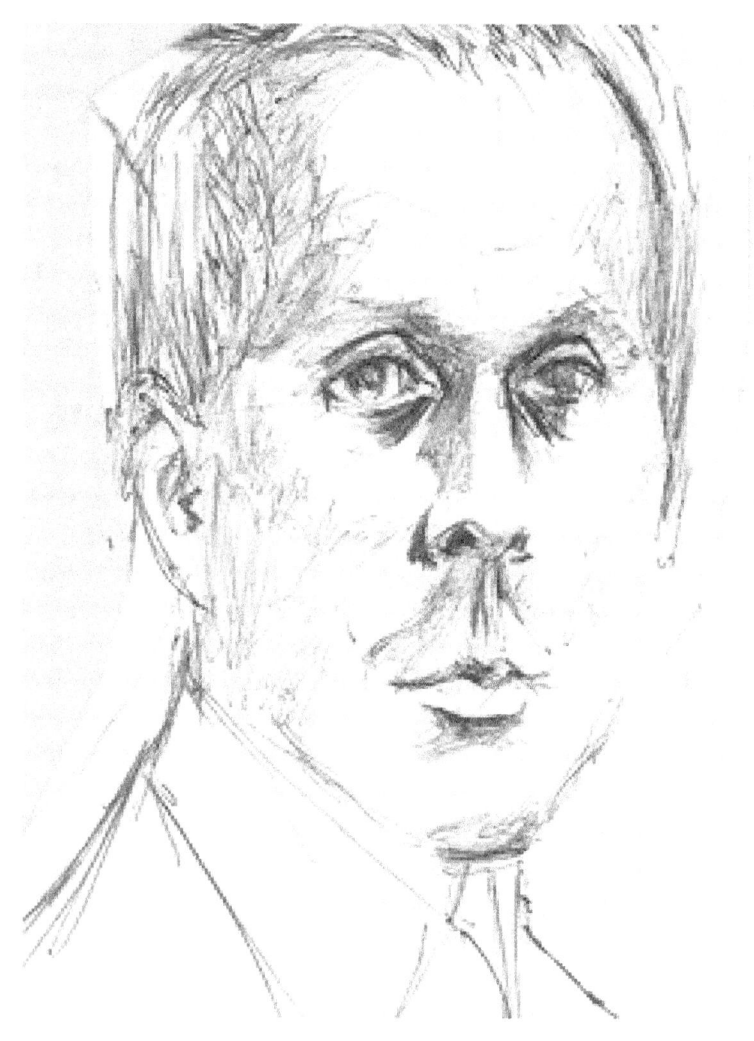

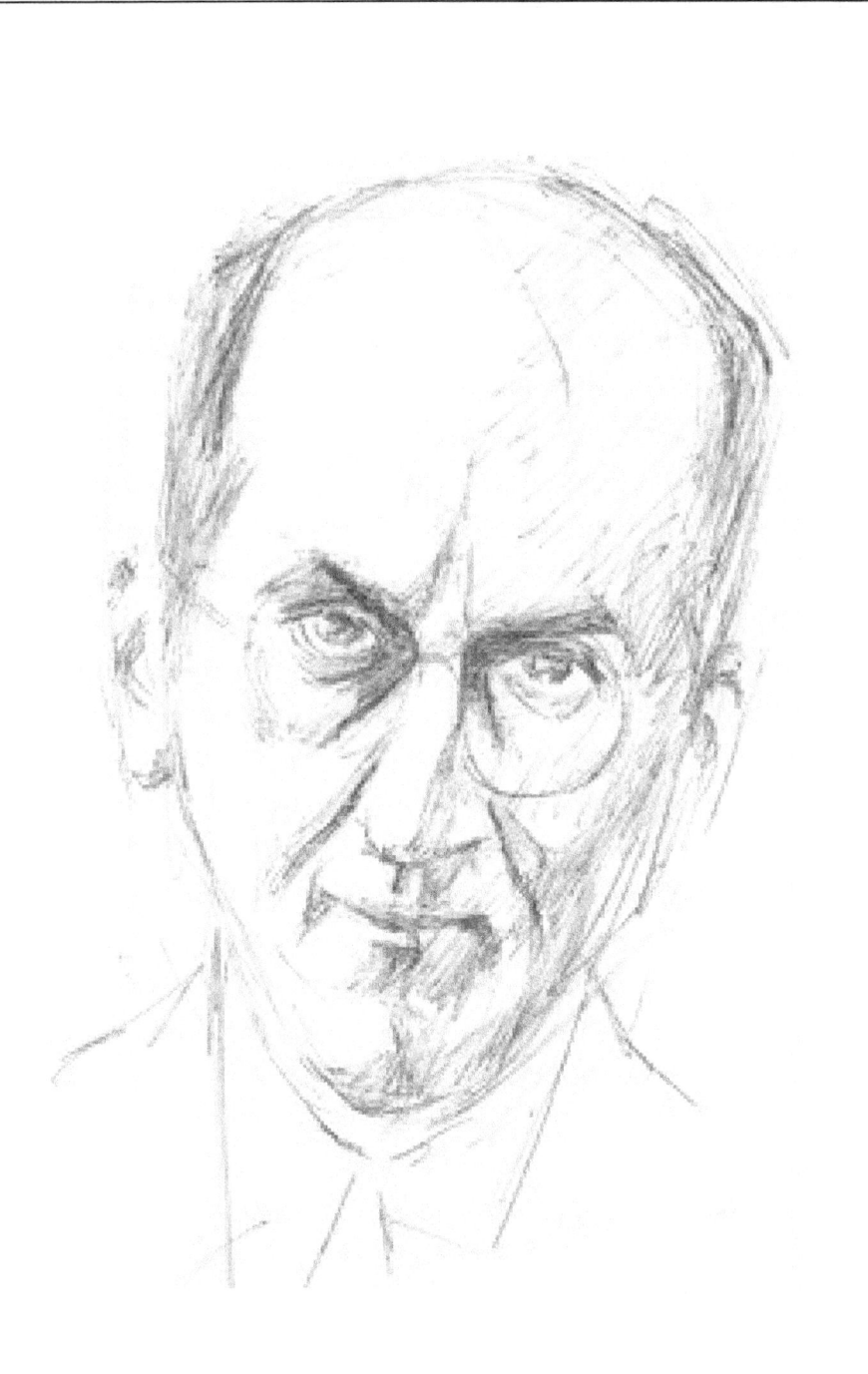

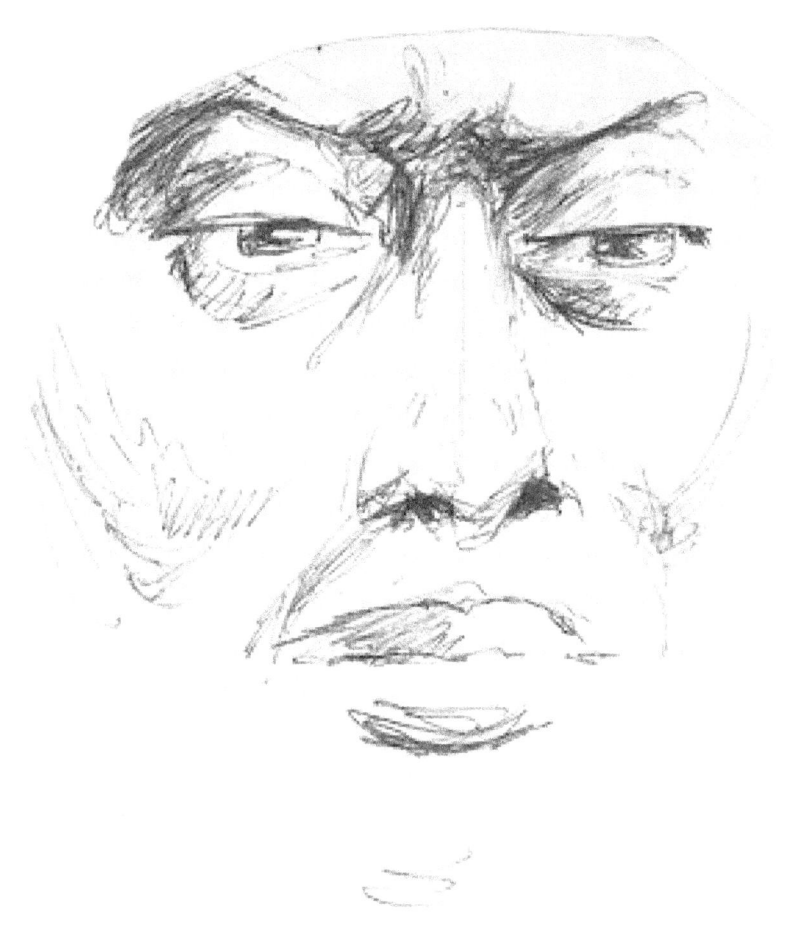

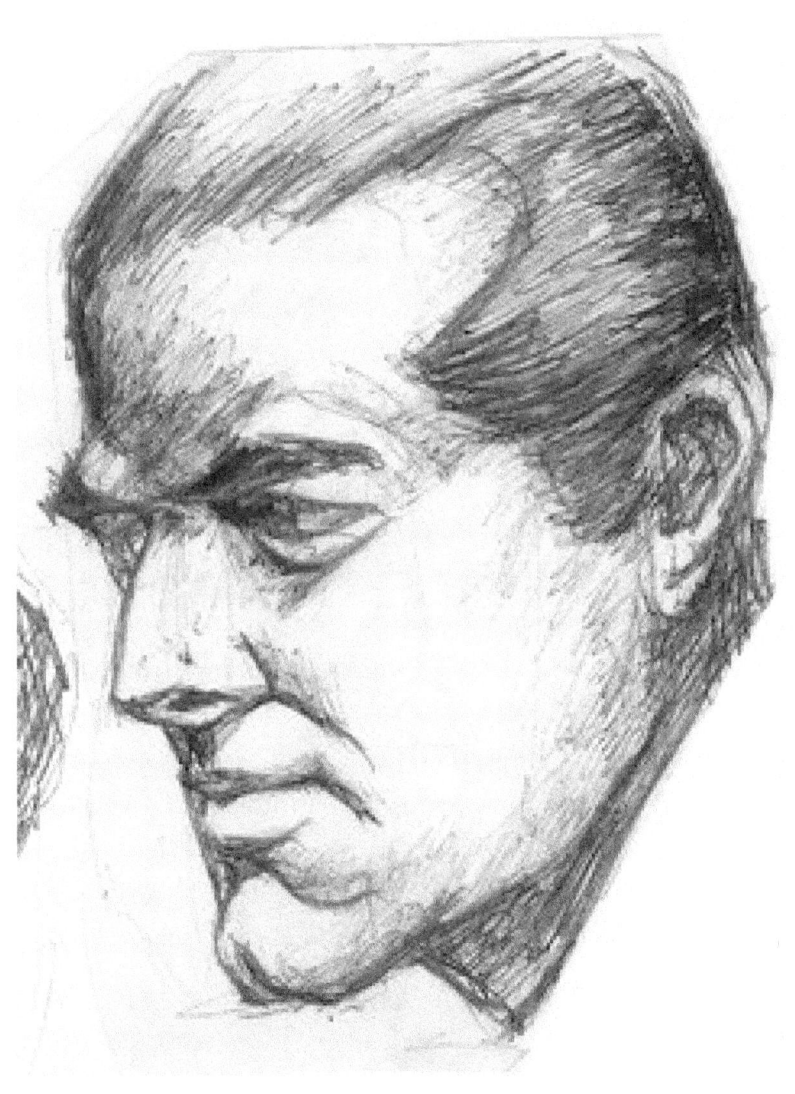

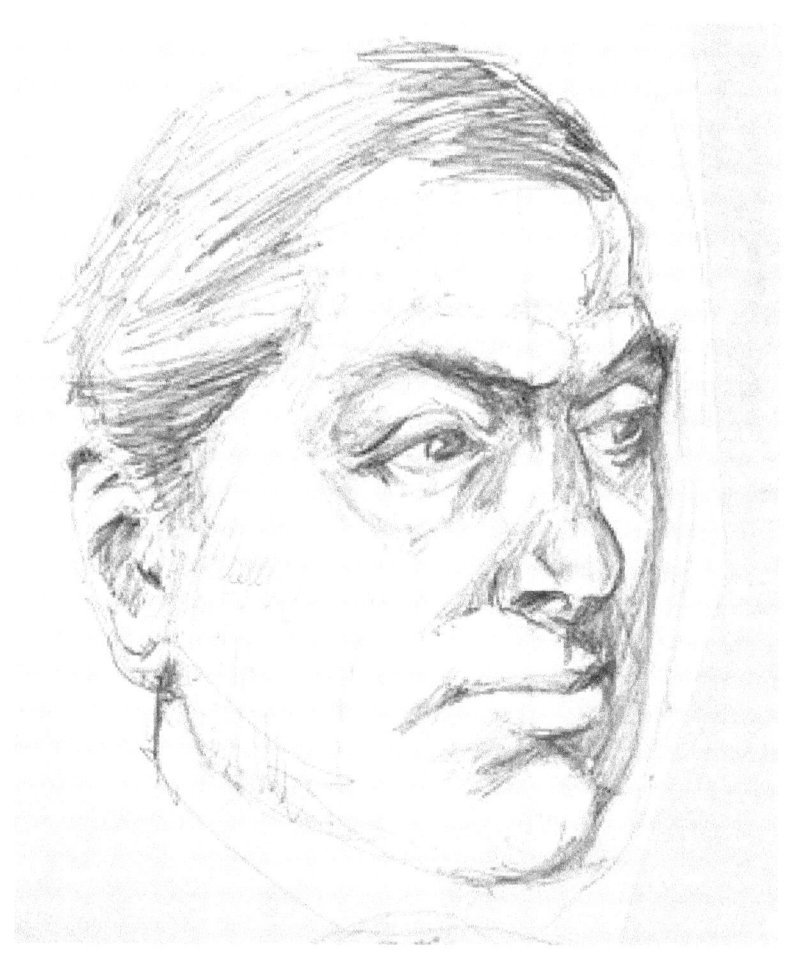

168

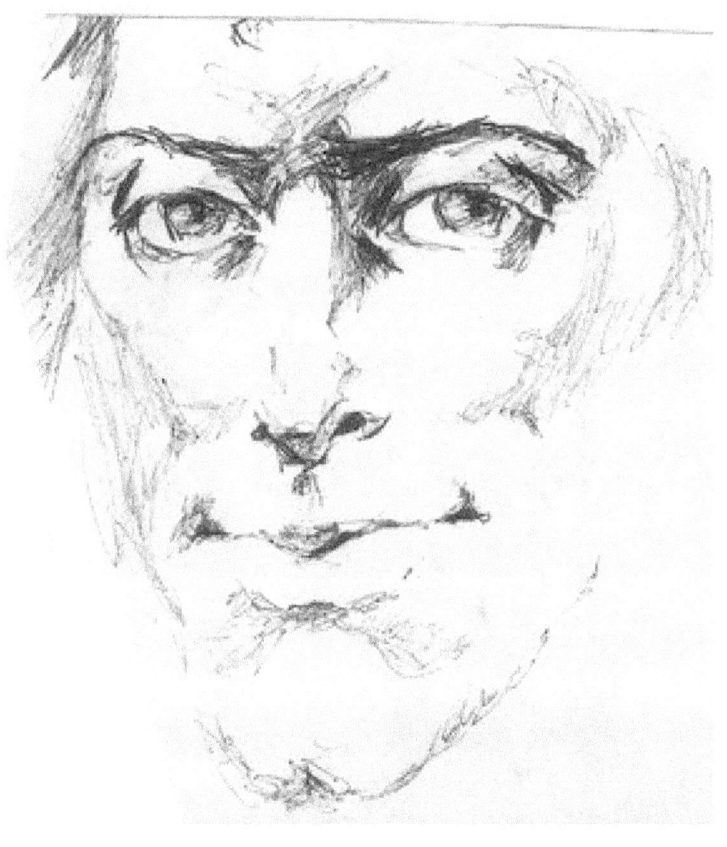

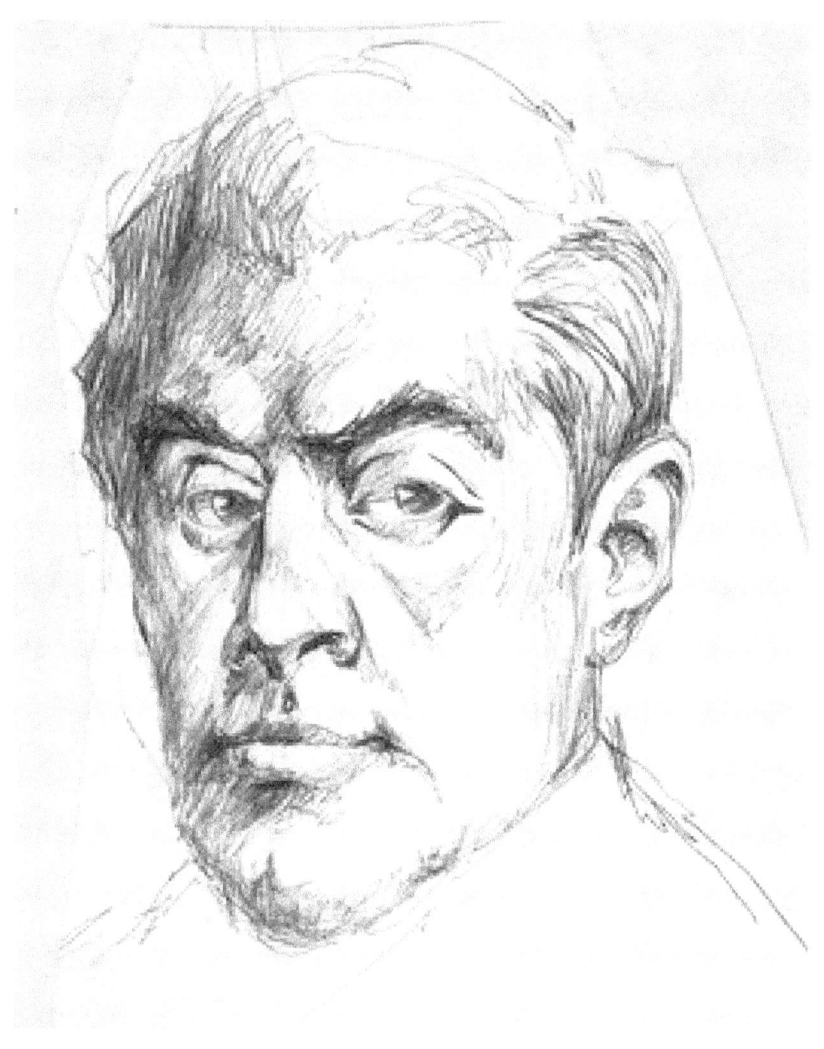

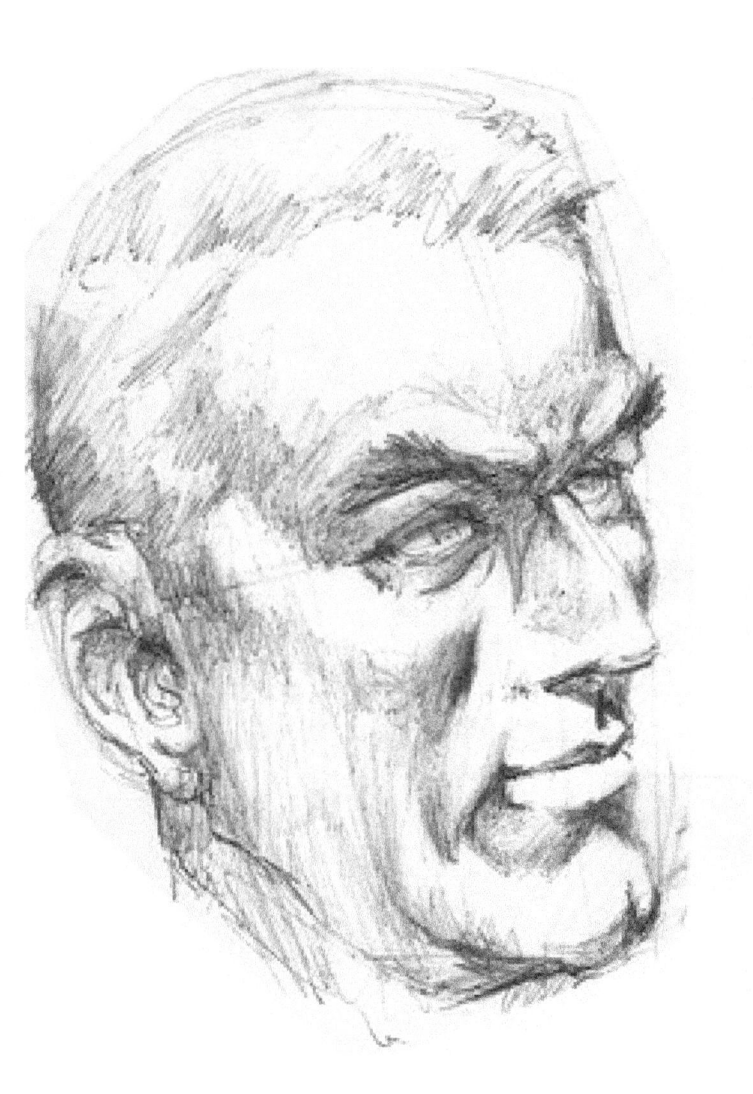

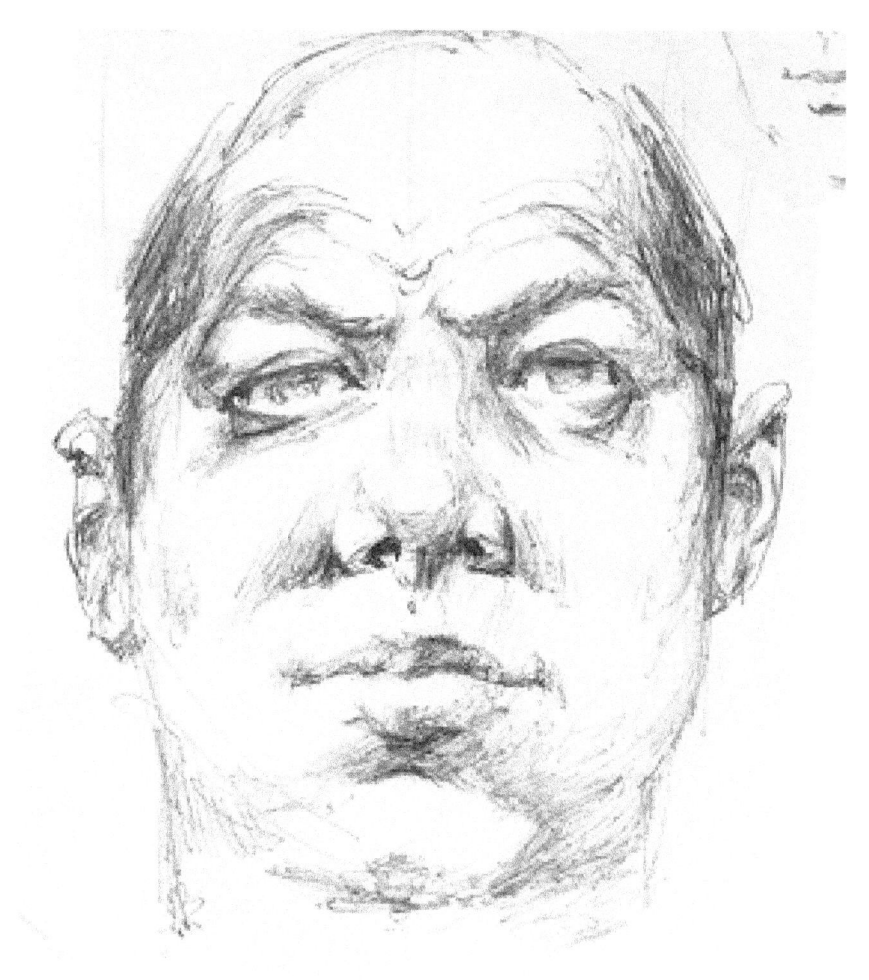

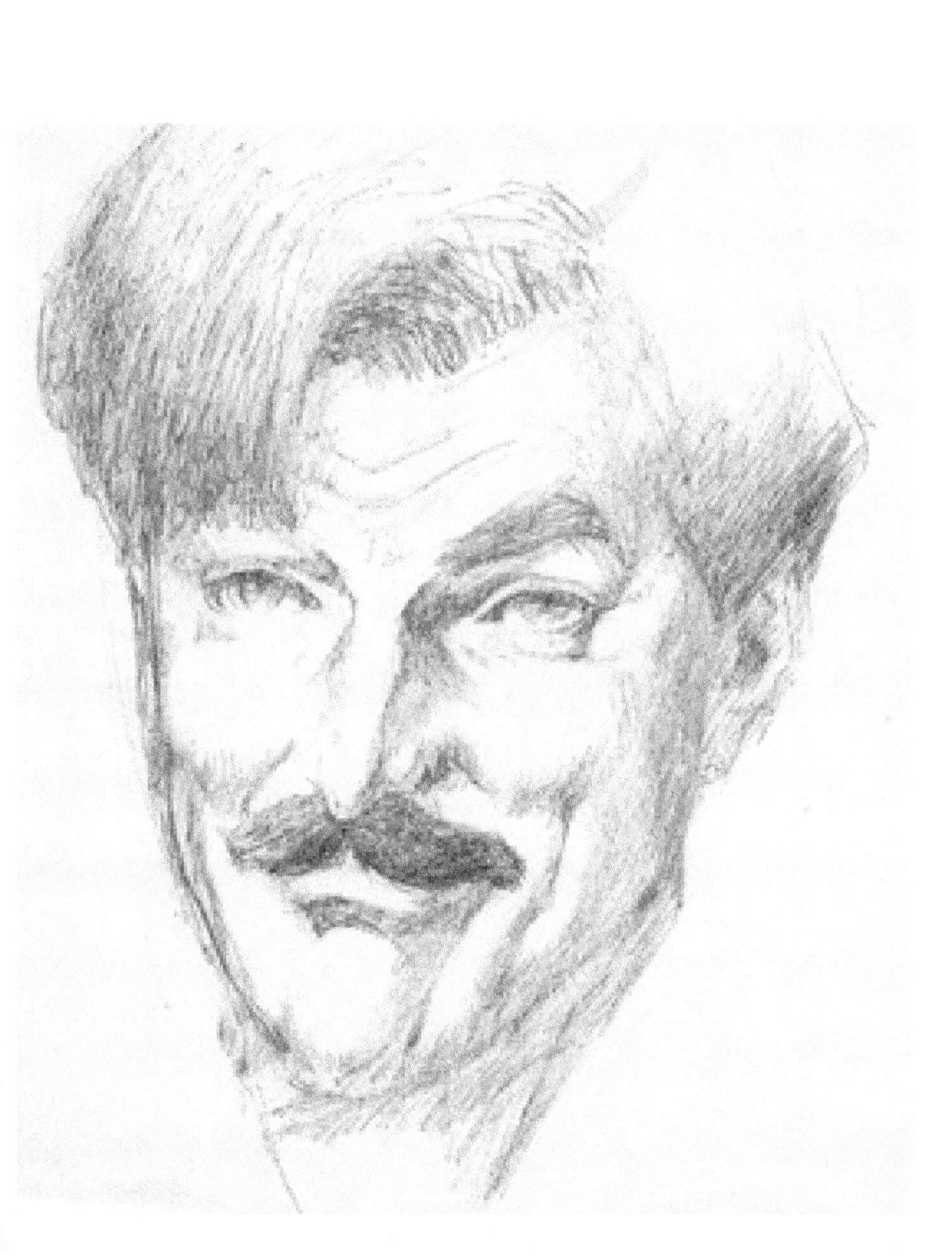

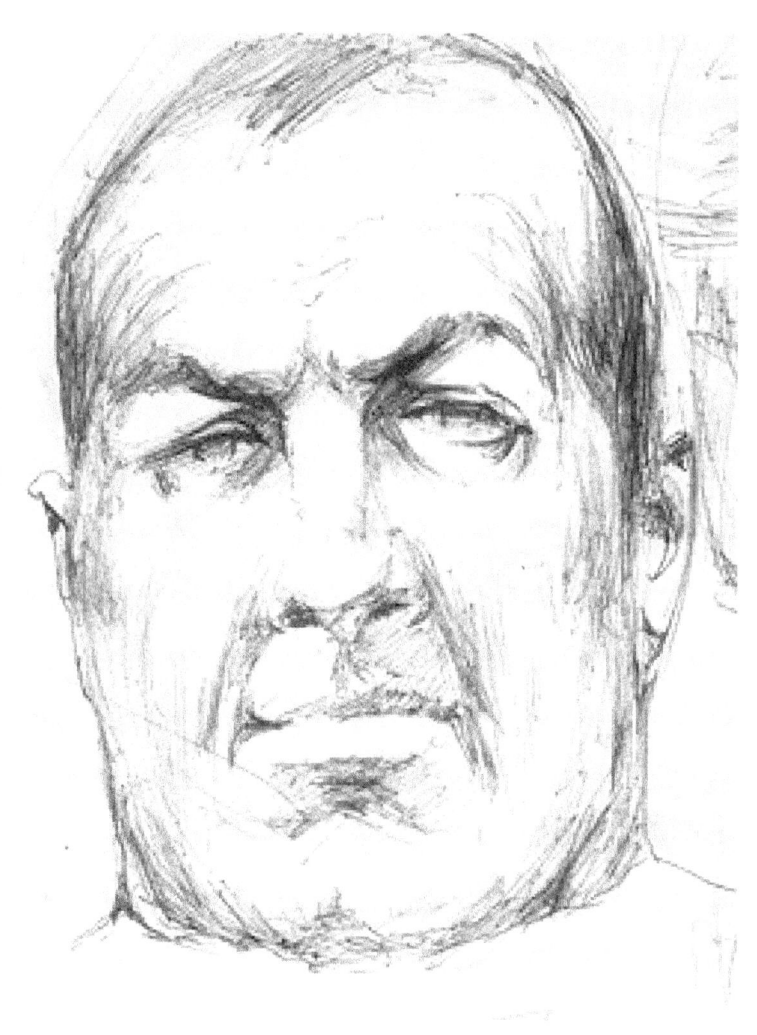

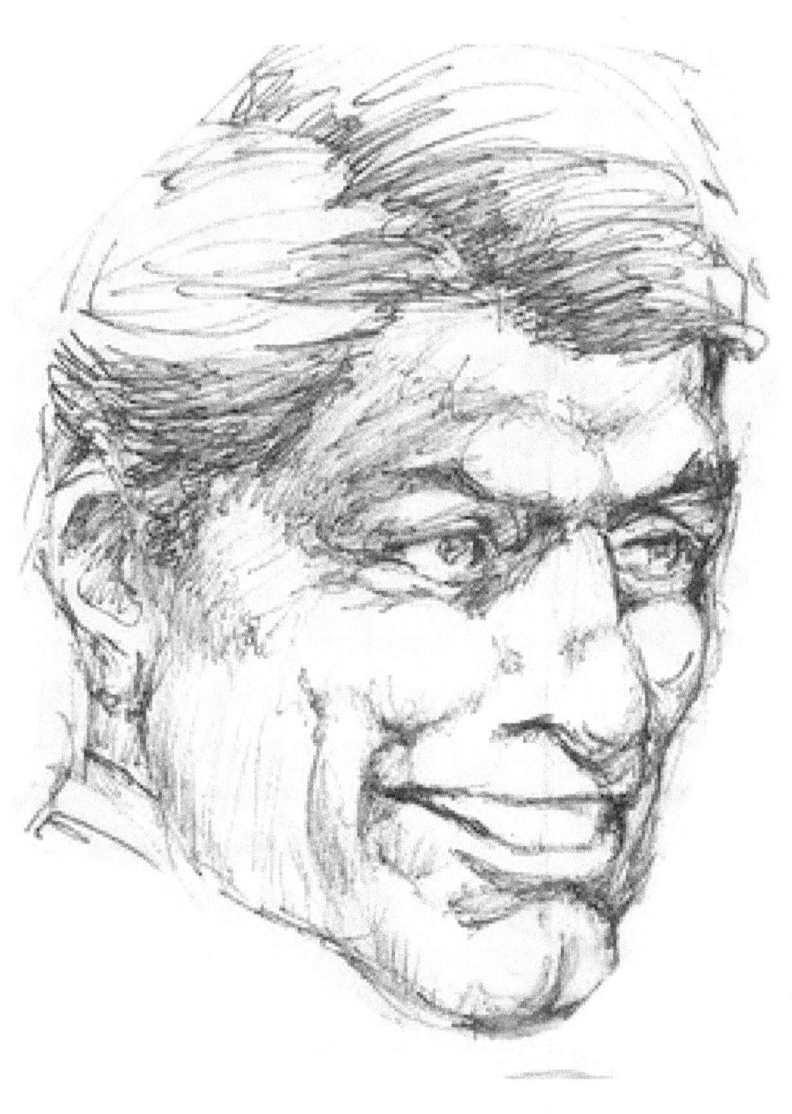

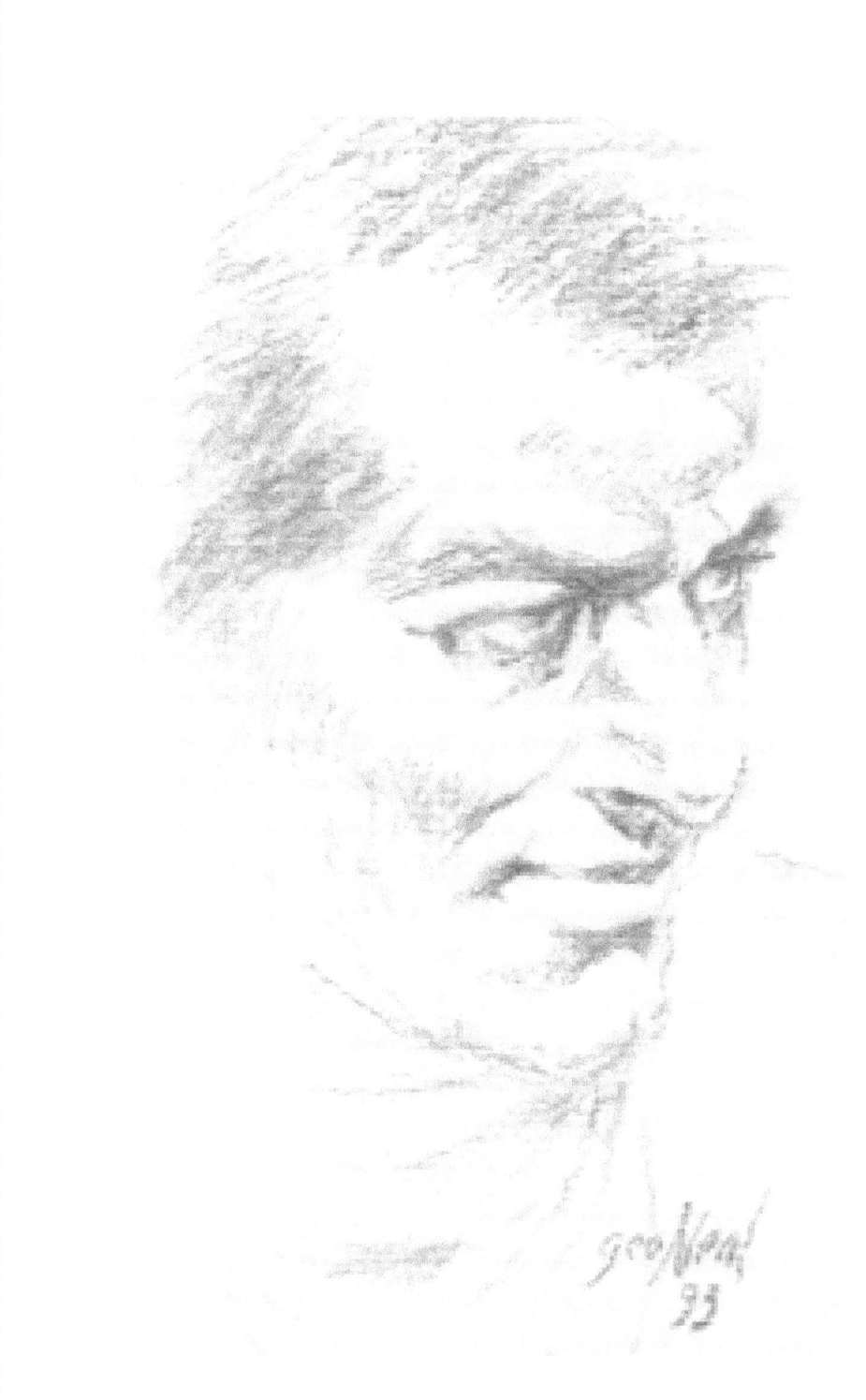

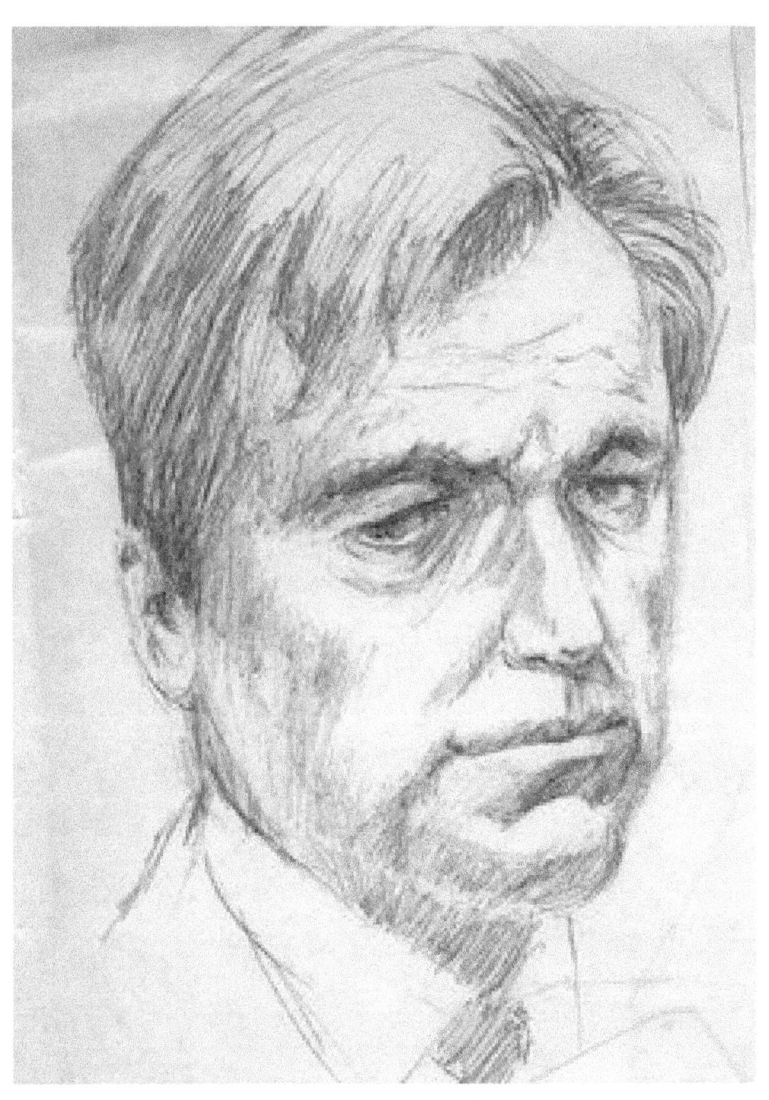

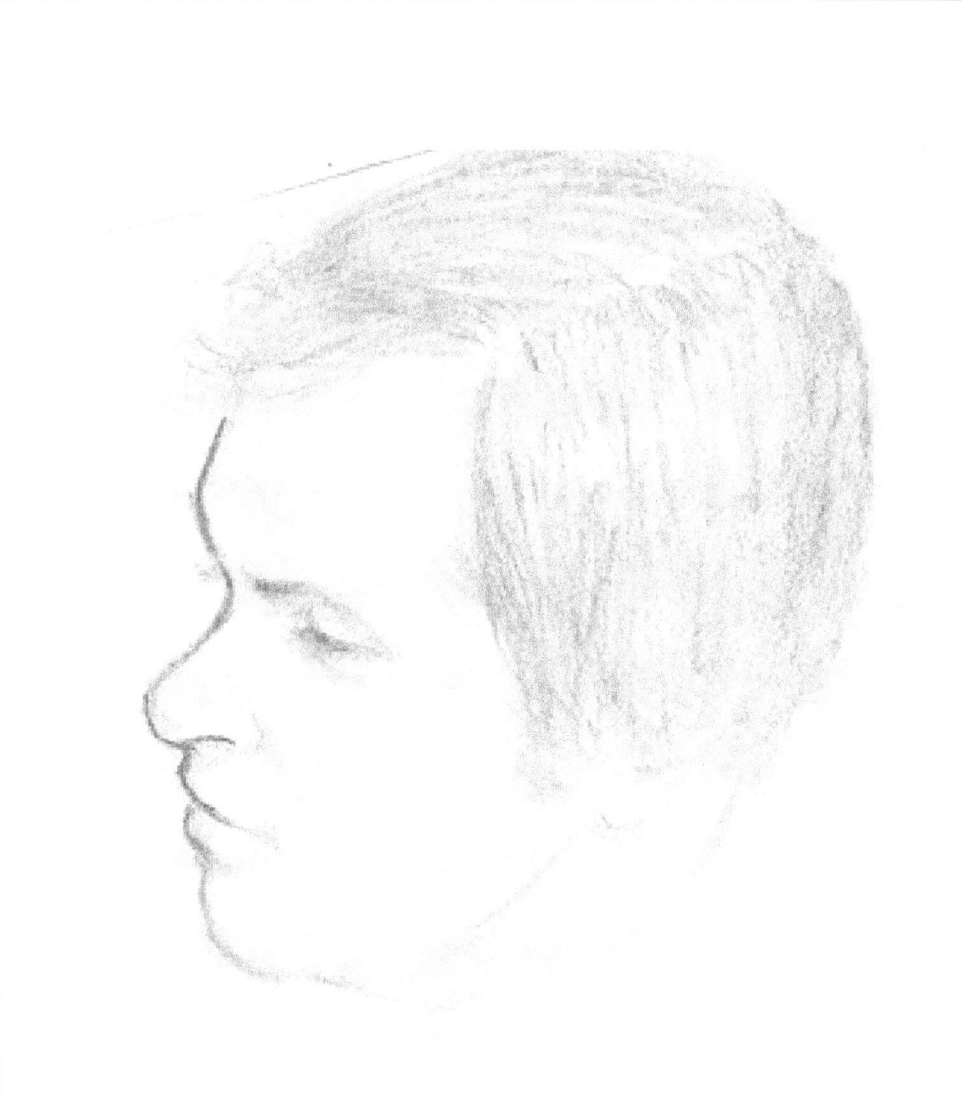

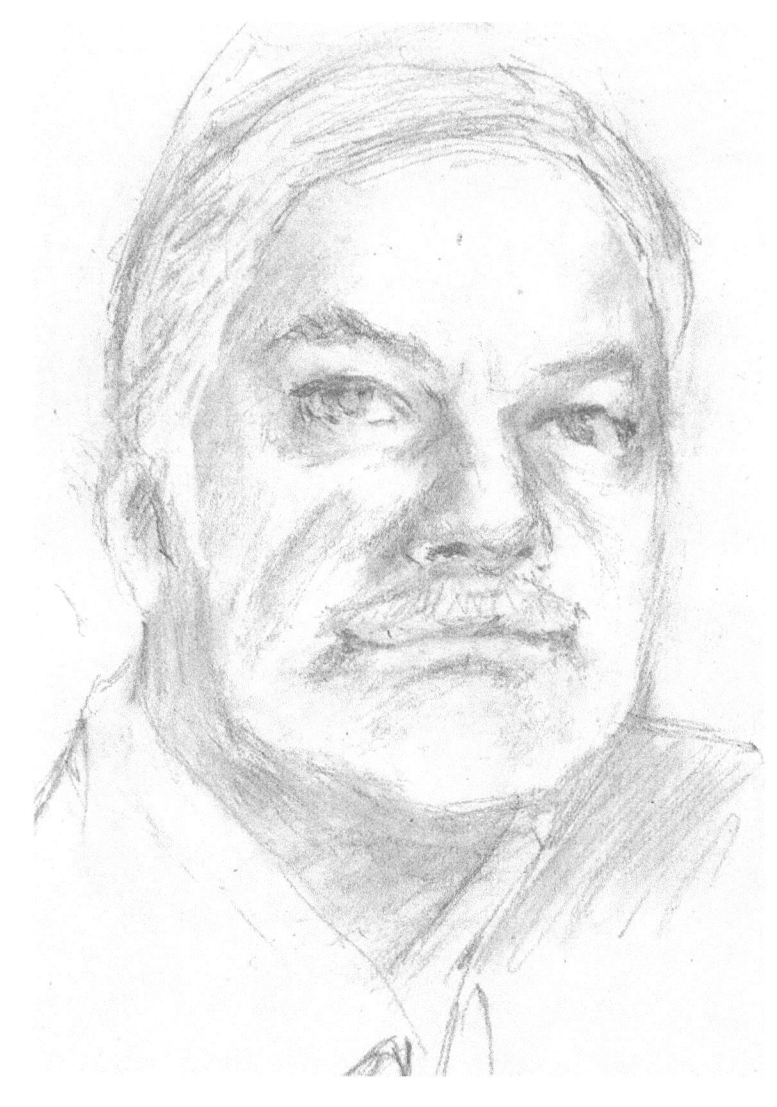

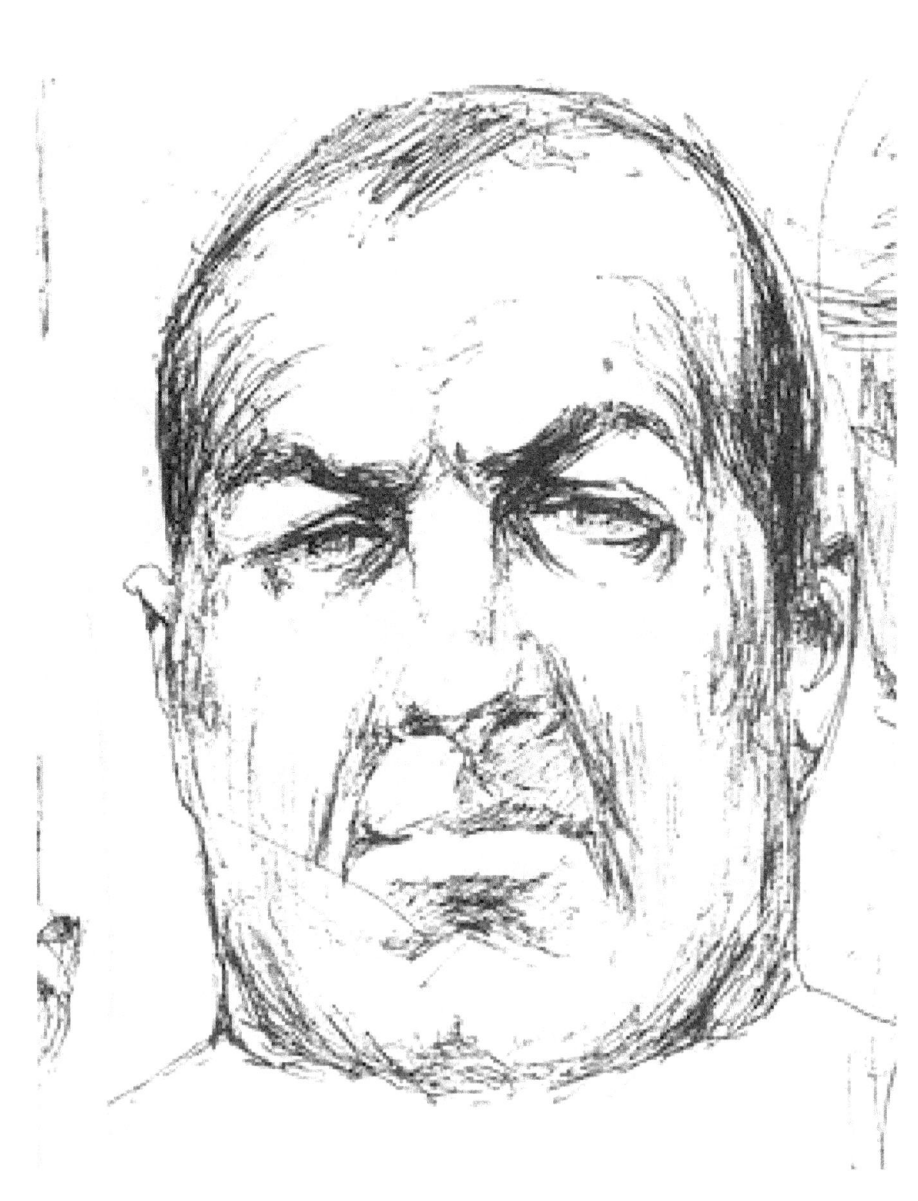

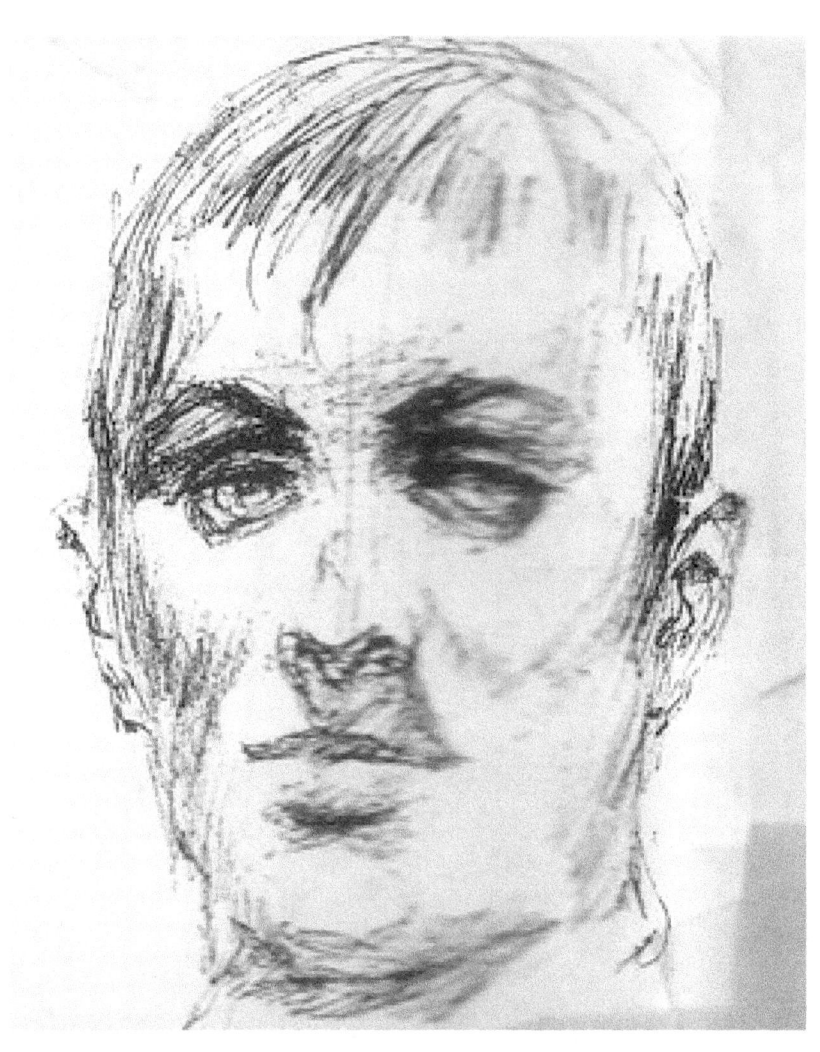

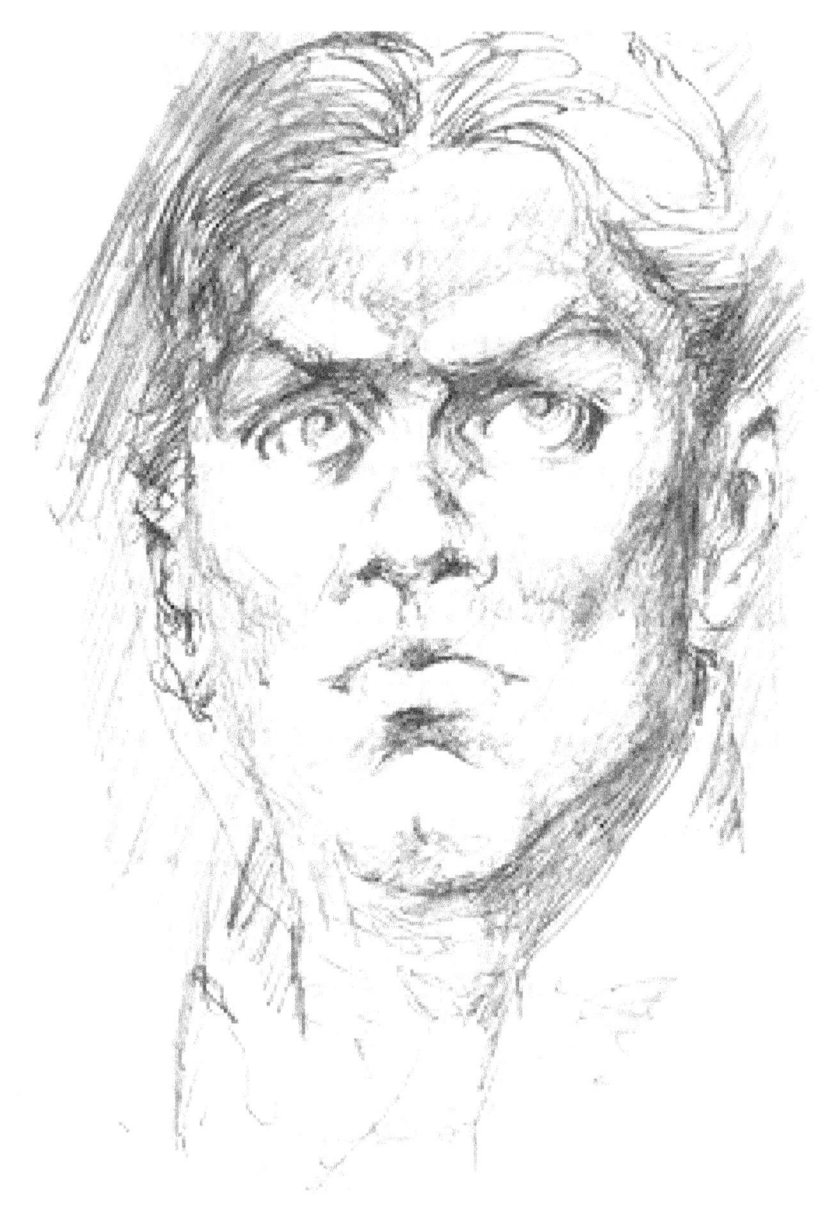

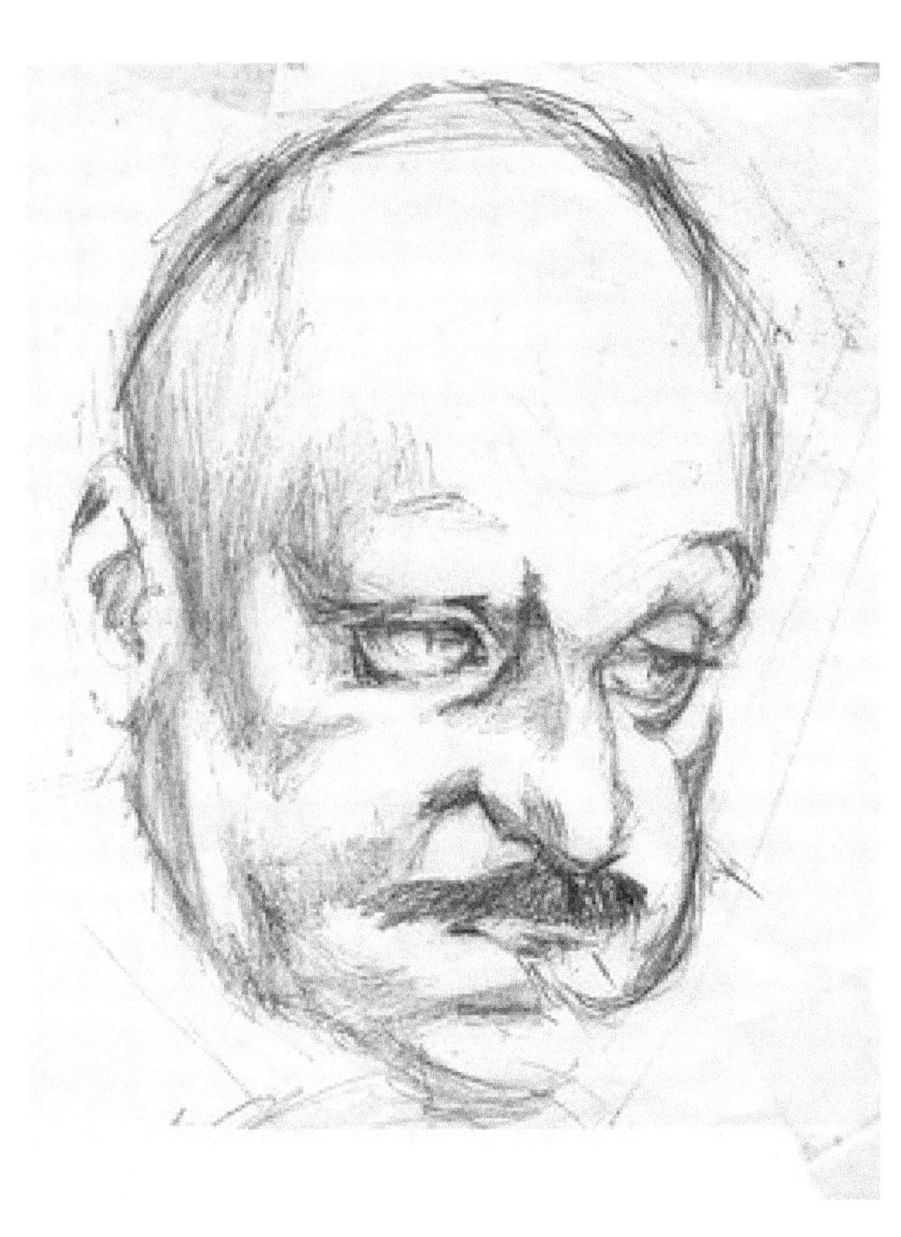

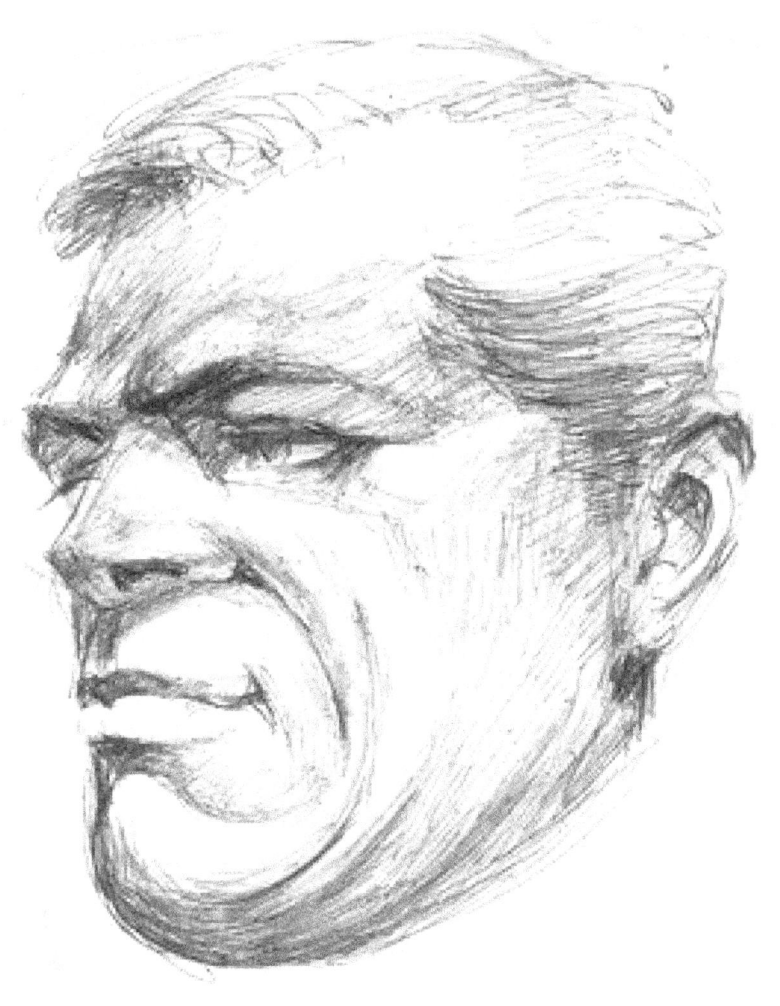

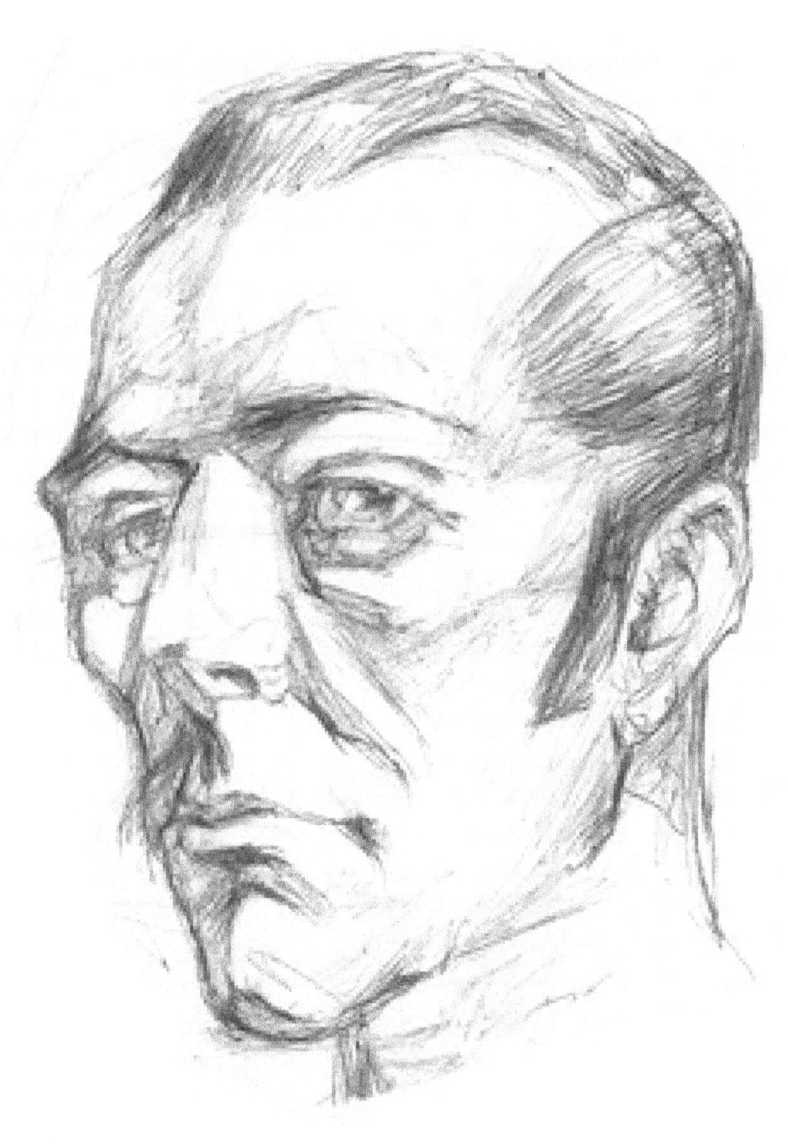

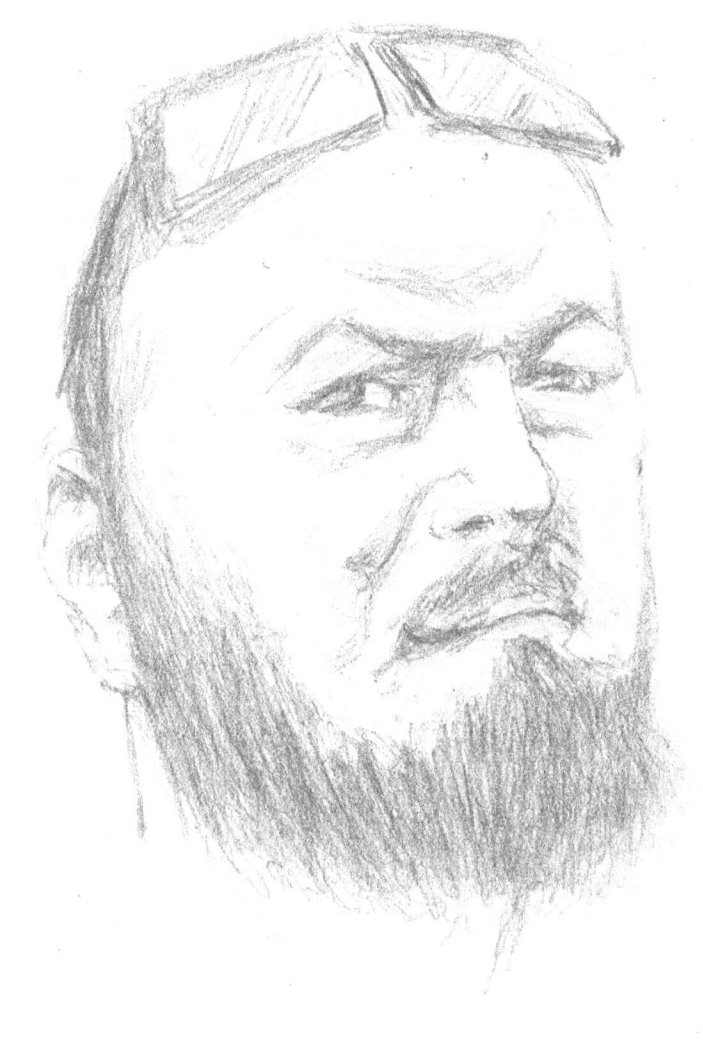

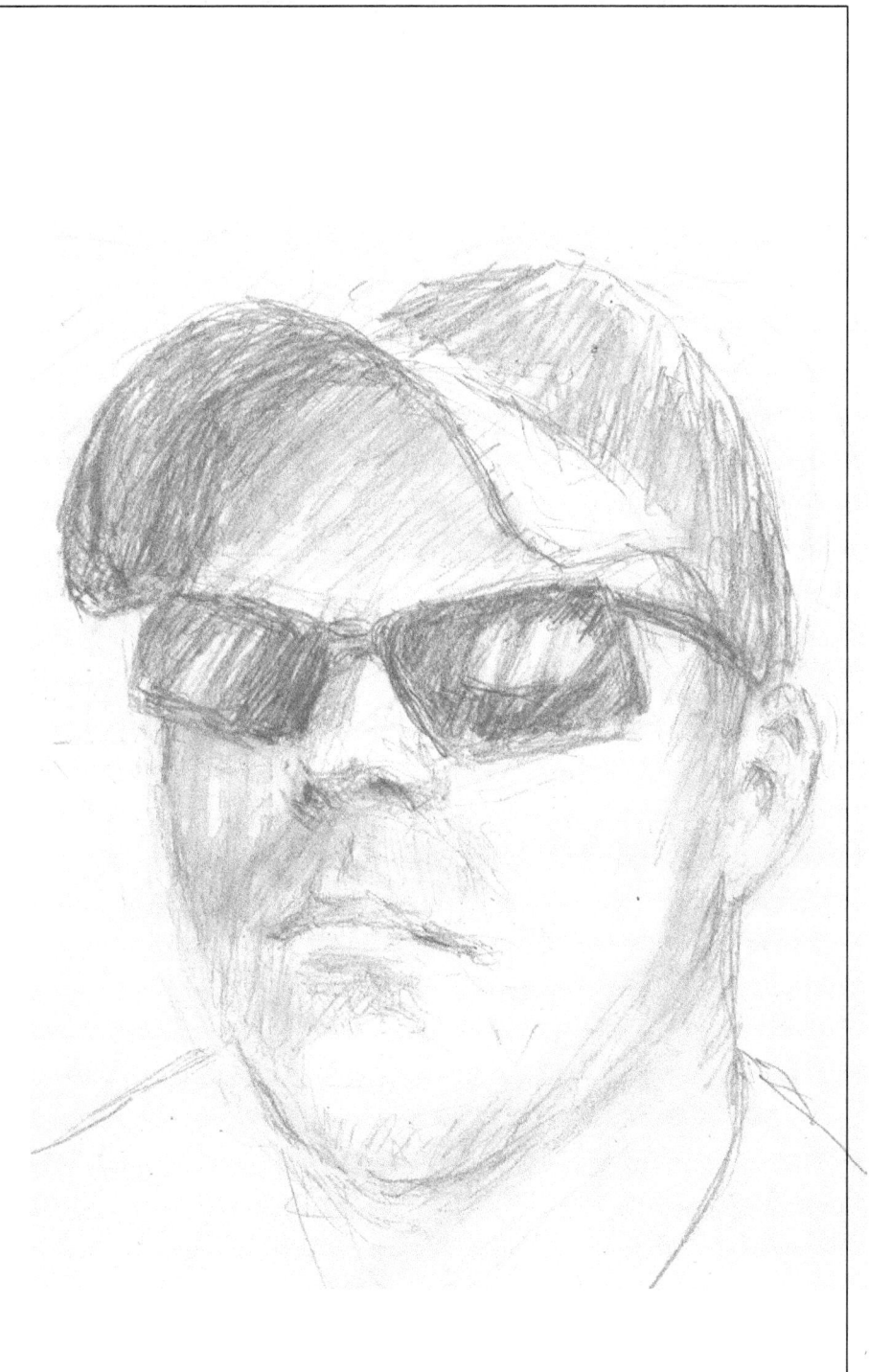

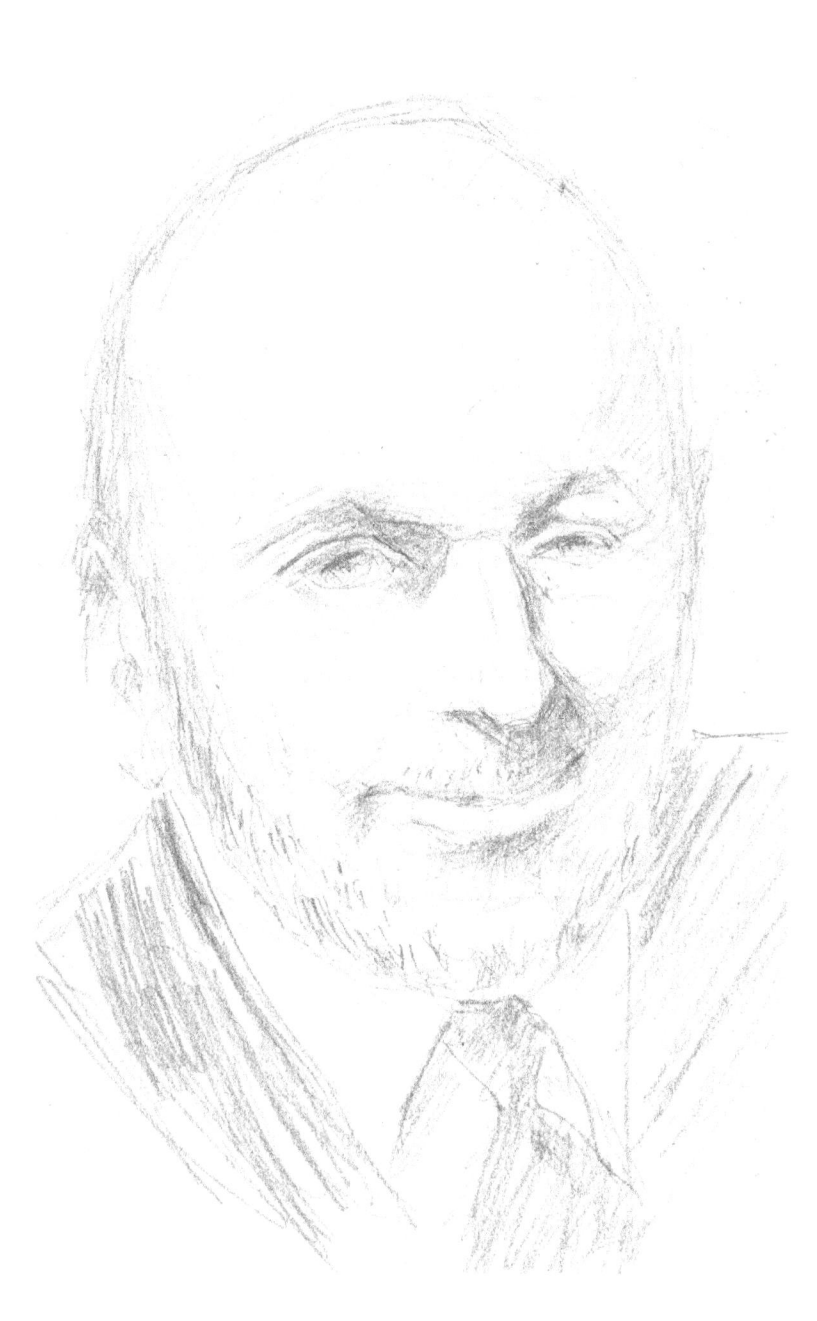

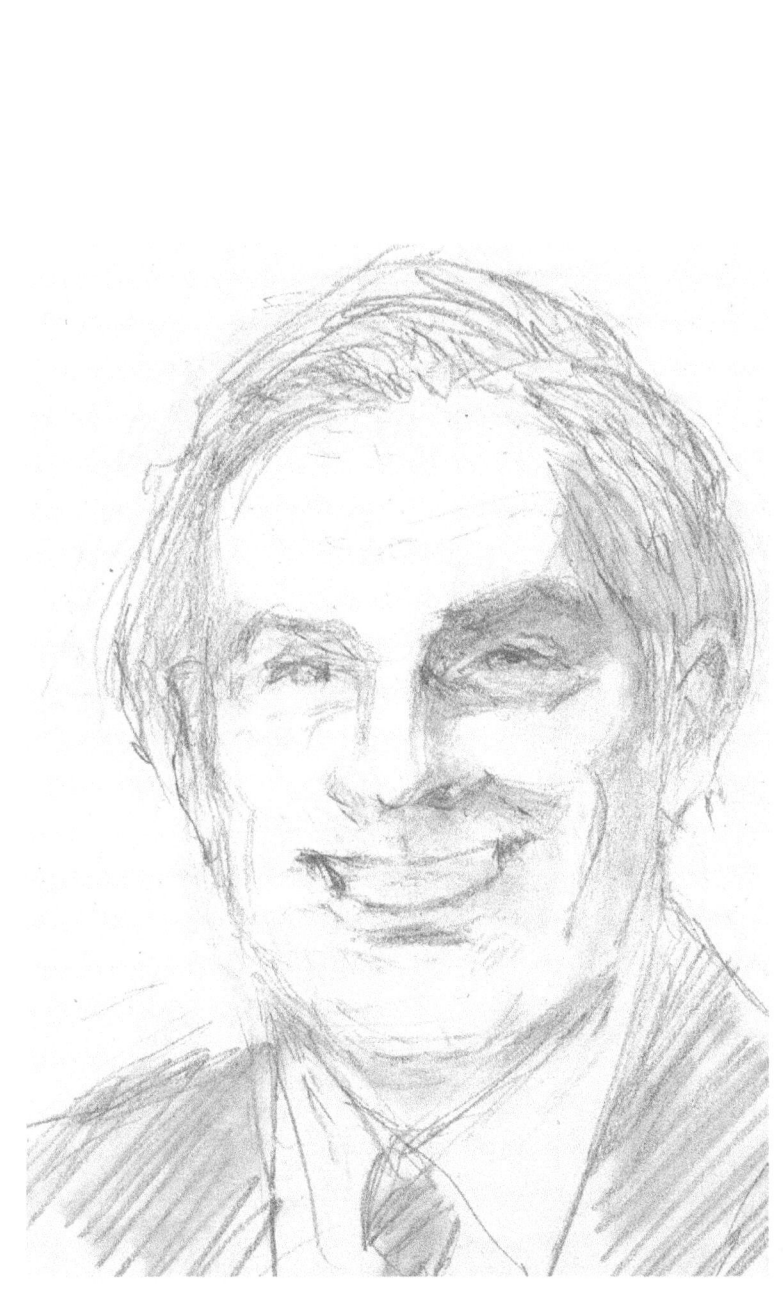

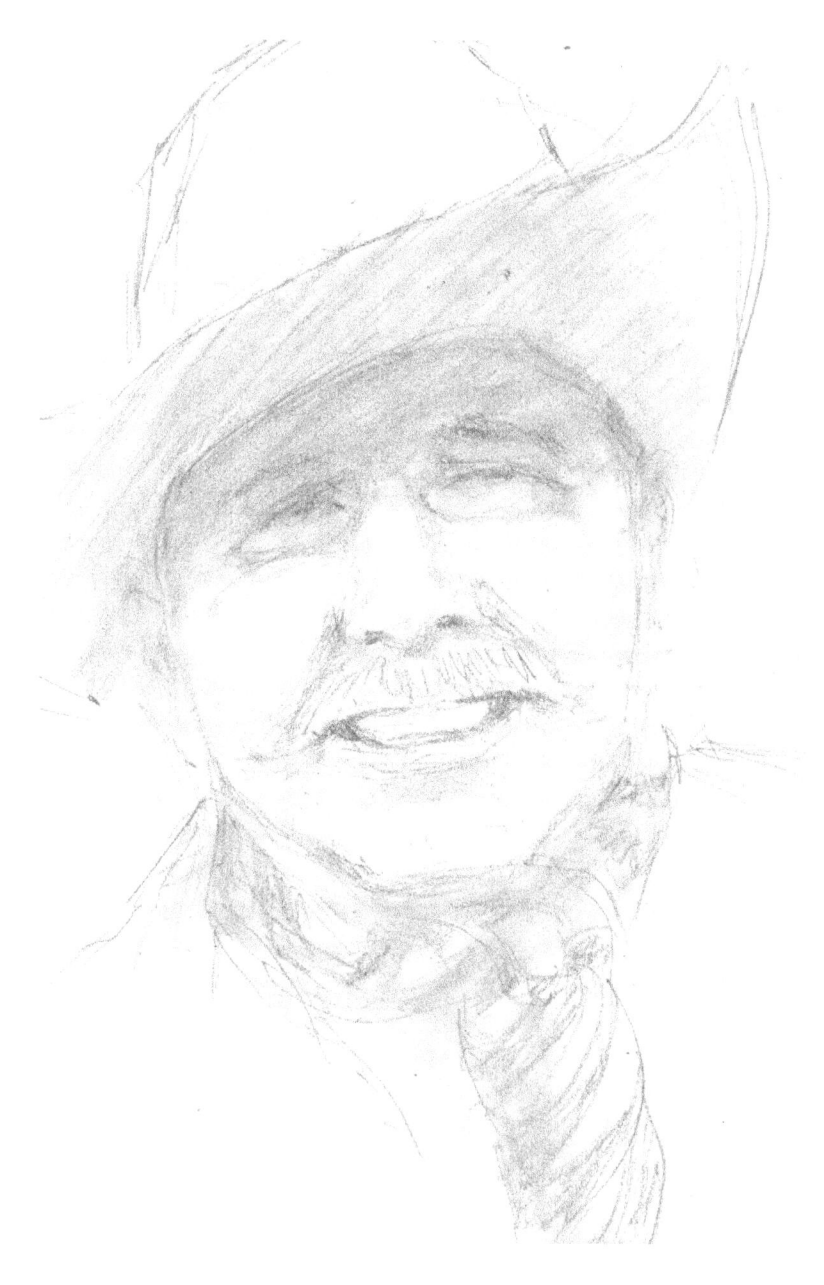

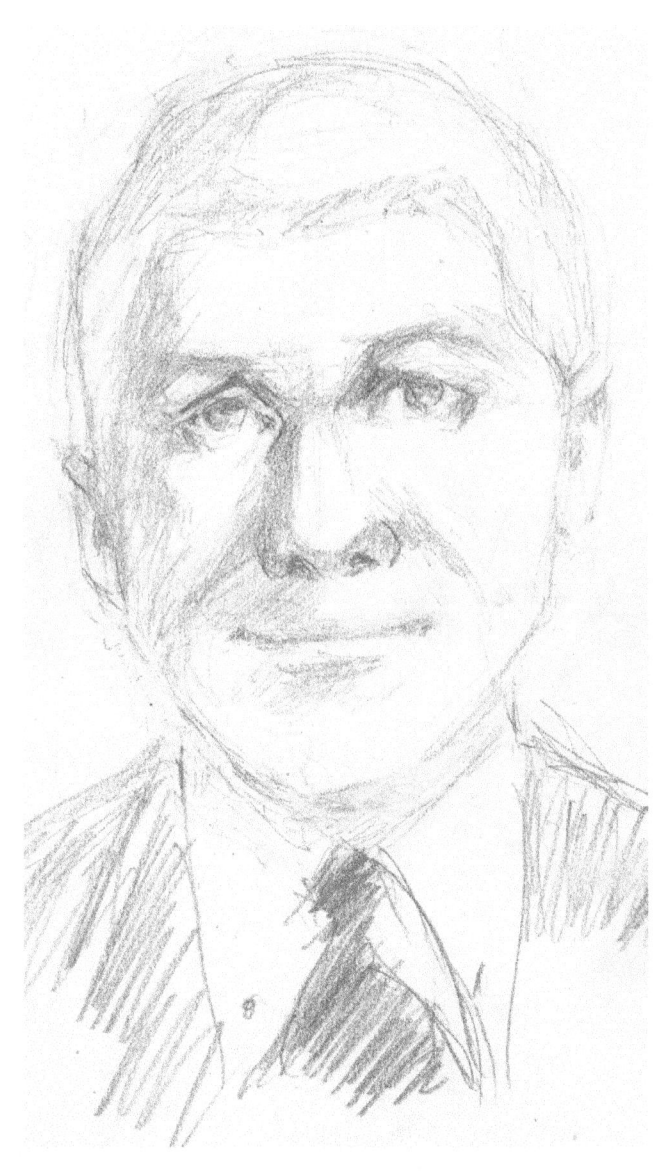

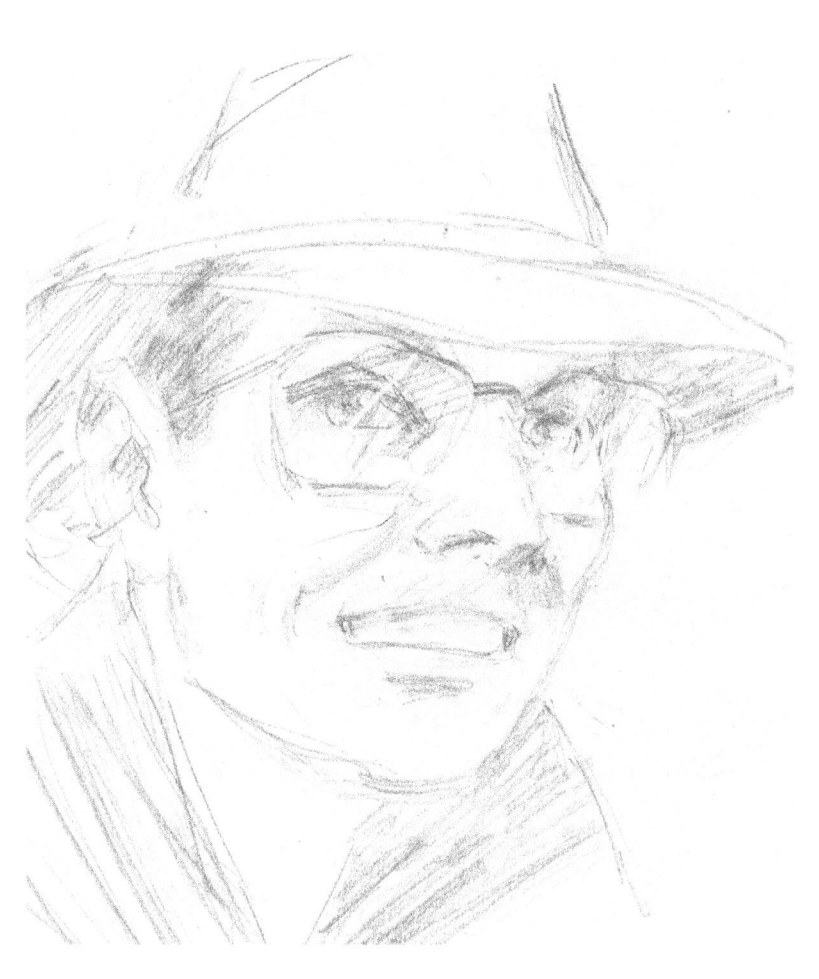

www.ingramcontent.com/pod-product-compliance
Lightning Source LLC
Chambersburg PA
CBHW051501170526
45166CB00001B/342